THE IMPOSSIBLE DREAM

By the same author:

RED DUSTER, WHITE ENSIGN
WINGS OF THE MORNING
LODESTONE AND EVENING STAR

Novel
THE LOST ONES

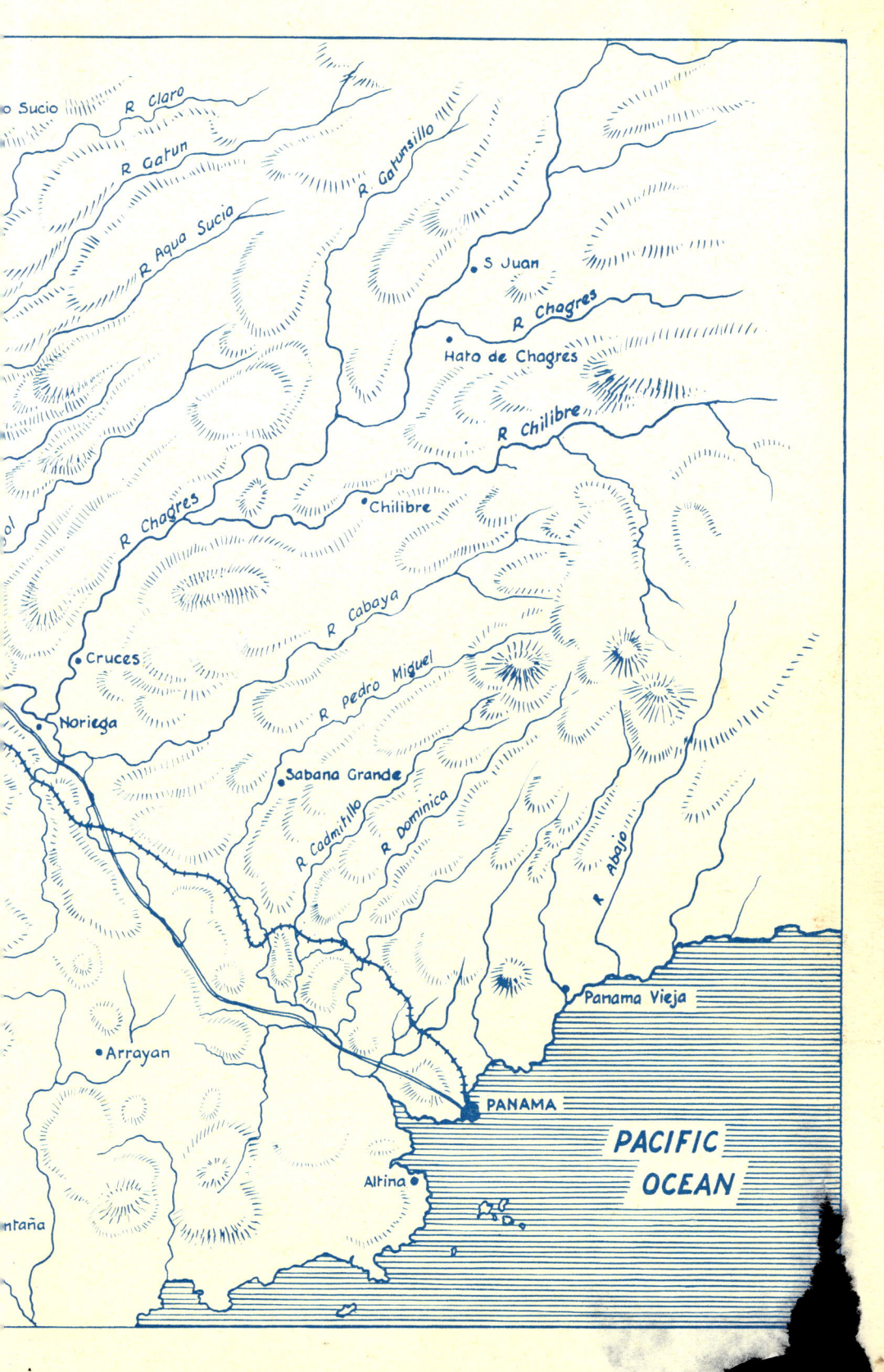

End of the day, Gatun Lock

THE IMPOSSIBLE DREAM
The building of the Panama Canal

by

IAN CAMERON

HODDER AND STOUGHTON
LONDON SYDNEY AUCKLAND TORONTO

London Borough
of Enfield
Public Libraries

J37605

627.137 Panama

Gr 6273

Copyright © 1971 by Donald Payne. First printed 1971. ISBN 0 340 04304 0. All rights reserved. No part of this publication may be reproduced or transmitted in any form or by any means, electronic or mechanical, including photocopy, recording, or any information storage and retrieval system, without permission in writing from the publisher. Printed in Great Britain for Hodder and Stoughton Limited, St. Paul's House, Warwick Lane, London, EC4P 4AH, by Ebenezer Baylis and Son Limited, The Trinity Press, Worcester and London

Never before have so much labour, so much scientific knowledge and so much administrative skill been concentrated on a work designed to serve the interests of mankind.

Sir James Bryce,
British Ambassador to Washington

The title of this book, *The Impossible Dream*, is from the musical play *Man of La Mancha* (words by Joe Darion, music by Mitch Leigh), © 1965 by Andrew Scott Inc., Helena Music Corp. and Sam Fox Publishing Co. Inc., and is used by special permission of Sam Fox Publishing Co. Inc., sole agents.

ACKNOWLEDGMENTS

I should like to thank the many societies, organisations and individuals who helped me with writing and illustrating *The Impossible Dream*: especially The Panama Canal Company, The Royal Geographical Society, The Surrey County Library (Dorking), Mrs. Joan St. George Saunders and Mr. A. Spark; also Miss Elizabeth Radice for proof-reading and indexing.

Grateful acknowledgment is made to the following for permission to use material.

Photographs. Culver Pictures, New York: Illustration Research Services, London: The Victoria and Albert Museum, London: Radio Times Hulton Picture Library, London; and Mr. John Freeman.

Drawings. The Panama Canal Company: Mr. Gerstle Mack: Macmillan and Co. Ltd. for permission to reproduce a drawing from *Problems of the Panama Canal* (1905) by H. L. Abbot: McGraw-Hill Book Company for permission to reproduce drawings from *The Panama Canal*, Vols. I and II (1916) by G. W. Goethals: E. P. Dutton and Co., Inc. for permission to reproduce drawings from the book *Who Built the Panama Canal?* by W. Leon Pepperman, illustrated by Joseph Pennell, copyright 1915 by E. P. Dutton and Co., Inc., renewed by W. Leon Pepperman 1943: and the Bucyrus-Erie Company for permission to reproduce a drawing of one of their steam-shovels.

Text. The Panama Canal Company for permission to quote a large number of extracts from the *Canal Record*: G. P. Putnam's Sons for permission to quote passages from *The Strength to Move a Mountain* (1958) by W. Storrs Lee and from *Mosquito Control in Panama* (1916) by J. A. Le Prince and A. J. Orenstein: Macmillan and Co. Ltd. for permission to quote a passage from *Problems of the Panama Canal* (1905) by H. L. Abbot: Alfred A. Knopf, Inc. for permission to quote passages from *The Land Divided* (1944) by Gerstle Mack: Collins, Publishers for permission to quote passages from *The Golden Isthmus* (1966) by David Howarth: Duke University Press for permission to quote a small passage from *Physician to the World* (1950) by J. M. Gibson: Frederick Muller Ltd. for permission to quote from *The Panama Canal* (1966) by Rolt Hammond and C. J. Lewin: Constable and Company Ltd. for permission to quote passages from *Panama: The Creation, Destruction and Resurrection* (1913) by Philippe Bunau-Varilla: Jonathan Cape Ltd. for permission to quote a passage from *Suez and Panama* (1940) by André Siegfried translated by Doris H. Buchanan: Ernest Benn Ltd. for permission to quote from *The Panama Gateway* (1913) by Joseph Bucklin Bishop published by Fisher Unwin: Hawthorn Books Inc. for permission to reprint selected quotations from *Construction of the Panama Canal* by W. L. Sibert and J. F. Stevens, copyright 1915 renewed 1943, by D. Appleton and Company: McGraw-Hill, quotations from *The Panama Canal*, Vols. I and II by G. W. Goethals, copyright G. W. Goethals 1916, used with permission of McGraw-Hill Book Company.

CONTENTS

		Page
Prologue: "Silent upon a peak in Darien"		17

PART ONE: THE FRENCH CANAL

1	Land of Fever and of Flood	23
2	The Dream of a Great Man	30
3	"Very Different from the Sands of Suez"	39
4	"Only the Drunk and the Dissipated will Die of Yellow Fever"	53
5	Death of a Dream	80
6	"It is No Crime to Grow Old"	97

PART TWO: THE AMERICAN CANAL

7	"I took the Canal Zone and left Congress to debate"	105
8	Chaos	116
9	The Foundations of Success	127
	(a) Reorganisation of Public Health	129
	(b) Reorganisation of Living Quarters and the Commissariat	142
	(c) Reorganisation of Transport	147
	(d) Reorganisation of Equipment	153
	(e) The Final Plan	159
10	The Transfer of Power	165
11	The Atlantic Division	173
12	The Central Division	201
13	The Pacific Division	225
14	The Land Divided	253
Epilogue: Return to Darien		265
Bibliography		271
Index		275

LIST OF PLATES

	Facing page
"A View through the Culebra Mountain"	80
Comte Ferdinand de Lesseps and some of his family	81
Jules Dingler	96
Charles de Lesseps	96
Lucien N.-B. Wyse	96
Gatun	97
Comte Ferdinand de Lesseps	176
Adolphe Godin de Lépinay	176
Philippe Bunau-Varilla	176
William Crawford Gorgas	177
John F. Stevens	177
The Cucaracha Slide	192
Theodore Roosevelt	193
George Washington Goethals	193
William Nelson Cromwell	193

LIST OF MAPS AND LINE-DRAWINGS

		Page
	The isthmus of Panama in 1880	Front endpaper
	End of the day, Gatun Lock	Frontispiece
1	Geological section across the isthmus of Panama	25
2	A typical freshet of the River Chagres	27
3	Incidence of malaria and yellow fever in the Canal Zone	28
4	The *Comte de Lesseps*	59
5	A French ladder-dredge	61
6	Additional excavation in the Culebra Cut	65
7	A self-propelling dredge	71
8	French cableway at work in the Culebra Cut	74
9	A mosquito-proof water-barrel	132
10	A portable fever-cage	133
11	Decline of malaria among employees	136
12	Three methods of destroying mosquito larvae	139
13	Mosquito-screened verandahs	141
14	Track layout in the Culebra Cut	151
15	Bucyrus steam-shovel	155
16	Longitudinal section of the canal	163
17	Annual excavation in the Culebra Cut	172
18	The Atlantic Division	174
19	The sea-going suction-dredge *Ancon*	178
20	Gatun spillway	191
21	Cableway for laying concrete	197
22	The guard gate at Gatun	199
23	The Central Division	202
24	Gamboa Dam	203
25	Cross-section of rocks in Culebra Cut	206
26	The Cut at Bas Obispo	208
27	Excavation in the Culebra Cut	217
28	The Cut at Paraiso	219
29	The Pacific Division	226
30	The sea-going ladder-dredge *Corozal*	232

31	The floor and gates at Pedro Miguel	238
32	Berm-crane at Pedro Miguel	240
33	Chamber-cranes at Miraflores	242
34	The walls at Miraflores	246
35	Cross-section of the culvert system	249
36	Electric towing locomotive	251
37	Possible routes for a new canal	266
	The isthmus of Panama in 1914	Back endpaper

PROLOGUE

"Silent upon a peak in Darien"

September 26th, 1513. The isthmus of Panama veiled in mist. The rivers in spate. And the conquistadors in heavy armour sinking up to their waists in mangrove swamp and freshet.

There were sixty-six of the conquistadors. For more than a month they had struggled through some of the most difficult country in the world, plagued by fever, heat-stroke and the poisoned arrows of the Indians. They had covered on average less than a mile a day, and they were close to the limit of their endurance. But their leader, Vasco Nuñez de Balboa, urged them on: "Soon," he told them, "we will come to the shore of the fabled sea, where men ride camels and even the cooking pots are made of gold." And because Balboa was a leader whom the Spaniards trusted and admired they followed the trail that he blazed.

In the early morning of September 26th they came to the lower slopes of an inconspicuous hill. It wasn't a high hill—no more than seven hundred feet; but from its crest, their Indian guides assured them, they would be able to see what no white man had ever seen before: the Great Ocean.

They started the climb, hacking their way through jungle lush and intransigent as any in the world; and by midday were approaching the summit. Here Balboa ordered them to wait.

> Then he went forwarde alone [we are told in *De Orbe Novo*] to the toppe. And there, prostrate upon the grounde and lyfting up his eyes towards heaven, he poured fourth his humble prayers before almightie God. And when he had made his prayers, he beckoned to his companions, pointing out to them the great maine sea, heretofore unknown to the inhabitants of Europe, Aphrika and Asia.

It was one of the great moments in the history of exploration.

The Spaniards struggled down to the shore of the new-found ocean on the afternoon of September 29th; and that evening Balboa in full armour waded into the muddy waters of a gulf that he named San Miguel, and laid claim to the Pacific in the name of Ferdinand of Castile. His expedition then spent the better part of three months exploring, trading and winning friendship of the Indians. They found no camels—the animals which the Indians had drawn for them in the sand were in fact llamas—but they did find almost unbelievable quantities of pearls and gold; and early in 1514 they made their way back, laden with treasure, to their base on the Caribbean.

Balboa, who was probably the ablest and certainly the most honest and humane of the conquistadors, at once sent Ferdinand of Castile his fifth share of the treasure, together with a report on the expedition. In this report he recommended that a fortified trail be established from ocean to ocean. He also added, rather as an afterthought, that one of the Castilian engineers who had made the crossing with him, a certain Alvaro de Saavedra, had suggested that a strait connecting the two oceans should be sought, and that if such a strait were not found, *"yet it might not be impossible to make one"*.

Four hundred years were to pass and tens of thousands of men were to die on the isthmus before the dream of this little-known Castilian engineer was realised.

In 1517 Balboa was executed, victim of the cruelty and treachery which all too often ended the career of the conquistadors. In 1529 Saavedra died in the Moluccas, his vision little appreciated and soon forgotten; and for centuries no one took up his suggestion of building a canal. Indeed for the better part of three hundred years Spain's attitude to the idea of cutting a waterway through the isthmus was summed up in the dictum of the Dominican Friars to whom Philip II turned for advice—"what God has joined together let no man put asunder"—and it was not until the early nineteenth century that the idea of a canal was seriously revived.

Two factors led to its revival: the impetus given to construction projects by the industrial revolution, and the waning of Spanish influence in Central America.

Before the nineteenth century building projects had depended almost entirely on manual labour; but in the years of technical progress which followed the Napoleonic War, the machines of the industrial revolution became harnessed and adapted to construction work. Dredgers, drillers, spreaders and cranes replaced shovels and picks, and it was largely due to the efficiency of these new machines that in the mid-nineteenth century a great network of roads, tunnels, railways and canals began to fan out over almost every country in the world. By 1870 it seemed as though no project was beyond the compass of the engineers' skill, no terrain too difficult for them to conquer.

And as the machines advanced over prairie, steppe and hill, so the power of the once omnipotent Spanish empire declined. For three hundred years Spain had enjoyed a virtual monopoly in Central America; but for reasons allegedly religious but largely in fact economic she had opposed the pioneering of better trade routes across the isthmus, and a veil of secrecy had prevented the land being mapped let alone developed. With the decay of the Spanish empire, however, this veil was gradually lifted, and between 1840 and 1870 a large number of adventurers flooded into a part of the world which had long been inaccessible. A few of these adventurers were genuine explorers; but most of them were visionaries, charlatans or cranks, and between them they produced a wonderful crop of outlandish schemes for linking ocean to ocean.

For without exception they underestimated the isthmus.

They arrived in Colon armed with the knowledge that the neck of the continent was less than forty miles wide—"no more than might be walked by a healthy man in a day"; they convinced themselves, after the most superficial of surveys, that they had found a way across which was devoid of mountains or linked by streams; they rode post-haste to Bogota, the capital of New Granada, and obtained a concession to build a railroad or canal along the route of their choice; they then returned to Europe with a scheme as grandiose as it was impractical.

Most of these adventurers—and this perhaps was fortunate—lacked the money and influence needed to get their schemes off the ground, but in 1876 there came to the isthmus a man who was short of neither. Lieutenant Lucien Napoléon-Bonaparte Wyse of the French navy was a great-nephew of Napoléon, a man of considerable private means, and an acquaintance of Ferdinand de Lesseps, the builder of Suez.

PART ONE

THE FRENCH CANAL

1

LAND OF FEVER AND OF FLOOD

The myth has grown insidiously in the English-speaking world: the myth that the French failed to build the Panama canal because of chicanery and inefficiency. This is not so. A worth-while canal through Central America could not have been built in the 1870s by the engineers of *any* nationality. For although the isthmus was low and a mere forty miles in width, its defences were the more formidable for being neither visible nor understood.

Exactly how formidable these defences were Lieutenant Wyse was soon to learn to his cost. In 1876, together with a handful of engineers and technicians, he struck into the interior optimistically declaring that three to four weeks would be sufficient to choose a route along which to build a canal. Yet in two years he never managed to survey a way across with any degree of accuracy.

Why?

What was the quality, we have to ask ourselves, of this narrow neck of land that it defied the onslaught first of intelligent explorers armed with compass, plane-table and theodolite, and then of tens of thousands of labourers backed by the resources and technical expertise of two of the greatest nations on earth?

In the south-west corner of the Caribbean a range of low green mountains rises over a coral shore. Most of the time the mountains are veiled in thunderheads and barred with alternate swathes of sunlight and rain; mist clings to their valleys, and up their slopes writhes a jungle, lush and impenetrable as any on earth. At first sight the mountains appear to be a continuous range, but as one approaches them closely they are seen to be a succession of individual hills: a formation of bewildering complexity; the isthmus's first line of defence. Most mountain ranges (including the near-by Rockies and Andes) were originally formed by folding, due to lateral pressure. The mountains of Central America, however, were formed by the upthrusting of individual volcanic cores—in other words little islands of hard rock, such as basalt, diorite and andesite, were pushed up through a conglomeration of lava and ash. As a result, a cross-section of the isthmus shows not an orderly arrangement of strata, but a confusion of faults, dikes, sills and cores. A glance at Figure 1 shows that in the forty-odd miles between Colon and

Panama there are six major faults, five major volcanic cores and seventeen fundamentally different types of rock. A further source of confusion is that the isthmus has been several times depressed below sea-level, and pockets of marine limestone coral and carb are now sandwiched between the layers of volcanic rock. The result is a geologist's nightmare.

The nuances of this peculiar formation and the heart-aches it would one day cause the construction gangs were little appreciated by the original survey teams. All *they* understood was the net result: that they quickly became lost in a maze of steeply undulating hills which followed no recognisable pattern but were likened by one of the surveyors to "a choppy sea with the wind knocking up random cross waves against the line of the swell": a defence of bewildering complexity.

The fact that the hills were choked from base to summit in tropical rain forest increased the surveyors' difficulties; and it was this rain forest which formed the isthmus's second line of defence.

Panama lies nine degrees north of the equator; its annual rainfall is a hundred and five inches, and its average temperature eighty degrees. These conditions are ideal for the growth of hygrophytic forest of a type which flourishes in the Amazon, Congo and South-East Asia—indeed the Panama jungle was recently used as a training ground for troops for Vietnam. It is hard for anyone who has not set foot in this sort of jungle to appreciate its density; but one of the original French surveyors has left a fair description: "The difficulties that beset us are enormous. For every line of our survey has to be cut slowly and laboriously through a wilderness of jungle so thick that it is impossible to see ten feet in any direction, and so gloomy and stifling that it is difficult to breathe. The ground is a quagmire of decomposing vegetation and the rain beats down on us day after day." The sheer physical labour of clearing a base, setting up a survey post and taking a bearing was enormous. Certainly it turned out to be beyond the capabilities of Wyse, whose maps were a compound of observation, guesswork and wishful thinking. The Panama jungle in fact proved an adversary which could be tamed only with patience, foot by foot; and even today if guard is relaxed it will creep back over land which man can not claim to have conquered, only borrowed.

The isthmus's third line of defence was the propensity of its rivers to flood. This flooding is brought about by two factors: the precipitous structure of the valleys, and the high rainfall. What happens is nicely described in the official words of *The Hydrology of the Panama Canal*:

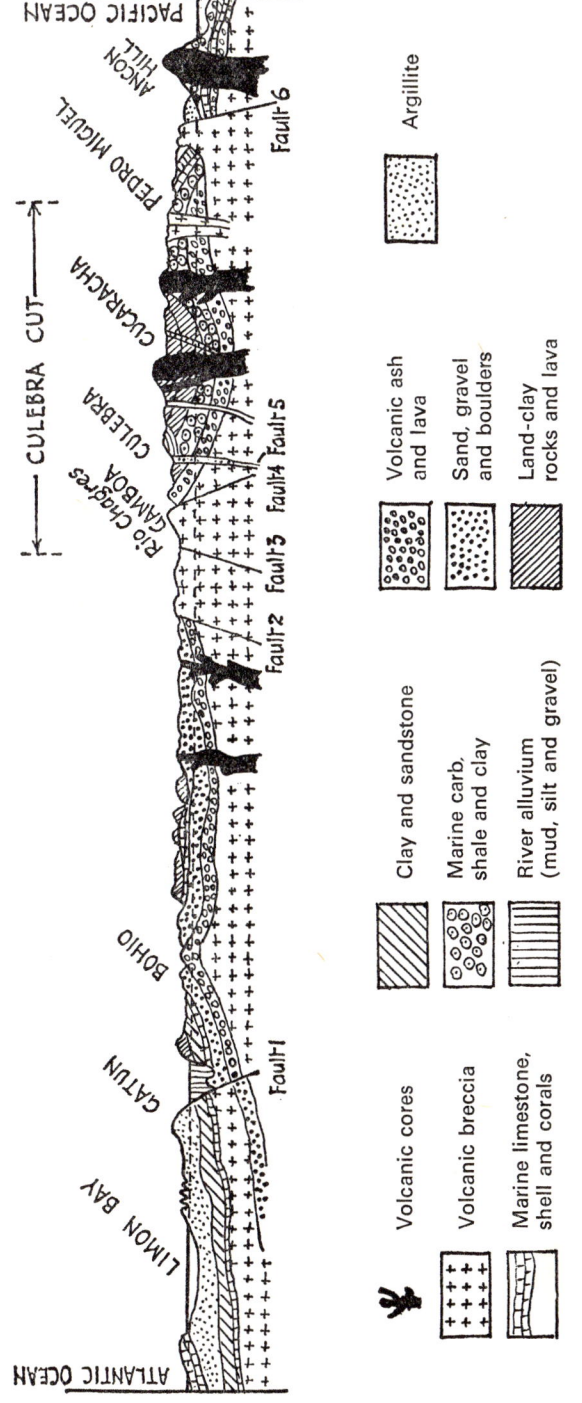

Figure 1. Geological section across the isthmus of Panama

> Although the entire country is clothed with dense vegetation, the slopes of the valleys are so precipitous and the rock lies so close to the surface, that tropical rainstorms convert the river banks into a series of small torrents and cascades; these cause the Chagres, and other rivers, to rise suddenly and to discharge an almost incredible volume of water.

As an example, the Chagres at Gamboa is normally a placid slow-flowing stream some forty feet above sea-level and discharging at the rate of 3,000 cubic feet a second; but after two days of torrential downpour (on July 19th and 20th, 1903) the river had risen to sixty feet above sea-level, and was discharging at a rate of more than 31,000 cubic feet a second (see Figure 2). And such a rise was typical rather than exceptional.

This susceptibility to flooding was noted by Wyse, but only *en passant*. Yet here in fact was one of the rocks on which French hopes were eventually to founder. For not in all their eight years' work were de Lesseps' engineers able to tame the Chagres, whose floods time and again swept away bridges, tracks and equipment, and spewed thousands of tons of debris into the canal they were so laboriously constructing.

The isthmus's final weapon was its most deadly. It was an endemic centre of yellow fever and malaria.

For more than three hundred years this south-west corner of the Caribbean had been known as the fever coast. British, French and Spanish seamen had died here in their tens of thousands of a disease thought at the time to have its origin in the miasmal mists which hung like a pall over the low-lying marshes and swamps.

> When the trade wind dies [wrote a visitor to Colon in the 1860s] and the sultry air of the isthmus ceases to move, a white mist will rise out of the ocean and hover like a fog over land and sea. This is the precursor of fever, and those who know the isthmus stay within doors. For the mist carries with it the poison of putrefaction, and wherever it encloses its victim death will follow.

We can, in the 1970s, recognise this as so much nonsense. But in the 1870s no one doubted it; for no one in those days suspected that fever was caused by the bite of the mosquito—indeed by the bite of two species only, *Stegomyiae* for yellow fever and female *Anopheles* for malaria. Bearing in mind therefore the current state of medical knowledge, it was inevitable that when the French came to build their canal they should suffer a crippling death rate. The Americans would have suffered likewise if it had not been for one important

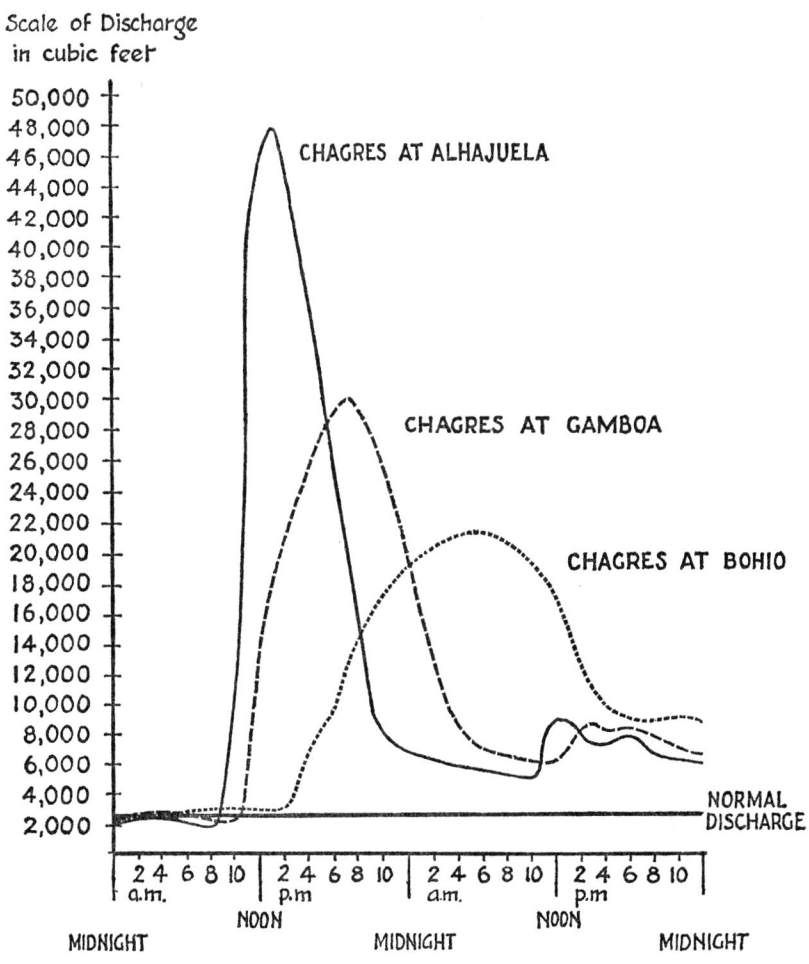

Figure 2. A typical freshet of the River Chagres

fact: at the turn of the century a group of doctors—Ross, Finlay, Reed, Lazear and Gorgas—discovered the connection between mosquitoes and malaria, and in 1904 one of these doctors, Gorgas, was appointed Chief Sanitary Officer to the newly-formed Isthmian Commission. A glance at the graph below (Figure 3) will show more eloquently than words the amazing results which stemmed from Gorgas's campaign against the fever-carrying mosquitoes.

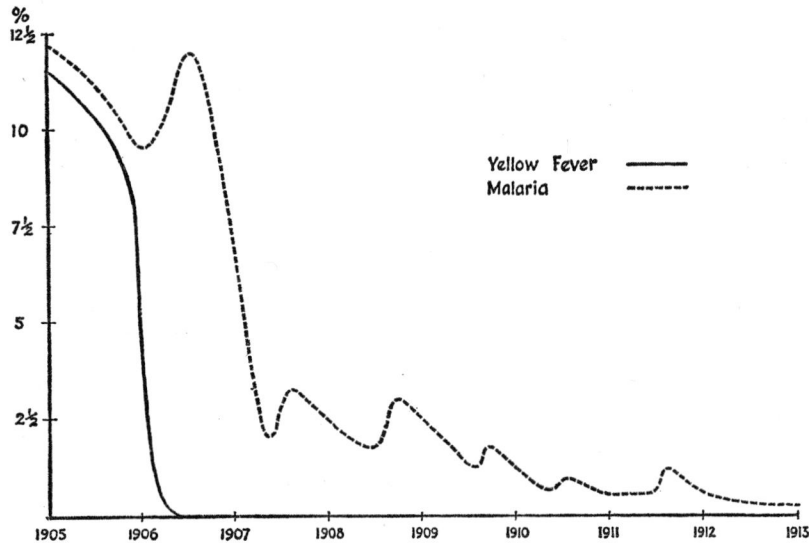

Figure 3. Incidence of malaria and yellow fever in the Canal Zone, 1905-13

Complex hills, dense forest, flooding rivers and a high incidence of fever: these were the problems facing the French. Each of the problems might by itself have been solved—by hard work, technical ingenuity or sacrifice; but together they added up to an obstacle which, in the nineteenth century, it was almost certainly beyond the compass of man to overcome.

And in this lay the seeds of tragedy. For the French were determined to achieve the impossible: determined no matter what the cost to build a sea-level canal.

Their determination had its roots in an unfortunate coincidence. In 1878 Wyse, after two abortive years on the isthmus, at last achieved something worth-while—although in the field of diplomacy rather than exploration. He obtained from both the Colombian government and the hitherto obdurate directors of the Panama railroad, a concession to build a canal along the line of the 1855 railway. Armed with this concession he sailed post-haste to France and put his proposal for a sea-level waterway to *Le Société de Géographie de Paris*. His proposal was vague and based on the very minimum of survey work. It would never have been pushed through if the president of *Le Société de Géographie* at this critical moment had not been Ferdinand de Lesseps, the hero of Suez.

2

THE DREAM OF A GREAT MAN

Ferdinand de Lesseps was neither an engineer nor a financier; he referred to himself as a diplomat, though today we would more likely classify him as a promoter or entrepreneur. When in 1878 he became president of *Le Société de Géographie* he was seventy-four years old and the most celebrated man in Europe, known simply as *le grand Français;* for to the glory of France and in the face of the most intransigent difficulties he had built the Suez Canal. Nor was de Lesseps merely respected, he was genuinely loved: loved for his gallantry with women, his spontaneity with children and his zest for living. Physically his energy was amazing—as proof of his perennial virility he loved to draw attention to his large family: fourteen children, nine of them born after his sixtieth birthday—*et quel enfants! Beaux comme des pursangs et sauvages comme eux!*—while mentally he had the optimism and resilience usually associated with extreme youth. It would be hard to imagine a more attractive personality. De Lesseps, however, had his Achilles' heel. Overconfidence. For in the sober words of Gerstle Mack (whose weighty volume *The Land Divided* is the definitive work on the canal) "he had been right so often that he had begun to think of himself as infallible; he had a profound almost mystical belief in his own intuition . . . (and) with Suez behind him he could not imagine failure at Panama".

The tragedy was that Suez and Panama were not comparable; and it was de Lesseps' over-confidence which led him to plunge headlong into an enterprise with which a more cautious man would have hesitated to become associated.

Looking back, one can see now that the French débâcle had its roots in the convening in 1879 of a special assembly (*Le Congrès International d'Études du Canal Interocéanique*) to debate the possibility of building a canal through Central America. For this assembly was rigged. It was rigged by de Lesseps and Wyse: not as some people were later to claim for reasons either fraudulent or dishonourable, but simply because as soon as de Lesseps read Wyse's report he decided that Panama was the place to build a canal, and that he was the man to build it. So when it fell to him as president of the Geographical Society to convene an assembly, he not unnaturally invited as delegates men who were his friends and associates, a hard core of them promoters and public officials with whom he had worked at Suez. There was nothing *per se* dishonest in this; but it did mean that at the heart of the assembly was a bloc of de Lesseps' admirers who were to support him, right or wrong, with adulatory blindness.

The assembly met on May 15th, 1879 in the hall of *Le Société de Géographie* in the boulevard Saint-Germain. It was an impressive gathering: a hundred and thirty-six delegates from twenty-two nations plus a galaxy of distinguished spectators. After the usual formalities the assembly split into five committees of which the fourth or Technical Committee was the most important. Its terms of reference were all-embracing: "to decide upon the most advantageous route and the most practical type of canal, to estimate costs of construction . . . and to devise means of ensuring safe and easy transit from ocean to ocean". More than half the members of this committee were French: less than a quarter of them were engineers.

They began by discussing the alternative routes: Nicaragua, Sapoa River, the Tehuantepec, San Blas and Panama. It soon became clear that the Nicaraguan route was likely to prove the cheapest; it, however, necessitated locks. And de Lesseps, from the moment he read Wyse's report made up his mind that he would build his canal through Central America as he had built it through the Middle East, at sea-level—for this, he insisted, was the only sort worth building. When Wyse was called to give evidence he supported de Lesseps and told the committee that a sea-level canal from Colon to Panama would be "perfectly feasible". His opinion was not accepted without misgivings; for having a vested interest in the Panama concession, he was naturally anxious to sell it; also his survey work had been sketchy in the extreme. In particular Wyse was challenged by Godin de Lépinay, a little-known engineer from the Department of Public Works whose contribution toward building the canal has seldom been given the recognition it deserves.

Adolphe Godin de Lépinay was, in the assembly, a small fish in a large pond; but he was a first-class engineer, he knew the isthmus and he was a man of integrity. He realised from the start that Wyse's proposal for a sea-level canal was impractical, and the alternative scheme which he now put forward had the simplicity of genius.

> Dam back the Rivers Chagres and Rio Grande [he pleaded] as close to the sea as you can so that their waters form a vast inland lake. Raise the water level of this lake to eighty feet above the sea and construct locks at either end. You will then have to do virtually no excavation in the valleys of the Chagres and Rio Grande, your

cut through the mountains of the continental divide will need to be eighty feet less deep, half the length of the canal will consist of a lake, and this will enormously reduce the volume of work.

Twenty-eight years later this scheme, almost down to the last detail, was successfully adopted by the Americans. But in the 1879 assembly it was passed over without so much as a debate. For de Lesseps vetoed any proposal involving the use of locks.

It is easy today, safe in the knowledge of hindsight, to point out that the Panama canal was an engineering project, and that de Lesseps ought to have listened to the advice of engineers. But it must be remembered that in building Suez *le grand Français* had time and again overruled his engineers—and been proved right. And so now, over-confident in the magic of his intuition, de Lesseps blocked de Lépinay's proposal, and, on an afternoon when only half the committee was in session, pushed through a proposal of his own.

As a result, on May 29th a rump of the assembly was asked to vote on the following resolution: "that this congress believes the excavation of an interoceanic canal at sea-level to be feasible; and that the canal should extend from the Gulf of Limon to the Bay of Panama."

The voting was *viva voce* in alphabetical order; and as delegate after delegate rose to speak in favour of the resolution it soon became clear that de Lesseps' supporters had won the day. De Lépinay, however, was vehement in his opposition. "Though unable to make my advice triumph," he cried, "I will not abandon it. And in order not to burden my conscience with unnecessary deaths and useless expenditure I vote 'No'." He sat down to a cacophony of booing.

When de Lesseps was called on to vote he answered in ringing tones which were heard in the farthest corner of the hall, "I vote 'Yes'. And I am willing to accept the leadership of this great enterprise." His announcement was greeted with such enthusism that polling was held up for nearly a quarter of an hour.

When the votes had been counted, it was announced that seventy-four delegates were in favour of the resolution and eight against. These figures, however, are misleading: for no fewer than fifty-four delegates were diplomatically absent or abstained, and of those who voted in favour only one (Pedro Sosa) was an engineer who had ever worked on the isthmus.

De Lesseps had triumphed. His victory, however, was Pyrrhic; and those who appreciated the technicalities of engineering and the difficulties of the terrain were aware from the start that he had bitten off a great deal more than he could chew.

One of the United States delegates, William Edward Johnston, was subsequently to accuse de Lesseps of having "packed and manipulated the congress so as to run through an impossible scheme". This was true. Yet de Lesseps' wire-pulling was prompted by the noblest and most altruistic of motives. He genuinely believed that he would be able to build the canal to the glory of France and the benefit of mankind. "It has been suggested by my friends," he told the congress in a light-hearted valediction, "that after Suez I ought to take a rest. But I ask you: when a general has just won one battle and is invited to win another, why should he refuse?"

The delegates left Paris in a glow of roseate enthusiasm, and de Lesseps, undeterred by the murmuring of a handful of engineers, planned his campaign. His programme was simple: first he would raise the necessary funds, second he would visit the isthmus, and third he would initiate the work of construction. His priorities epitomise his confidence. For before he had even set foot in Central America and before he had studied a single detailed survey of the proposed route, he proceeded to try to launch his *Compagnie Universelle du Canal Interocéanique* with a proposed capital of 400 million francs.

A lesser man would have been warned by what happened next. For in spite of de Lesseps' reputation, the public fought shy of his new company. The subscription took place on August 6th and 7th, 1879; but it wasn't 400 million francs which were raised, it was thirty million—less than a twelfth of what had been hoped for.

De Lesseps now displayed all the resource, energy and refusal to admit defeat which had characterised his leadership at Suez. He arranged a whirlwind series of lecture tours; he founded an official company magazine (the *Bulletin du Canal Interocéanique*); he took his family on a visit to the isthmus; and he appointed a special syndicate whose task was to ensure favourable publicity.

His lecture tour started uncertainly but, after a few weeks, turned into a triumphal procession. For de Lesseps was an inspired speaker—fluent, lucid and witty—and carried away by the tide of his own enthusiasm he carried others with him. It was an idealistic gospel he preached: the vision of "an even grander Suez, an oceanic Bosphorus whose waters will unite the nations of the world". And before the flood of his enthusiasm all obstacles seemed capable of being swept aside. The continental divide?—it was only a matter of digging. The floods of the Chagres?—they would be diverted. The climate?—"it lends itself admirably to cultivation and industry". And he was appealing to an audience who *wanted* to believe. For France in the 1870s was the France of St.-Simon and the doctrine of regeneration through work, and universal peace through the undertaking of great public works devoted to the good of mankind. No wonder that charmed by oratory, philosophy and a manipulated press, tens of thousands of Frenchmen were persuaded to invest their savings in an enterprise which seemed not so much a gamble as a crusade.

The *Bulletin du Canal Interocéanique* was another silver-tongued persuader. Published in September 1879, it was to prove, in the ten years of its life, a typical company magazine, disseminating to the public a great mass of semi-technical propaganda. Its editors, however, went to such pains to spotlight accomplishments and gloss over short-comings, that it eventually fell into disrepute and became dubbed *le Moniteur des Chimères*. As soon as this magazine was successfully launched de Lesseps prepared to visit the isthmus.

In the autumn, a party of surveyors had been sent ahead to examine the proposed route and to make sample borings; and on 30th December *le grand Français* himself stepped ashore at Colon, together with his wife, three of his younger children and a coterie of distinguished engineers.

From the point of view of climate de Lesseps couldn't have arrived at a more misleading moment. The seasonal rains had ended—literally a couple of days before he landed—the skies were cloudless, and the north-west trades blew pleasantly in from the Caribbean. De Lesseps was delighted both with the invigorating air and the warmth of his reception. He spent twenty-four hours in Colon, attending a banquet and a firework display and briefly inspecting the harbour; then he boarded the train for Panama. En route he was greeted with scenes of "indescribable enthusiasm", for the people of the isthmus saw in his proposed canal a guarantee of their future prosperity. At Barbacoas, however, in the upper reaches of the Chagres valley, there took place an incident which a less optimistic man might have taken for an augury. The ever-tactful *Bulletin* simply records the fact that "at Barbacoas Bridge the party were met by the President of the state of Panama . . . and after a short walk they boarded another train to continue their journey to the Pacific." What the *Bulletin* fails to make clear is that the "short walk" was necessitated by the fact that three weeks earlier the Chagres had risen forty-eight feet in as many hours and swept away the central span of Barbacoas bridge!

De Lesseps arrived in Panama on the first day of 1880, and he at once embarked on a round of parties, inspections and ceremonial engagements which reduced his staff to a state of physical and mental exhaustion. For a man of seventy-five his energy was phenomenal: in the words of a local reporter, "he worked all day, danced all night, and infused a new vigour and animation into the life of the isthmus." He loved official occasions—pomp and circumstance, parades and speeches, red carpets and brass bands; but he also loved people, and it wasn't long before he was sharing the sorrows and joys of those who lived in the isthmus, visiting their sick and becoming godfather to their children. His beautiful young wife, who came from Martinique, and his children also made a host of friends—although the children caused some bewilderment at first because they were "all dressed like girls but all behaved like boys!"

For six weeks the pace was frenetic: fireworks, bull-fights, tattoos, concerts, dances, dinners and ceremonies of initiation—the first symbolic blow of a pickaxe wielded by de Lesseps' daughter Totote, and the first exploding of dynamite at the summit of the continental divide. Some writers, indeed, have suggested that there was too much revelry and too little work. Rodrigues of the New York *World*, for example, ever eager to disparage the French, wrote that "they looked more like a picnic party than a scientific committee . . . the writer was with them for twelve days and he can safely say that there was not a stroke of earnest work done, and many of the young men were more interested in fishing in the Bay of Panama than in testing rocks." Rodrigues, however, had a chip on his shoulder and acid in his pen; and his sneer is typical of the ill-informed criticism which has cast a quite unmerited stigma on the reputation of the French engineers. For the scientific committee appointed by de Lesseps were competent men who did their job conscientiously and well—witness the weighty opinion of Joseph Bucklin Bishop, later secretary to the American Isthmian Commission: "the French report was a very thorough and scientific document." It has been suggested that six weeks was too short a time in which to prepare so important a dossier. And there is some truth in this. It ought, however, to be remembered that French surveyors had been working all autumn along the line of the canal, and that the committee had a vast amount of data already in its possession—the surveys of Wyse and the Railroad Company for example—and their task was therefore verification and analysis rather than research.

As soon as de Lesseps and his entourage were settled in Panama, the committee was divided into eight groups, each under a specialist engineer and each with its own particular field to report on. For five weeks there was much checking and collating of data; then on February 7th the groups' findings were handed into a central board whose members included George Totten, chief engineer of the Railroad, and Jacob Dirks, an authority on the canals of Holland. This board dovetailed the findings of the various groups into an overall plan, a document of more than 300 closely reasoned pages and diagrams, which was handed to de Lesseps on February 14th.

The plan conceived by the board was basically simple: for a sea-level canal seventy-two feet wide and twenty-eight feet deep, with its banks set back at an angle of approximately forty-five degrees. Starting at the Atlantic terminal of Colon, the canal was to run for five miles through mangrove swamps as far as Gatun: then for twenty-one miles up the valley of the Chagres: then, curving right, it was to pass *via* the Obispo watershed through the hills of the continental divide: and finally to follow the valley of the Rio Grande to the Pacific terminal of Panama. The stumbling block was the Chagres. It crossed the proposed route no less than twenty-seven times, and when in flood its water might be anything up to eighty feet *above* the finished canal. To hold it back the French planned a gargantuan dam 110 feet high at Gamboa, plus diversionary channels to lead the river east to the Atlantic. The amount of excavation was estimated at 93 million cubic yards, the cost at 843 million francs, and it was thought that "with good and judicious management the canal ought to be completed within eight years".

This report has been the subject of much criticism. If, however, we accept the basic premise that the canal had to be at sea-level, it is difficult to fault it except in its lack of a detailed plan to contain the Chagres. De Lesseps, at any rate, was delighted; and within twenty-four hours of reading it he was on his way to New York. "Panama," he told the people of the isthmus, "will be easier to build, easier to finish, and easier to maintain than Suez."

There followed a six months' promotional tour which would have taxed the strength of a professional athlete. During the spring and summer of 1880 de Lesseps visited the great cities of the world—Philadelphia, San Francisco, Chicago, Boston and New York; Liverpool, London, Paris, Lyons and Rheims; Brussels, Amsterdam, Ghent, Barcelona and Madrid—and wherever he spoke his vigour and enthusiasm confounded the sceptics and won him a host of new devotees: *vide* the New York *Herald*: "with the eagle glance of genius he stands upon the summit where dawn casts its earliest light, and sees, in advance of the sleepers in the valleys below, the illumination which the climbing sun will shed upon them also." His tour, both in the New World and the Old, was an unqualified personal triumph. And when in the autumn he returned to France he judged that conditions were right for floating another loan. With press and *Bulletin* now united in his praise and his successful tour still fresh in the public's mind, the result was very different from the last time. He raised not 30 million francs but 600 million.

There was, however, a price tag. To ensure success, de Lesseps was forced to stoop to deception and chicanery.

The deception stemmed from a flaw in his character: his congenital over-optimism. The moment he left the isthmus, for example, he began to "adjust" the estimates prepared by his scientific committee. He reduced the cost of construction from 843 million francs to 658 million; he reduced the amount of excavation from ninety-three million cubic yards to eighty-six million and he reduced the time of completion from eight years to six and a half. This was totally unwarranted; and it set an unfortunate precedent.

The chicanery stemmed from the fact that the syndicate whom de Lesseps had appointed to ensure favourable publicity found that the support of the press wasn't given freely; it had to be bought. Newspapers and magazines, in other words, had to be bribed (to the tune of more than 1,500,000 francs) in order to boost the canal. This, given the conditions of the time, may have been inevitable. It was none the less reprehensible. And de Lesseps was later to learn to his cost the truth of the adage that "he who touches pitch shall be defiled therewith".

As soon as the loan had been successfully floated, the *Compagnie Universelle du Canal Interocéanique* was incorporated and its administration fixed by statute. Ferdinand de Lesseps was to be president; there were five vice-presidents, a secretary-general and a board of twenty directors: there was also a sub-committee, with Charles de Lesseps (Ferdinand's son) as chairman, which consisted of a consulting engineer, a consulting contractor and a panel of fifteen technical advisors. The salaries of all these officials were remarkably low; although a captious critic might have scented a trace of nepotism in the inclusion on the board of four members of the de Lesseps family— Ferdinand himself, his brother Jules, and his sons Victor and Charles.

At least one of the de Lesseps, however, was a reluctant participator. Charles—Ferdinand's elder surviving son by his first wife—was cautious and level-headed, and he saw all too clearly the dangers which lay ahead.

> What [he asked his father] do you hope to gain from Panama? Money?—You will bother with it no more than you did at Suez. Glory?—Surely you have had a surfeit and can leave that to somebody else . . . The Panama project is indeed a magnificent one, but think of the risks. At Suez you only succeeded by a miracle; so why not be content with one miracle in your life time rather than hope for another?

De Lesseps, however, was unmoved. And Charles, having made this one plea, never made another. He worshipped his father, and though his head cried warning his heart was soon to lead him into the thick of the fray. "If," he wrote, "you feel you have to go ahead, and if you want me to help, I shall do so cheerfully and will never complain, no matter what may happen. All that I am I owe to you; and what you have given me, you have the right to take away." For ten years Charles was to serve his father loyally, with never a word of recrimination; and when the disaster which he had foreseen came to pass, it was the son rather than the father who paid more dearly. History has few more moving examples of filial devotion.

With the formation of his company de Lesseps was committed: committed beyond recall to an enterprise which was foredoomed to disaster as surely as a Greek tragedy. For with the engineering equipment and the medical knowledge of the 1880s, a sea-level canal through Central America simply could not have been built: yet it was not in de Lesseps' nature to admit defeat.

Defeat, in any case, was not a prospect which crossed many people's minds in 1881. At the end of January de Lesseps' company was launched amid paeans of praise—"never before has there been so happy a marriage of capital and science" (*Journal des Débats*): "Success is certain. Enthusiasm is universal" (*Le Gaulois*): "Oh ye of little faith! Hear the words of genius, and believe!" (*La Liberté*)—and on February 1st de Lesseps read to an enthusiastic press a telegram from the isthmus which he described as eloquence in few words. It read simply, "TRAVAIL COMMENCE."

3

"VERY DIFFERENT FROM THE SANDS OF SUEZ"

There was hardly a hint to start with of the Calvary to come; for success in 1881 seemed not only possible but assured.

No one did more to propagate this early optimism than the contractors whom de Lesseps initially put in charge of construction. Couvreux and Hersent were among the largest civil engineers in Europe; they enjoyed an excellent reputation based on their work in three continents, and one would have expected so experienced a firm to tread warily on unfamiliar ground—not one of their directors had ever worked in Central America. In fact they did the opposite. And in 1880 Abel Couvreux made a speech at Ghent in which he was guilty of a series of quite remarkable *faux pas*. He said the so-called deadly climate of Panama was "nothing but an invention of the canal's adversaries"; he said the total excavation for a canal at sea-level "definitely need not exceed 75 million cubic metres": he said his firm "estimated that costs could be reduced from 168 million dollars to 102 million": and, most remarkable of all, he said that the slopes of the Culebra Cut could be set back not at forty-five degrees but vertically—"Do we not in Europe often see quarries a hundred and eighty feet deep with their sides completely vertical? Why shouldn't the same be possible in Panama?" On each of these fundamental points Couvreux was utterly wrong—indeed one can only agree with Bunau-Varilla (who was subsequently in charge of excavation in the Cut) that "it would be difficult to condense into fewer words a greater number of errors". Yet Couvreux was typical of the "practical men" in whom de Lesseps and the public put their trust. These men had triumphed at Suez. There seemed in 1881 no reason why they shouldn't triumph at Panama, where the canal—as de Lesseps never lost the opportunity of pointing out—need be only half as long.

So the first of the French engineers arrived on the isthmus in a glow of roseate optimism. Nor was their optimism immediately dispelled. For they, like de Lesseps before them, had their first glimpse of Panama at the most favourable time of the year, the start of the dry season.

There had been virtually no rain for a month when on 29th

January the *Lafayette* hove-to beside the rickety quay in Limon Bay. Aboard her were forty engineers, led by Armand Reclus who had previously surveyed the isthmus with Wyse. Several of the engineers brought their wives to a land which had been described in France as "among the healthiest regions in the world"; and although they were somewhat dismayed by the heat and the formidable nature of the jungle, their early impressions were not unfavourable.

The task of this vanguard was to stake out the line of the cutting, and this they did in little more than a month, helped by the extremely accurate surveys made the previous spring by de Lesseps' scientific committee. In February they were joined by Gaston Blanchet, senior representative of Couvreux and Hersent, an able and conscientious engineer whose reports in the months to come were models of lucidity. Under Blanchet's guidance a force of native labourers set to work with machete and axe to clear the line of the canal; and by 1st May a ribbon of open ground some fifty to sixty feet wide had been hacked and levelled from coast to coast. This was a considerable feat; for, to quote one of the engineers in charge, "the heat was oppressive, the jungle so thickly matted that one could see only a few yards in any direction, and of the sky overhead there was seldom a trace".

Meanwhile the terminals at Colon and Panama were transformed from sleepy backwaters to bustling ports.

> Colon [wrote a correspondent in the May issue of the *Bulletin*] is no longer recognisable. In its harbour is a constant coming and going of steamers bringing in technicians and engineers. It is easy for everyone to find work, but not so easy to find lodgings ... A few weeks ago there was only one hotel; now there are three, and an excellent restaurant with a French chef from New York; but even these are nothing like enough.

In Panama, the Company bought the Grand Hotel in Cathedral Plaza, which it converted into its administrative headquarters; while sites were cleared for intermediate towns at Gatun and Emperador. By midsummer some two hundred French engineers and eight hundred native labourers were at work on the three preliminaries to construction: surveying the route and its environs in detail; erecting working quarters and hospitals; and testing and ordering equipment.

Anyone today who studies the maps, graphs and statistics pieced together by Blanchet and his surveyors cannot fail to be impressed by their thoroughness and accuracy. This is confirmed by Bishop: "the

French left an extremely valuable collection of maps, surveys, drawings and records. All their work of this kind was done in an admirable manner and proved of the greatest use." Witness also Goethals: "Whenever I wanted guidance on a specific point I consulted the French records. They were first rate." The surveying was carried out by Blanchet himself and a small group of engineers, never more than thirty of them, sometimes less than a dozen. On the purely physical level their achievements were amazing; for carrying heavy plane-tables, theodolites and tachymeters they hacked their way through literally thousands of miles of unmapped and complex jungle; while technically the excellence of their work is proved by the fact that even today the ordnance maps of the isthmus are based on the observations they took.

They concentrated first on delineating the line of the cutting: above-ground mapping contours which were accurate to within ten centimetres, and below-ground sinking test-wells to the depth of eighty feet. Data gleaned from the latter amazed them. For every well told a different story: layer after layer of breccia, limestone, coral, carb, sand, gravel, volcanic lava, argillite or clay, all piled higgledy-piggledy in random drifts and faulted planes—it was their first hint of the heart-ache which lay in store for them in the Culebra Cut. When Blanchet had surveyed the line of the canal itself, he turned his attention to what he began to realise would prove the heart of the problem: the rivers which emptied into it. The course of these rivers had been plotted with reasonable accuracy by de Sosa, Reclus and Wyse; what hadn't been plotted was their propensity to flood. By the spring of 1882, however, observation posts had been set up on the Chagres, Trinidad, Obispo and Rio Grande; these were equipped with fluviographs, and it wasn't long before alarming statistics were reaching the Company's headquarters in the Plaza: statistics which showed rivers rising twenty feet in as many hours and their rate of discharge increasing overnight from 3,000 cubic feet per second to 60,000. The chief offender was the Chagres. And in the autumn of 1882 Blanchet and a party of twelve surveyors set out to map its headwaters.

It was a reconnaissance shrewdly aimed. But in the hills between the Chilibre and the Gatuneille, Blanchet felt one evening unnaturally cold; next morning his face was flushed and his body damp with sweat; he had contracted malaria. A lesser man would have given the survey up; but Blanchet struggled on, plagued by heat, near-incessant rain and recurrent bouts of shivering. By the end of the month the survey was finished. But Blanchet was dead: one of the first of the many who (to quote Bunau-Varilla) "as surely as those who fought at Lodi or Marengo laid down their lives for France".

And the tragedy was that the efforts of Blanchet and his surveyors were largely in vain. More than fifty per cent of the cutting which they delineated with such care was subsequently submerged, the dam which they planned was resited, and the channel which they surveyed through Limon Bay was dug elsewhere. Time, new techniques and the abandonment of a canal at sea-level made much of their work of no more than academic value. But they have their memorial: a whole series of maps of the isthmus, which are recognised today as models of the surveyor's craft.

In the sphere of building, the work of the French was equally sound but even more ephemeral.

Two stories have grown up about de Lesseps' housing programme: the first that the labourers' quarters were "shoddy, ramshackle and ill-suited to the tropics", the second that they were "unreasonably luxurious [and that] the architects never spent one thousand francs if two were available". Both stories can't be true; and both in fact are a long way wide of the mark; for in the light of the medical knowledge of the time, the quarters erected by the French were as good as it was possible to make them.

Negro workers were housed in barracks, which were built on low concrete piers, to counter flooding and the ravages of ants. The buildings were constructed of well-seasoned timber and roofed with corrugated iron; they were waterproof, well-ventilated and contained fifty bunks apiece arranged in two tiers. There is no evidence to suggest that the labour force were in any way dissatisfied with them.

The houses of the whites were well-sited, sensibly designed and soundly built: witness the subsequent reports of Lieutenant Kimball of the U.S.N. and Armand Rousseau of the Parisian Department of Public Works: "the buildings are as convenient and comfortable as conditions allow" and are "constructed with proper regard for comfort and health". Indeed in almost every respect the French buildings compare favourably with those erected twenty years later by the Americans. They were not, however, screened. For no one in the 1880s suspected the connection between mosquitoes and malaria and yellow fever. And because of this one omission, the quarters which were designed and assembled with so much care proved in the event to be little more than elegant death traps.

As for the French hospitals, they were "without doubt the finest and most perfect ever set up in the tropics"—such at any rate was the opinion of the Canadian doctor Wolfred Nelson who was resident on the isthmus at the time.

De Lesseps may have genuinely believed that Panama was among the healthiest regions in the world, but specialists in tropical medicine knew otherwise; and in January 1881 Dr. Companyo, a veteran of Suez, arrived in Colon with a competent and well-qualified staff. Within a year they had erected a complex of hospitals in Ancon (a suburb of Panama) and another in the outskirts of Colon overlooking Limon Bay; smaller dispensaries were later established along the canal, and a convalescent home on an island in Panama Bay. The terminal hospitals were magnificent establishments—carefully sited, built in accordance with the latest medical theories, and staffed by skilled doctors and devoted nurses. Gorgas described the Ancon complex as "a very much better institution than any (comparable) hospital in America ... it consisted of sixteen detached wards, theatres and living quarters, the buildings being light, airy and surrounded by tropical gardens of great beauty." Unfortunately these magnificent buildings (like the barracks) proved a death trap. For they too were unscreened; and malaria-and-fever-carrying-mosquitoes, not only flew through them at will, but were actively if unwittingly encouraged to breed in the surrounding gardens, where thousands of pottery rings full of water protected the plants from ants but at the same time provided an ideal resting place for the ovipositing *Aëdes Calopus*. "Probably," wrote Gorgas, "if the French had been trying to propagate yellow fever they could not (unwittingly) have provided conditions better adapted for this purpose." It is tragic that so much careful and devoted work should have been negated through lack of medical knowledge—a lack which was of course universal in the 1880s.

The French had better fortune with their equipment, much of which survived the interregnum and was used by the Americans right through to 1915.

It was fashionable at one time to believe that in ordering equipment de Lesseps' engineers were guilty of careless lavishness—"Everything imaginable was sent [to the isthmus] from hairpins to grand pianos, including ten thousand snow-shovels* to a land where snow never falls" (Helen Nicolay). This is myth. The truth is that the work at Panama was both complex and novel, and a great deal of experimenting was unavoidable. To start with Couvreux and Hersent drew on their experience at Suez, ordering the type of strong lightweight machinery which had done wonders in shifting

---

*This story is typical of the ill-informed criticisms which it was fashionable at one time to level at the French. In fact, the number of shovels ordered was not 10,000 but 1,050; and they were intended not for shovelling snow, but for scooping ash out of the boilers of the steam-shovels—for which work they were ideally suited.

the sands of Bitter Lake. When this broke down in the heavy clay of the Chagres Valley, they not unnaturally began to experiment by trial and error. And if, to quote Gerstle Mack, their

> programme sometimes appeared to involve more error than trial, most of the mistakes were due to inexperience rather than ineptitude, [and] it would be grossly unfair to ascribe the shifting policies of the French company to sheer stupidity. The construction of the Panama canal was an engineering work unprecedented in scale and altogether exceptional in conditions, and it was only to be expected that various methods of attack would be tried and discarded in the search for a solution. When the United States government undertook the task it too fumbled and shilly-shallied for some time before it developed an organisation that worked efficiently.

Indeed, in their first year on the isthmus the French amassed far more and far better equipment than the Americans in theirs (see table below); and it depends perhaps on one's temperament whether one condones more readily the excesses of Blanchet or the parsimony of Wallace.

Equipment ordered and used by the French in their first 18 months of excavation (1881/2)		*Equipment ordered and used by the Americans in their first 18 months of excavation (1904/5)*
Steam-shovels	32	8
Flat-cars and trucks	3,300	560
Locomotives	49	35
Drills	169	390
Dredges	14	7
Boats, barges, tugs, lighters, etc.	92	48
Miles of railway track	80	6
Pumps	96	–

Yet excesses is perhaps too harsh a word. There was, without doubt, the occasional spree of ill-advised spending and the occasional speculator making a kill; but bearing in mind the technology of the 1880s the French equipment was, by and large, as good as could then be brought together—there is not much point in condemning Couvreux and Hersent for working with lightweight machinery when they used the heaviest that was available at the time.

There is, however, one criticism which can with justification be levelled at the French engineers: their equipment was too diversified.

The Americans succeeded in building a canal largely because they were able in the end to standardise both equipment and technique—

they simply dug out the soil by steam-shovel, loaded it onto flat-cars and towed the flat-cars away via the Panama Railroad. The French failed to build a canal, at least in part, because even after five years of experiment they were still excavating and disposing of the soil by a great variety of methods: by bucket-dredge, suction-dredge, shovel, elevator, cableway and even by hand; they then loaded this soil onto one of eleven different types of flat-car running on one of six different gauges of track. They were forever modifying and adapting their plant, until hardly two machines were alike. Some of the methods they devised were ingenious and technically brilliant; they worked far longer hours than the Americans under far worse conditions; they performed almost unbelievable feats of endurance in a cause they believed to be noble, and on parts of the canal their achievements were heroic. Yet they were never able to knit their efforts into a homogenous whole. This was largely due to the fact that after 1882 (when Couvreux and Hersent withdrew) the work of construction was split up among a series of sub-contractors, each of whom had his own ideas on how to cope with his own particular section of the canal. This in turn led to further diversification, the evil effects of which can be seen especially clearly in the layout of track.

The track initially put down by Couvreux and Hersent was Belgian rail, 19.7 feet long, $4\frac{7}{8}$ inches high, and $3\frac{3}{4}$ inches wide at the base; it weighed fifty-six pounds and was laid on unballasted sleepers without tie-plates. Such track might have been suitable for marshalling yards in Europe, but it proved inadequate for carrying heavy loads through the tropic rain forest, tearing out or subsiding on even the gentlest curve. Couvreux and Hersent were well aware of this; but they were unwilling to lay new track until they gained control of the Panama Railroad, and by the time this came about they were thinking of withdrawing under an escape clause in their contract. Track therefore soon became the responsibility of individual firms, each of whom was only interested in its own section of the canal. The result was a multiplicity of layouts, lacking uniformity and overall plan. Chief Engineer Wallace may have been exaggerating when he said years later that, "in the French cars the wheel gauge varied with almost every individual car"; but there is no doubting the sober words of the railroad engineer M. Raggi who worked for the French Company for almost a decade: "The chief difficulty facing us was supplying our excavators regularly with a sufficient number of cars. A large percentage of lost time was due to 'waiting for cars'; and this in turn was due to the poor condition of the track."

What was true of track was true to a lesser degree of other

equipment: locomotives, cars, steam-shovels, cableways and drills: they were all too diversified. Only in the field of dredging could the French equipment be described as ideally suited to the work it was expected to do—witness Goethals: "the French dredges were excellent. In this sphere alone did their equipment approximate ours." Dredges work as individual units; and it is perhaps indicative of the French assault on the isthmus that it was this highly individual field in which they achieved the best results.

By the end of 1881, little construction had been attempted on the canal itself, but a sound start had been made on preliminaries. The line of the cut had been cleared and surveyed, and research was under way on the inflowing rivers. Living quarters had sprung up at selected sites—notably Colon, Gatun and Emperador—and the hospitals were finished "except for a lick of paint". Equipment was piling up in the assembly sheds, and the strength of the working force, both unskilled labourers from the West Indies and skilled technicians from France, was increasing according to plan. In short, 1881 was a good year for the French. They avoided the pitfalls of bureaucratic red-tape and divided control which later bedevilled the Americans; they had few labour problems; and there is every indication that workers and technicians alike felt that the Company was taking good care of them, and that as the trees were felled and the houses rose and plans took shape on the drawing boards they experienced a sense of exhilaration and achievement. Nature, it appeared, was bowing yet again to the assault of Man.

Appearances, however, were deceptive; and even in 1881 the writing, for those who had eyes to see, was on the wall. At the end of the year, for example, there appeared in the *Bulletin* a letter from "an anxious shareholder". The *Bulletin* dismissed this letter with a mixture of condescension and disdain; but in fact the unnamed shareholder hit on precisely the four points which were to prove the Company's undoing. "In France," he wrote, "an average of three years' work is considered essential before a major construction project is put under way. Is it wise, in unknown Panama, to embark on the greatest ever project after only a single year of research?" He went on to query, as a corollary to this, the wisdom of a canal at sea-level. He also accused the *Bulletin* of "vagueness, evasiveness and lack of knowledge on matters of a technical nature". Finally he pointed out that in spite of the small size of the working force there had already been more than thirty deaths from malaria and yellow fever. The *Bulletin*'s reply to this very sensible analysis of danger is indicative of those qualities of vagueness and evasiveness of which the shareholder complained:

We know you have confidence in us [the editors wrote] and you have expressed this confidence in the most tangible way, by giving us your money. If we say there is no illness on the isthmus, this is because there is none, and anyone who asserts the contrary is a gossipmonger who is merely trying to undermine your confidence so that he can take over himself. Remember Suez!

Remember Suez! How many times in the years to come was this nostalgic *cri de coeur* used to boost morale. But without justification. For Suez and Panama were not comparable, and triumphs past were no guarantee of triumphs to come.

This, however, was not generally appreciated in 1882—the year which saw the gradual change-over from preliminary study to actual construction.

On 20th January the first spadeful of earth was dug out of *la grande tranchée* (the actual line of the canal) at Emperador; and within ten days a cutting 250 feet long, fifteen feet wide and six feet deep had been excavated by steam-shovel, bucket-dredge and hand. The work was easier than had been expected; for the earth was soft, and on the few occasions when the working party hit rock, this was quickly dynamited.

The next site to get under way was at Colon, where a great earthen platform, sixty acres in extent was pushed into Limon Bay. By the end of April this had been encased in a stone wall so that ships could tie up alongside, and work was started on dredging a deepwater-channel to the sea.

By midsummer excavation was under way at Gatun, Gamboa, Bas Obispo, Culebra and Paraiso, and a start had been made on the terminal channels in both Panama and Limon Bay.

All this made good news for the Company at its first Annual General Meeting which was held on 29th June, 1882.

This meeting was a personal triumph for de Lesseps. Never had *le grand Français* been in more ebullient form, enthusing over his Company's many and very real achievements, light-heartedly refuting its handful of critics and in the end inspiring the shareholders to give him an overwhelming vote of confidence. It was, however, the last carefree meeting he was to hold; for already there were signs of two of the shoals on which his enterprise was eventually to founder: disease and the proliferation of contracts.

Disease was not considered a serious problem in 1882. There had, it is true, been eighty-five deaths among 1,150 employees during the first twelve months of construction, but de Lesseps claimed that this was a lower mortality-rate than on the average work-site in Europe.

However, during the second year of construction British and American journalists began to paint an increasingly gloomy picture of an isthmus ravaged by disease. There is seldom smoke without fire; and it seems clear that even at this early stage malaria was rife and yellow fever very much in the offing. To this undoubted fact, however, the French authorities turned a blind eye, the official attitude being summed up in the *Bulletin:* "We sent a well-qualified doctor to the isthmus and this is his report: 'I certify that the town of Panama and the port of Colon are exempt from yellow fever, smallpox and any other contagious illness. I base this declaration on information gained from the most reliable sources as well as from research and personal observation'." Truth has many faces—there certainly *was* malaria; there certainly wasn't smallpox; yellow fever isn't contagious. Those in Paris may have genuinely believed that reports in the English-speaking press were maliciously exaggerated; but those on the isthmus, as they saw their friends being carried one by one into but never out of the hospitals, must have smelt death with every shift of the tropic wind.

As for contracts, these were soon put out to international tender because of the defection of Couvreux and Hersent.

Couvreux and Hersent are something of an enigma. They entered the fray with almost light-hearted optimism, agreeing to construct the canal for 512 million francs within seven years; for eighteen months they worked on the preliminary studies with meticulous care and efficiency; then, quite suddenly, they withdrew. It was a turning point in the history of the canal; and one wonders what prompted so sudden a change of heart? The truth is hard to pin down; but the basic fact seems to be that Couvreux and Hersent realised that the Company had failed during its preparatory period to produce a plan which got to grips with the isthmus's two most obdurate technical problems—the propensity of the Chagres to flood, and the tendency of the canal banks (especially in the Culebra Cut) to slide in. De Lesseps, for example, promised frequently and glibly that the Chagres was going to be tamed, but he never once said *how;* while even in 1885 he still clung to the belief that the sides of the Cut could be sloped back as steeply as forty-five degrees—whereas in fact they had to be sloped at less than twenty degrees. These were fundamental errors. And their significance is brought home by the words, thirty years later, of the greatest of all engineers to work on the isthmus, John F. Stevens: "only an engineer can fully appreciate the far reaching effects of a mistake during the preparatory period. For a mistake then, as to a general principle or as to the relationship of plant to work, is a basic mistake and can never be fully overcome." Couvreux and Hersent were experienced engineers; they saw the mistake that was being made; and they took the view that discretion was the better part of valour.

At the time, their withdrawal (under a perfectly legal escape clause in their contract) assumed the guise of altruism; for they wrote to de Lesseps expressing their willingness to undertake the rest of the work on terms to be agreed, but pointing out that such an arrangement "would be burdensome to the Company", since in their opinion the system of offering the work to small subcontractors had given good results during the trial period and ought to be extended; their continued employment (they said) as general contractors drawing a fixed percentage on all sums paid, would only be a needless expense. De Lesseps accepted this withdrawal with apparent gratitude—"I appreciate the value of your renunciation and render you all our thanks."

Couvreux and Hersent's actions were, however, interpreted later in a far less favourable light: *vide* the report of the *Chambre des Députés* of 1893:

> This firm exhibited great ingenuity in abandoning their contract, and disguising their action under the cloak of a desire to aid and oblige the Company. The truth is that during the trial period they had been able to form a shrewd idea of the difficulties which lay ahead, but were unwilling to undermine the Company's position by a frank admission of their motives.

Vide, too, Bunau-Varilla, who was chief engineer in the vital years 1885/86: "The responsibility of MM. Couvreux and Hersent is immense. Nor did they redeem their presumption [in taking the job on] by sacrificing themselves to the enterprise. They completely deserted the battlefield . . . leaving the works without a precise programme." When the French Company eventually went bankrupt and Panamist became a word of abuse, efforts were made to discredit Couvreux and Hersent even further: their fees, critics said, had been exorbitant, and why had Hersent been retained as a consultant long after his firm had withdrawn? Chicanery there undoubtedly was among some of the later contractors; but there is not the slightest evidence that Couvreux and Hersent were in any way guilty of sharp or dishonest practice. They received for their work from March 1881 to December 1882 one million two hundred thousand francs net, certainly not an excessive sum for the work they performed; while there is no reason to doubt the sincerity of Hersent's reply when he was asked to justify his subsequent remuneration—

"I gave the Company useful advice, and I am convinced it was well worth the 60,000 francs I received for it; I resigned when I thought my co-operation no longer helpful." Couvreux and Hersent's contribution to building the canal may have been inglorious: it was never in any way dishonourable.

Indeed it was not thought, in 1882, that the proliferation of contracts which stemmed from their withdrawal, would be anything but beneficial. For on 1st December the *Bulletin* wrote as follows: "The work of boring a canal through the isthmus is about to embark on its most critical phase, that of constructing the channel itself. The contracts signed during the past year mark the beginning of this second phase which now succeeds the period of studies and installations." All this is entirely in keeping with what the Commission originally had in mind. The *Bulletin* goes on to say that excavation was already under way at the following sites—Colon, Gatun, Gorgona, Gamboa, Bas Obispo, Emperador, Culebra, Paraiso and Panama; and that initial digging indicated the work would be easier than anticipated because the amount of hard rock (and hence of dynamiting) was less. Then came the key passage:

> And so, less than two years after the Company's formation, the working force is in position all along the line of the canal, the sites are open, and most of the cubage to be excavated has been allocated to a series of different contractors—Colombians, Americans, French, etc.—all of whom have proved themselves in their own country in the carrying out of great public works, and all of whom have undertaken to finish their particular task within a specific period. When these contractors have dug to a certain depth along the whole line of the canal, the rest of the work will be easy.

It sounds delightfully simple. The agreements made with the various contractors were, however, often carelessly worded and full of ambiguities and loopholes. Several of the French firms, inspired by patriotic fervour, worked heroically to fulfil the near-impossible tasks they had been set. But several of the American, British and Dutch firms, when the going got tough, exhibited no little ingenuity in extracting from the Company the maximum of money for the minimum of work.

Looking back, it is easy to say that the French ought to have foreseen the danger of subcontracting work to a series of individual firms. Yet this was the system which had worked at Suez; and there seemed, to those in Paris, no reason why it shouldn't equally well work at Panama. Those on the isthmus, however, had their doubts: for they, by 1882, had begun to appreciate the vital fact which de Lesseps seems never to have grasped: that Suez and Panama were as different as chalk from cheese.

Gerstle Mack puts the case very clearly:

The experimental nature of the work was something that de Lesseps failed to foresee. He had envisaged another Suez—in fact an easier Suez since the experience gained in Egypt could be applied to the American isthmus. Yet the similarities between the two projects, upon which he insisted, were . . . less apparent than the differences, which he refused to recognise or at least to admit. In one feature only—total length—did a comparison favour Panama: the Suez waterway extended about 100 miles from sea to sea and required some eighty miles of artificial excavation while the Panama canal measured less than fifty miles. In every other respect Panama presented far more difficult conditions. The maximum elevation on the Suez line was but fifty feet above sea-level, at Panama 330 feet. At Suez most of the digging took place in sand and soft earth; at Panama much hard rock was encountered, and slides vastly increased the total amount of excavation. The problem of the Chagres River with its erratic floods had no counterpart at Suez. Although labour had to be imported, housed and cared for at both places, Suez lay much nearer large centres of population, and the prevailing wage was lower. Both regions suffered from excessively high temperatures, but the dry desert heat of Africa had no such enervating effects as the moist sultriness of the tropical jungle. Lastly the deadly fevers of Panama were almost unknown at Suez . . . It soon became evident that experience at Suez was more of a drawback than an asset at Panama. Almost everything had to be unlearned.

And in this last sentence lies the basic reason for the failure of the *Compagnie Universelle*. For de Lesseps was too old to unlearn.

Long after his seventieth birthday he remained the most charming, alert and gifted of men. Young at heart and blessed with a robust constitution, his physical and mental vigour were phenomenal. But in one respect age had crept up on him. He lacked mental elasticity. He was still able to shift his ground on small issues—say in manipulating a meeting of shareholders; but on the big issues he had made up his mind. And there was no shifting him. He had built a sea-level canal at Suez. He intended to build a sea-level canal at Panama. And nothing on earth would persuade him to settle for less. He could never bring himself to admit the simple truth expressed by one of his engineers in a letter home to his wife: "The work at Panama is almost entirely new work, and very different from the sands of Suez."

4

"ONLY THE DRUNK AND THE DISSIPATED WILL DIE OF YELLOW FEVER"

It was alleged by Bunau-Varilla that Couvreux and Hersent "deserted the battlefield . . . leaving the works without a precise programme". This is exaggeration; for the contractors stayed on the isthmus until preparations were virtually complete, and other firms had been awarded contracts for excavation along the greater part of the canal. What *is* true is that Couvreux and Hersent themselves carried out little work which wasn't strictly investigatory or preparatory, as is clear from the February (1883) issue of the *Bulletin:*

> Work along the proposed line of the canal has now reached the following state:
> At Colon the earth platform has been completed with soil excavated from Monkey Hill, and this platform is already covered with warehouses and streaked with railway track. Dredges have cleared 6,900 cubic metres of silt from the approaches to Folks River and dumped it far out to sea. The goal here is for a channel fifty feet wide and eleven feet deep, so that the enormous dredges of Huerne, Slaven and Co. can be towed inshore of Telfers Island to start work on the canal itself.
> Between Folks River and Tiger Hill (Gatun) the land has been completely cleared of forest and the line of *la grande tranchée* staked out. Borings and test wells are completed, and this region can therefore be put at the disposal of the contractors who have undertaken to excavate six miles of channel within three years at a cost of 1-franc-50 per cubic metre (a far lower figure than was originally estimated by the Technical Commission). The first of the three great dredges to be used by these contractors has already left the United States for Colon, and the others will arrive in April; these dredges have been designed to excavate 3,000 cubic metres of silt per day.
> Between Tiger Hill and Matachin the line of the canal will keep as close as possible to the centre of the Chagres valley so that digging can take place in the lowest of the alluvial beds which have been carefully surveyed; in this region the canal will cut the river a great many times but will cross the railway only twice . . .

Another section of the Company has cleared land for diverting the rivers Chagres and Trinidad in the loop above Gatun; this work is ready to be carried out by the Company's third and fourth dredges now being assembled in Limon Bay ... Studies concerning the damming of the Chagres (at Gamboa) have been continued without interruption; surveys and soundings had been made of the site; the hills of the upper Chagres valley, which will form the walls of a reservoir, have been triangulated; and fluviographs are helping to gauge the flood-potential of rivers emptying into the reservoir which will eventually be formed in the upper valley.

Between Matachin and Paraiso, in the hills of the continental divide, excavation-ditches for study have been opened up along the proposed line of the cutting, and the ground has been staked out among individual contractors. At Gorgona unloading bays have been constructed and pilot track laid for the first of the steam-shovels. At Bas Obispo, the highest hillocks have been "topped", and a forfeit clause [for not completing the work on time] has been written into the contractor's agreement. At Emperador the work is especially well advanced; the preliminary ditches have all been opened up, and a contract has been signed for shifting 2,500,000 cubic metres—this will entail digging out *la grande tranchée* to its full width and a depth of seventeen feet. At Culebra too the Company has been able to negotiate a favourable contract for the whole of the excavation.

Between Paraiso and the Pacific, the Company has considered the several plans for an outlet into Panama Bay. We believe it important that the final choice of a route is not delayed any longer, so that work in clearing can begin during the present dry season.

(It was finally agreed in March that the outlet should be via La Boca and the valley of the Rio Grande, finishing about a third of a mile to the south of the river mouth and continuing into the sea until level with the Island of Perico.)

This summary confirms that by January 1883 excavation had either started or was about to start along virtually the whole canal. At this vital moment Couvreux and Hersent withdrew, and the Company was obliged to appoint a new director general. The man they chose was Jules Dingler, a forty-seven-year-old engineer who had served with distinction as Chief of Bridges and Roads in France, but who had no first-hand knowledge of the isthmus. The wonder is not that he failed, but that he came as close as he did to success.

Dingler has never been accorded the recognition he deserves; for in the eyes of the world he was a failure. He was also a whipping boy for the Company's enemies, who in the witch-hunt that followed defeat were ready to believe even the most unlikely calumnies. Hardly a book on the isthmus contains his photograph, and in several he is mentioned only in a footnote. Yet Dingler was a first-class engineer, a sound administrator, and a man of courage and loyalty who for more than two years served the Company devotedly under the most harrowing circumstances.

He arrived on the isthmus at the end of February, accompanied by Charles de Lesseps, and after the usual round of receptions he set about restoring order and confidence, both of which had been shaken by Couvreux and Hersent's defection. His first step was to inspect sites and study reports; he then submitted a detailed scheme for a sea-level canal to the Superior Advisory Commission in Paris. Much to his gratification, his scheme was approved at once and *in toto*. This was an important step, for it gave the contractors an overall plan towards which they could work; and indeed if we accept the supposition that the canal had to be at sea-level, it is hard to see how Dingler's scheme could have been bettered—certainly it was more realistic than that of the Technical Commission of 1880, for it reduced the slope of the cutting and raised the estimate of excavation from ninety-three million cubic yards to 157 million. Dingler had no illusions as to the magnitude of the task he was faced with.

His second step was to order sufficient equipment to undertake the work, and the table below shows that as regards quantity at least he did everything possible to provide his working force with adequate machinery:

Equipment in Use

	1882	1883	1884	1885
Steam-shovels	32	72	79	99
Flat-cars and trucks	3,300	6,119	8,961	10,461
Locomotives	49	92	122	147
Drills	169	194	206	206
Dredges	14	20	21	34
Boats, barges, etc.	92	144	320	357
Miles of track	80	170	260	260
Pumps	96	185	256	324

Equipment was bought by the Company and rented out at a remarkably low rate to the various contractors. This was a sound idea, for it enabled even the smaller firms to use top-class machinery which they might otherwise have been unable to afford. It did, however, lead to administrative difficulties—frequent payments, frequent inspections and frequent suits in the Colombian courts: *vide* Dr. Nelson, "there is enough bureaucratic work (in this system) to furnish a dozen first-class republics with officials for all their departments. The expenditure is something colossal." It should, however, be borne in mind that Nelson was a Francophobe.

Dingler's final step was to separate the work of construction into three divisions; and by considering these one by one we can see the problems he faced and the techniques he used to overcome them.

Limon Bay and the Lower Reaches of the Chagres
This was the largest division, and constructionwise the easiest. It extended from mile 0 at the earth platform at Colon, to mile 22 at Tabernilla. It was under the command of M. Clavenad, a specialist in dredging. And dredging, in the years ahead, accounted in this division for more than eighty per cent of the excavation.

The Atlantic entrance to de Lesseps' canal was beside the earth platform at Colon. This platform in other words had a dual purpose: to afford a sheltered mooring for ships, and to protect the mouth of the channel from silting up. It was massive in 1883, but Dingler enlarged it still further to provide seven deep-water berths; he also modernised the port's quays, warehouses and railway facilities, building what was virtually a new town on the shore of Manzanillo Bay. This work was pushed steadily forward throughout 1883 and 1884. The building programme however, was never able to keep pace with the vast influx of equipment pouring in from Europe and the United States, and before long wharves and platforms were strewn with a conglomeration of machinery, some of it discarded as unsatisfactory and some waiting month after month to be carried inland by the overloaded railway.

As for Colon itself, Bishop describes it with pious horror:

> The two ocean cities, Colon and Panama, were the permanent abode of disease, for they were without even the most elementary provisions for health-protection. They had no sewers, no water supply, no sanitary appliances. Their only scavengers were the huge flocks of buzzards which circled constantly above them . . . Colon was a collection of wooden buildings harbouring a population which contained more of the dregs of humanity than any other settlement of its size on the globe . . . [It] had a single main street, running along the waterfront, which was composed almost entirely of places for gambling, drinking and accompanying vices; and these diversions were in full progress day and night with such abandon as to make the town uninhabitable for decent persons. It was a veritable sink of iniquity.

Bishop goes on to deplore the superfluity of wine:

> Nothing like the supply of liquor which the French poured out upon the isthmus was ever seen before or since. It was well nigh unlimited in quantity and was sold to everybody at the prices at which it had been bought wholesale in France. Champagne, especially, was so low in price that it flowed like water ... The consequences were as deplorable as they were inevitable: the ingredients for a bacchanalian orgy being supplied, the orgy naturally followed.

What Bishop fails to make allowance for is that wine, on the isthmus, was a great deal safer to drink than water; also it is a Frenchman's natural beverage, and quantities which the Americans regarded as excessive were to Dingler's engineers no more than a pleasant modicum. Also there was another side to the picture—to quote de Lesseps: "[we] intend to open at Colon, assembly rooms provided with books, periodicals and various indoor games where our employees can gather in the evenings and during the siesta hour, thus strengthening the bonds of friendship which turn our staff into one large [one almost expects him to add 'and happy'!] family." Bishop and de Lesseps in fact saw Colon through glasses of a different tint; both, however, would have agreed that the port was sleazy, humid and a fountain-head of disease.

Excavation on the canal proper started in February 1883, when a pair of incongruous-looking machines pushed past the earth platform and into the mangrove swamps at the mouth of Folks River. They were small sixty-horse-power elevator dredges, with an endless chain of buckets, nine cubic feet in capacity, operated by sprocket-chain drive. They discharged the soil they dug up into hopper barges which carried it laboriously out to sea and dumped it through discharge vents in their hulls. Within a couple of months a channel ten feet deep and fifty feet wide had been extended past the mouth of Folks River and into the swamps inshore of Telfers Island. And it was here, in April, that the excavation of Dingler's canal started in earnest.

The dredges which started it were the gargantuan *Comte de Lesseps*, *Prosper Huerne* and *Nathan Appleton*. These formidable machines belonged to the only contractors who worked continuously on the isthmus throughout the whole regime of the *Compagnie Universelle*—Huerne, Slaven and Co., of San Francisco.

The Slaven brothers were Canadians who had settled in California about the middle of the century. They had little experience in dredging but were shrewd businessmen, and they submitted their bid to excavate in Limon Bay "with an audacity akin to inspiration";

for they promised to undertake the work at the flat rate of twenty-three cents per cubic yard. Since this was far less than the price suggested by the Technical Commission, the French company were delighted, and speedily negotiated a contract. Eighteen months later, in the spring of 1883, Slaven's three great dredges were towed into Limon Bay. They were the largest, heaviest and most complex pieces of machinery ever seen on the isthmus—120 feet long, thirty feet wide and eight feet in draught; their ladder was built in two sections, their belt-transmission was automatic, and the silt they excavated was funnelled into vast chutes (180 feet long) which dumped the debris well clear of the working site. To quote Tracy Robinson they were "so nearly automatic that one of them could be operated by a dozen men" (see Figure 4 opposite). They at once set to work on the mud flats inshore of Telfers Island; and to start with they kept pace with or even exceeded their promised 3,000 cubic metres a day. However, as the channel they dug progressed inland, from mud flats to mangrove swamps, from mangrove swamps to coastal plain, and finally up through the gentle gradient of the Mindi Hills, so the technical difficulties of excavation increased. In 1884 and again in 1885 the Company reduced its yardage and increased its prices. For although the dredges' long chutes for discharging soil worked well enough by gravity when the land on either side of the cut was low, as the land grew progressively higher and the slope of the chutes progressively nearer the horizontal, it became necessary to use pumps and hoppers to clear the excavated soil. Costs snowballed. Because of loose drafting in the original contract, however, no provision had been made for equitable adjustment to cover such a contingency, and this soon led to acrimonious disputes between Company and contractors.

Altogether Huerne, Slaven and Co. (later known as the American Contracting and Dredging Company) excavated about seventeen million cubic metres from the Atlantic end of the canal; for this they were paid 70,812,896 francs. There are two ways of looking at this. The French accused the Americans of overcharging and chicanery (though just how enormous Huerne Slaven's profits actually were the French never discovered, for the Slaven brothers prudently kept their books in the United States!). The American Company on the other hand, pointed out that they, alone among more than two hundred contractors, completed their allotted work on time, and in fact excavated very nearly as much as all the other contractors put together—albeit in the easiest part of the canal. Both arguments are tenable. And perhaps the investigating committee of the Chamber of Deputies hit the nail on the head when they subsequently castigated

Figure 4. The Slaven Brothers' *Comte de Lesseps*, the largest of the French dredges

the *Compagnie Universelle* for signing an agreement which was so full of loopholes and ambiguities—"what sort of contract is this, which leaves room for so many disputes?"

In 1883, however, and indeed throughout most of 1884, there was little hint of the trouble to come. These were halcyon years for the French. And as Huerne Slaven's enormous dredges bit steadily through the silt of Limon Bay, Clavenad had every reason to be satisfied.

The position in the lower reaches of the Chagres was not so easy to define. For in this inland section of Clavenad's division progress ebbed and flowed according to the level of the river. For longish periods excavation would be rapid; then the freshet of a couple of hours would undo the work of weeks.

The French never solved the problem of the Chagres. To start with, having no previous statistics to refer to, they were buoyed up by the hope that the river's freshets were, in the words of one of their engineers, "exceptional, and hardly likely to be repeated another year." Not until the catastrophic floods of December 1885 did they at last realise that containing the river was a *sine qua non* of success. Before this they merely nibbled at the problem (digging diversion channels and bolstering banks at the two dozen places where the river crossed the canal); and indeed they only achieved the success they did because of the ingenuity of their contractors and the excellence of their dredges.

Clavenad divided work in the valley among some dozen contractors. Typical of these were Artigue and Sonderegger, a small and virtually unknown firm who agreed to complete a mile and a half of *la grande tranchée* between Bohio and Soldado. They planned to excavate two million cubic yards, completing the canal to its full width (72 feet) and depth (29.5 feet) within two and a half years, and for this work they rented two dredges and some twenty subsidiary craft—mostly hoppers, scows, tugs and floating drills.

Their dredges were of the thirty-six-bucket, endless-chain variety—typical of those which did such sterling work first for the French and subsequently for the Americans. By the end of Dingler's regime more than twenty of these dredges were in operation (see Figure 5 opposite); they did the bulk of excavation in the valleys of the Chagres and Rio Grande, and their statistics are worth recording. They had rectangular box-type hulls, 112 feet long, 30 feet wide and 11 feet in draught; their towers were comparatively low, the hopper beneath the upper bucket being only twenty feet above water-level; their ladder was designed in one section, but could be varied in length according to the nature of the work; their buckets (thirty-two

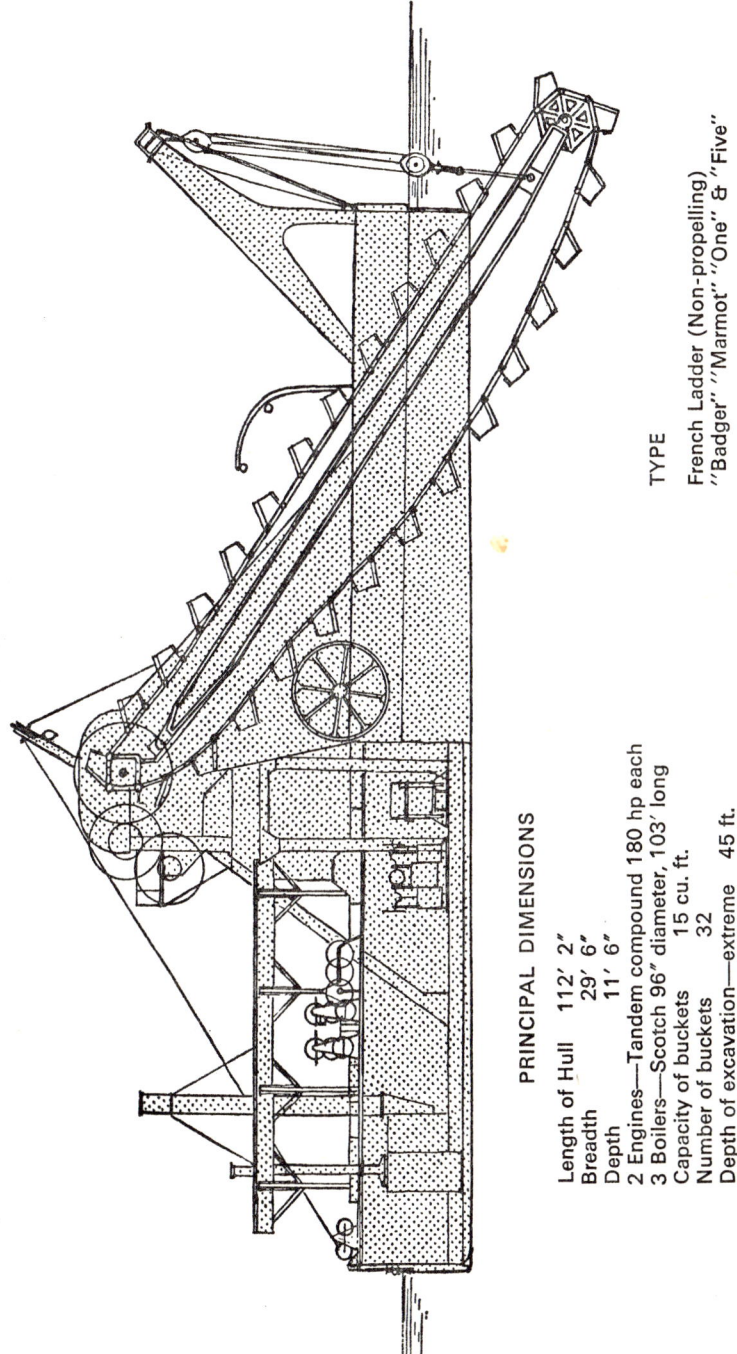

PRINCIPAL DIMENSIONS

Length of Hull   112′ 2″
Breadth   29′ 6″
Depth   11′ 6″
2 Engines—Tandem compound 180 hp each
3 Boilers—Scotch 96″ diameter, 103′ long
Capacity of buckets   15 cu. ft.
Number of buckets   32
Depth of excavation—extreme 45 ft.

TYPE

French Ladder (Non-propelling)
"Badger" "Marmot" "One" & "Five"

Figure 5. A ladder-dredge, typical of those which did sterling work for the *Compagnie Universelle*

to thirty-six in number and seventeen cubic feet in capacity) were made of iron, wrought in one piece and with the links forming an integral part of each bucket; they could dig to a depth of fourteen feet. Power for dredging was provided by a three-cylinder vertical steam-engine with direct gear transmission. All parts were interchangeable. The cost of each vessel was 115,000 dollars at Colon; this did not however, include the cost of erection—the machines being shipped in sections from France and assembled at the various sites—and it has been estimated that by the time they were actually at work each dredge cost not less than 150,000 dollars. When they were working in harbour or lake, discharge was via a floating pipeline; but when they were working beneath high banks, and soil had to be spewed out a long way both vertically and horizontally from the dredge, it was via hydraulic hopper.

This hopper was an ingenious arrangement whereby a barge, having three powerful horizontal engines in its stern, was moored beside the dredge. Each engine had a piston with a three-foot stroke, the rod being connected direct to the piston of a water-pump. Water, taken from beside the dredge, was thus forced at high pressure into the hoppers. At the neck of each hopper were iron gratings (set at right-angles to disintegrate the material forced in) and three jets of water converging on a common point, and these jets forced the excavated debris out of the barge and into a pipeline supported by pontoons. This pipeline ran up the bank and into the surrounding swamps, where material was spewed out at a distance of 200 or even 300 yards from the working site. The hydraulic hopper had two great assets: air (and hence the possibility of an air lock) was excluded, and excavated material was kept clear of the pump components. It worked perfectly, except when the soil passed into it contained a high percentage of clay, which tended to resist disintegration and form into hard balls which blocked the pipeline.

It was such dredges and such ingenious accessories which enabled Artigue and Sonderegger to excavate nine-tenths of their promised two million cubic yards. Several of the other contractors were less successful. But by and large the French in the Chagres valley did excellent work under the most trying conditions: trying not only because of the heat, but because the flood-plain of the valley was a breeding ground for mosquitoes, and malaria and yellow fever took a heavy toll of Clavenad's engineers.

Exact figures are hard to come by; but it seems probable that in this the wettest and unhealthiest section of the canal, six out of every seven Europeans contracted either malaria or yellow fever. "It was [to quote David Howarth] like a battlefield . . . two out of every three Frenchmen died ... yet there were always more who volunteered to come from home, because they looked on the task as a battle and themselves as soldiers fighting for France."

In the end even the evasive *Bulletin* was forced to admit that the incidence of disease was assuming dangerous proportions:

Year	Number of deaths in Ancon and Limon Bay Hospitals
1881	60
1882	125
1883	420
1884	1,230

By the winter of 1884/85 it was all too obvious that the isthmus was in the throes of a full-scale epidemic; and although, constructionwise, progress in Clavenad's division had been satisfactory, the future looked far less roseate than the past.

The Upper Reaches of the Chagres and the Hills between Matachin and Culebra

This was the smallest division, extending from mile twenty-two at Tabernilla to mile thirty-three at Emperador. It fell geographically into two regions: the upper part of the Chagres Valley, and the hills of the continental divide. It was under the command of Maurice Hutin, a forty-six-year-old engineer, who took over as director-general when Dingler was invalided to France.

In the Chagres, Hutin employed the same technique as Clavenad, allocating the work to a series of small contractors. Typical of these were Thirion and Percepied, who undertook to excavate a million cubic metres. Their site was between Mamei and Gorgona, where the river loops like a tired snake between embryo hills. Excavation here may have been technically simple, but flooding was an ever-present anxiety; silt and debris were frequently washed back into the excavated channel, and spoil, as a consequence, had to be dumped well clear of the working area. In spite of these difficulties, progress in the valley was generally good.

It was a different story in the hills.

Looking back, it is easy to see that the French, like the Americans a generation later, didn't do enough geological research. Couvreux had said airily that the slopes of the cutting through the hills could be "vertical"; de Lesseps had allowed for slopes of one in three, and Dingler had prudently altered this to one in four; but in fact the slopes had, in places, to be as gentle as one-in-ten (i.e. gaining one foot in height to every ten feet in length). This was due to the peculiar geological formation of the divide. Test borings had, of course, been made in both valley and hills; but these were nothing like deep enough, nor were they analysed with sufficient care. It was not therefore, until the autumn of 1883 that the French experienced the phenomena which finally put paid to de Lesseps' dream.

Landslides.

Gerstle Mack gives us a vivid description both of the cause and effect of these slides.

> Enormous masses of the upper stratum persistently slid into the cut, carrying with them rails, dump-cars, steam-shovels and often buildings. During the dry season the slopes held together fairly well, but with the onset of the torrential rains each year hundreds of thousands of cubic metres washed down into the open space below. The terraced dumps of previously excavated material proved no more stable as they softened and shifted under the rains and piled up in the laboriously dug channel. Excavation became a veritable task of Sisyphus. If the slides had merely added to the contractors' original allotment . . . the loss of time and labour would have been serious enough; but unfortunately that was only part of the difficulty. The crumbling talus slopes could be stabilised only at a very flat angle, which necessitated an enormous breadth of excavation at the top, and to make matters worse every foot added to the width of the cut also increased its depth. [For] the Culebra pass formed a narrow saddle flanked by steep ridges, so that whereas its summit along the axis of the canal reached an altitude of only 330 feet, the broad cut extended so far into the bordering hills that its sides rose almost 150 feet higher. The additional width and depth augmented the total cube to be excavated by many millions of metres. (See Figure 6 opposite.)

It is easy, armed with hindsight, to say that the French should have carried out sufficiently extensive tests to foresee and forestall these slides. But it must in fairness be pointed out that the geology of the isthmus was unique on two counts: its complexity, and the predisposition of its clays to decompose and slide. This unfortunate combination is described in detail by Henry L. Abbot, Marcel Bertrand and Philippe Zurcher, who at the end of the century submitted a geological appendix to the General Report of the 1898 Commission.

> One of the most conspicuous and widely distributed formations on the isthmus is a peculiar form of soft red clay which has much

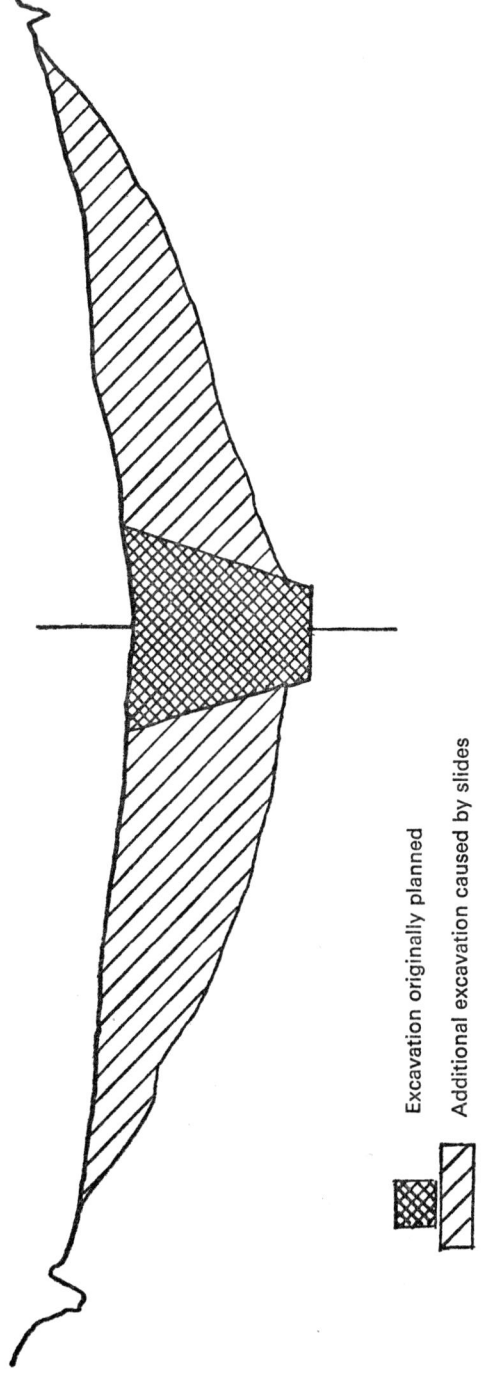

Figure 6. Additional excavation necessitated by the flat slopes of the Culebra Cut

Excavation originally planned
Additional excavation caused by slides

to do with the slides. These clays are the product of gradual surface decomposition under the influence of a tropical climate, and they naturally exhibit different stages of progress, the final form presenting the appearance of ferruginous unstratified mud. Indeed they might be mistaken for sedimentary deposits, and this the more so since intercalations of breccias sometimes appear between different layers. But this view would be erroneous. The red layers simply mark surface decompositions more or less advanced, which naturally terminate when lower impermeable clay strata have been attained. Such soft, red strata were often found at the levels where caving occurred in the cuts, and the sliding was usually assisted by abundant infiltrations which transformed the clay into a lubricator to favour movement when the slope of the under-lying strata was turned towards the excavation . . . Another noteworthy fact is that the beds of comparatively impervious clay do not entirely prevent the circulation of water in the lower layers, and this gives rise to a phenomenon, quite unusual, which is shown up when one examines small specimens. Rocks, apparently solid and compact, disintegrate when they are immersed for a few moments in water and are subjected to light pressure. This may occur even with eruptive specimens. Microscopic examination explains the cause. Such specimens when cut thin in oil are found to be traversed by argillaceous filaments which depolarise light, and which form with crystalline residues the body of the rock. These filaments appear to be the product of decomposition, although they are difficult to distinguish from true argillaceous deposits. But whatever the cause, the fact of disintegration is certain. *Rocks, apparently solid when they are taken from deep shafts, suddenly exhibit unstable cohesion when exposed to rain, separating like marl or granulating like sand.*

It is worth remembering that the Americans, who had the advantage of being able to study this report, nevertheless seriously underestimated the danger of slides. No wonder the unsuspecting French were ill-prepared to cope with them.

In the first part of 1883, however, slides didn't constitute a major problem. For the work was still either preparatory or confined to "topping" the highest points along the line of the prism. For some time therefore progress was satisfactory, with steam-shovels, cable-towers, locomotives and track being massed at the sites, and the highest points at Matachin, Bas Obispo, Camp Elliot, Las Cascadas, and Emperador being systematically removed. The *Bulletin* gives details of excavation:

January 1883	78,405	cubic metres
February 1883	111,082	,, ,,
March 1883	158,741	,, ,,
April 1883	152,000	,, ,,
May 1883	146,947	,, ,,
June 1883	156,080	,, ,,

These figures seem impressive—until we recall de Lesseps' promise that by the middle of 1883 excavation would be running at a million cubic metres a month. And one wonders why, after so promising a build-up the French assault failed to gather momentum?

The fact is that just as Clavenad's engineers were brought up short by disease and floods, so Hutin's were brought up short by disease and landslides.

To understand the seriousness of the slides, we have to understand the method by which Hutin carried out excavation. After removing the peak of the divide and the lesser summits, the French attacked the Cut in the direction of its length, thus enabling them to use simultaneously a number of excavators. The result was a series of trenches, lying one above the other, each with the natural surface of the ground as its point of beginning. A cross-section of the excavated area therefore appeared as a series of steps, each about sixteen feet high (the depth to which the excavators could work) and wide enough (perhaps another sixteen feet) to hold the excavator and the track for the train which served it. This was a thoroughly workmanlike technique, and one which was later adopted by the Americans. Hutin's method of soil disposal, however, was not so workmanlike. For the contractors were allowed to make their own arrangements for dumping; and naturally and without exception, in an effort to keep down costs, they simply carried the soil to the nearest valley, ran a railroad parallel to the slope and dumped the soil over the side. The result was a series of unstable banks, often perilously close to the working sites. Bunau-Varilla, writing from first-hand experience, has left us a description of these banks—and of what happened to them.

> First, a railroad line was run from inside the Cut to a convenient valley. Here the side of the hill was excavated to carry a railroad track, following the horizontal section of the valley. Trains were then run out along the line and their contents dumped onto the hillside below; so that little by little the hill under the railroad became covered with dumped soil. When this new mass was sufficiently thick, the track was taken up and relaid parallel to its original line only lower down the hill. So when the dump had

been formed, it resembled a series of large horizontal terraces, the sides of which plunged into the valley below while the hill above was left covered with virgin forest . . . During the dry season, this arrangement worked well. But as soon as the rains began in earnest, the dumps slid, the tracks were displaced, and the movement of the spoil trains became paralysed . . . Why did this happen? For two reasons: the excessive rainfall, and the peculiar nature of the soil. Rain which had fallen on the hillside above the dump flowed down in veritable streams. These streams were temporarily halted at the platform of the dumps, and the hollow places between the clay of the spoil bank filled with water. This water turned the clay soapy and caused it to disintegrate; so that after a while the whole bank lost its coherence and slid away in the form of a muddy morass.

Bunau-Varilla goes on to discuss possible remedies: the digging of drainage cuts, and (the scheme he eventually adopted) the building of spoil banks at right-angles to the valley rather than parallel to it. But he never mentions the remedy, later adopted by the Americans, which seems so obvious today: that of carrying the soil away via the Panama Railroad, and dumping it five, ten or even fifteen miles from the working site.

The French never solved the problem of what to do with their excavated soil. This was due in part to their failure to anticipate the soil's unstable nature, in part to their lack of control over the Panama Railroad (which remained an independent American-controlled corporation even after de Lesseps had bought a majority holding), and in part to the simple fact that there was not, among the senior French engineers, a single specialist in railways. The railway, in fact, was the key that the French never found. And it was a vital key; indeed the Americans, twenty years later, achieved virtually nothing until the arrival of John F. Stevens and the reorganisation of the Panama Railroad.

It was not long, therefore, before Hutin and his engineers became bogged down in the hills between Matachin and Culebra. And by the summer of 1884 the problem of disease was added to that of the slides.

It is impossible to say how many of Hutin's engineers succumbed to malaria and yellow fever. We don't even know the total number of deaths among employees of the *Compagnie Universelle*—although Gorgas's estimate of 22,000 is probably not far short of the mark— nor do we know what percentage of these deaths were French and what percentage West Indian. What we do know is that two out of three Frenchmen died, and that by the summer of 1884 an epidemic was sweeping the isthmus. Figures of deaths in the Ancon hospital are more eloquent than words:

In March, 1882	4 deaths
In March, 1883	19 ,,
In March, 1884	93 ,,

When Hutin first took over his division in the summer of 1883 prospects had seemed roseate. But by the summer of 1884 sickness and the never-ending slides had so reduced excavation that men were beginning to question not whether the canal would be completed on time but whether it would be completed at all.

Culebra Cut and the Approaches to Panama Bay
This division, from mile thirty-five at Culebra to mile fifty opposite Perico Island, consisted of three clearly defined sections: the Culebra Cut, the valley of the Rio Grande, and the channel through Panama Bay. It was under the jurisdiction of Bunau-Varilla, one of the most colourful and controversial characters associated with the canal.

It would be no exaggeration to say that Philippe Bunau-Varilla sublimated his life to one god: the Panama canal. He tells us that when he was ten and a student at the *Écôle Polytechnique*, his mother said to him: "Suez is finished, Philippe, but Panama remains to be built. Build it." Forty-five years later he proudly watched the first ship sail through what he had come to think of as "his" canal, and certainly no man ever worked with more single-minded purpose to make his dream come true. He arrived on the isthmus in the autumn of 1884, and after only three weeks under Dingler's tutelage, was placed, at the age of twenty-five, at the head of the Pacific division. "I devoted myself passionately," he wrote, "to the work entrusted to me." And the key word is "passionately". For Bunau-Varilla really *cared* about the canal; he considered it "the greatest conception the world has ever seen of the French genius"; its completion was, to him, a matter of national honour, and to admit defeat would have been tantamount to betraying his country. It is easy today to ridicule such an attitude: to decry Bunau-Varilla's overweaning vanity, his theatrical posturing and his inability to see any viewpoint other than his own: flag-waving patriots are out of fashion now, and there is indeed something both alarming and distasteful about Bunau-Varilla's obsessive crusade. But this shouldn't blind us to the fact that he was a brilliant engineer, a first-class administrator, and the sort of leader who inspired his men to prodigies of valour. His contribution to building the canal was nothing short of gargantuan—one can only wish that he hadn't pointed this out so frequently and so vehemently!

Of the three sections into which his division fell, the Bay of Panama was, as regards construction, the easiest. He describes the work as follows:

> The problem was to dig a channel three miles long between the mouth of the Rio Grande and Perico Island. The long submarine beach which had to be opened up consisted of soft mud. All the pundits prophesied failure. "It would be simpler to fill the pitcher of the Danaedes," they said, "than excavate a channel through such soil, for the action of the sea will fill in the cut as quickly as it is dredged." A careful study of local conditions, however, made me think otherwise. I noticed that although there were coastal currents, the sea was smooth; for the shape of Panama Bay protects it from the influx of ocean swell. Where there is no swell, the currents are usually surface currents, and mud and sand from the sea bed seldom become mingled with the water. I felt sure the channel wouldn't silt up. And facts confirmed my view. For even six months after it was dredged, the axis of the channel was precisely the same as after the passage of the dredge. It was a first battle gained: one so-called insurmountable difficulty overcome.

The work of excavating this channel was carried out by *A–1* and *A–3* (see Figure 7 opposite); probably the most successful of the many first-class dredges used by the French. They were marine-type, self-propelling dredges, built by Lobnitz and Company of Renfrew, Scotland. They had moulded hulls 170 feet by twenty-six feet, a single screw, direct inverted compound engines of 300 h.p., Scotch marine boilers, and thirty-two to thirty-six buckets; their dredging gear was driven through frictions by sprocket chain; because of their freeboard they were able to operate in the open sea, and they could dig to a depth of thirty-five feet. Both dredges were subsequently taken over by the Americans, who were amazed and delighted by their capacity for work. Indeed under their new names *Mole* and *Gopher*, *A–1* and *A–3* carried out valuable and more or less continuous excavation right through to the completion of the canal. Nor was their excellent record due (as has sometimes been insinuated) to the fact that they were rebuilt by the Isthmian Commission in the early 1900s; for during the first eighteen months of Bunau-Varilla's regime they excavated a permanent deep-water channel, seventy-two feet wide, the length of Panama Bay.

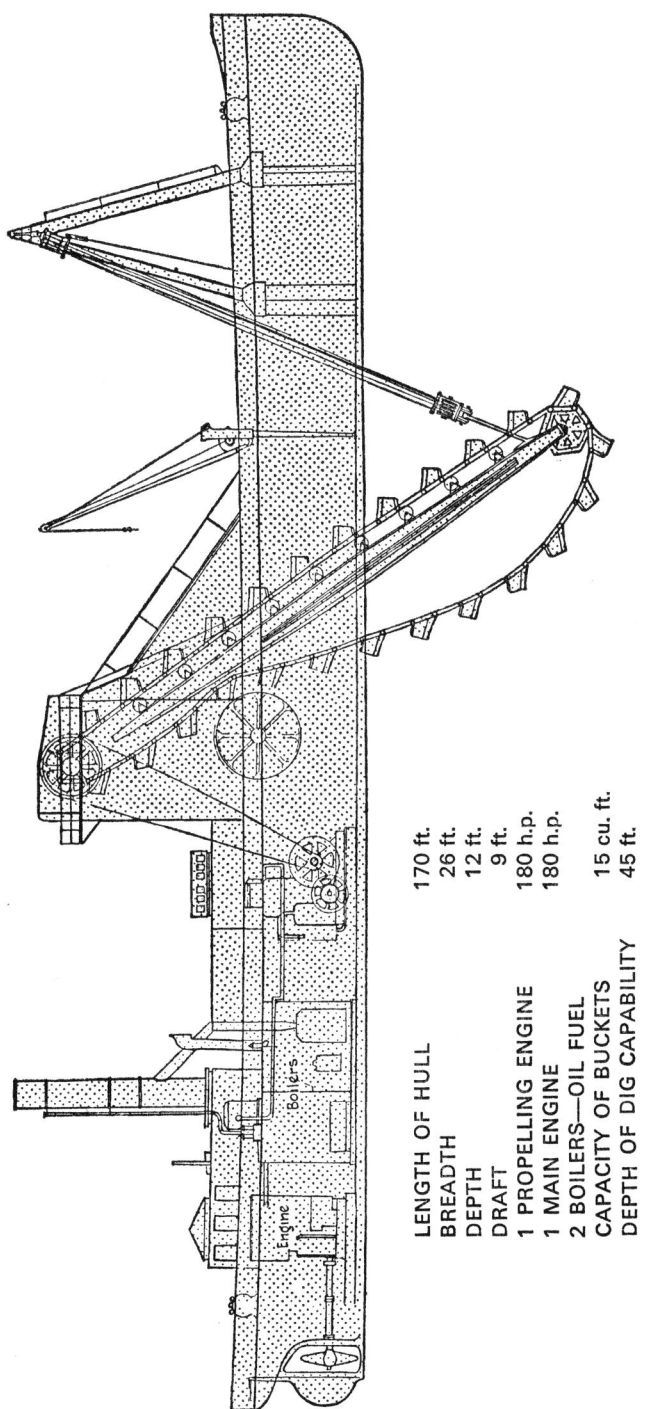

Figure 7. A-1 (subsequently renamed the *Mole*) self-propelling dredge

LENGTH OF HULL	170 ft.
BREADTH	26 ft.
DEPTH	12 ft.
DRAFT	9 ft.
1 PROPELLING ENGINE	180 h.p.
1 MAIN ENGINE	180 h.p.
2 BOILERS—OIL FUEL	
CAPACITY OF BUCKETS	15 cu. ft.
DEPTH OF DIG CAPABILITY	45 ft.

Meanwhile in the valley of the Rio Grande, lighter dredges pushed inland from La Boca wharf, excavating a channel toward the hills. Progress here was slow and unspectacular. This, however, was because the work was accorded a low priority, rather than because of technical difficulties; and in fact a good deal of valuable excavation was, over the years, carried out quietly and unobtrusively in the Rio Grande, while events a few miles inland stole the limelight.

For inland lay the Culebra Cut*: the mile-long saddle across the highest point of the hills: the immovable mass which had, somehow, to be moved before de Lesseps' dream could come anywhere near reality.

Bunau-Varilla has left us a good description of the Cut. It was, he tells us, a well-defined indentation through the hills, a wooded pass some 300 feet above sea-level. Its rocks consisted of volcanic breccia, overlaid with a soft red clay which proved at first so delightfully easy to move that the main problem in excavation would, it was thought, be heat and the congestion caused by working in a restricted space. By the end of 1884 the woods had been cleared, pilot trenches had been run the length of the Cut, and a contract had been signed with Cutbill, de Longo, Watson and Van Hattum (usually referred to as the Anglo-Dutch Company) for the excavation of thirteen million cubic yards.

This Company amassed an impressive array of equipment and a working force of 2,000 men, and in the spring of 1885 they attacked the Cut with vigour. Their equipment has been described by Goethals.

> The principal machines used by the French [in the Cut] were excavators mounted on trucks. On the body of the truck was a frame supporting a ladder which projected over the side, with a tumbler at either end, about which worked an endless chain of buckets with a capacity of six cubic feet. The contents of the buckets were dumped into a hopper from which, by means of a chute, the material was loaded into cars alongside the excavator. These cars were six-metre cars, holding $4\frac{1}{2}$ cubic metres in place. There was also a large number of dump buckets of $1\frac{1}{2}$ cubic metre capacity which were handled by cranes mounted on trucks. In addition there was a system of cableways, consisting of four

---

*The French used the term Culebra Cut to describe the saddle at the highest point of the hills; the Americans used it to describe not only the saddle but also the adjacent valleys of the Obispo and Rio Grande. To the French, therefore, the Cut was one mile long, whereas to the Americans it was ten.

American cables and two French, both handling buckets of one cubic metre capacity. These cableways [see Figure 8 on page 74] extended across the Cut, supported by towers on either side; the buckets were filled by hand, and were then drawn to the bank of the Cut and dumped into cars. The French also resorted to a large amount of task work, which was performed by West Indian negroes; each man was required to do a specific amount of work per day, could do it in his own time, and do as much more as he saw fit. This work was paid for by the bucket.

At first all went well. But after some 250,000 cubic yards had been removed in the spring of 1885, the dry season came to an end; the spoil banks which had been built above and parallel to the Cut became saturated and slid into the excavated channel, and work ground to a stand-still.

Bunau-Varilla was in a difficult position. He had very decided views on how to remedy the slides; but the contractors (to quote his own words) "were absolute masters when it came to choosing their method of work, and [he] was powerless to force upon them a solution". So the Anglo-Dutch Company toiled on, often performing prodigies of excavation, only to see the spoil banks disintegrate under the influence of rain and spew back into the Cut the debris they had so laboriously taken out. It was not (as has often been claimed) their equipment which was inadequate, it was their method of soil-disposal. They never recognised the fact—which seems so obvious today—that the basic problem in excavating the Culebra Cut was one of transportation.

It was because of this failure that the Anglo-Dutch Company achieved such meagre results. They undertook to excavate thirteen million cubic yards: in fact they excavated 810,000, less than one-sixteenth of their target. Small wonder that after eighteen months their contract was annulled, and the work handed over to Artigue and Sonderegger, a company directly controlled by Bunau-Varilla.

If one reads Bunau-Varilla's book, *Panama: the Creation, Destruction and Resurrection*, one gets the impression that the moment his firm took over they achieved fantastic results, and that only the liquidation of the *Compagnie Universelle* denied them the honour of completing this vital section of the canal. Nothing could be further from the truth. For in fact Bunau-Varilla's "solution" to the Culebra problem was basically unsound, and resulted in a comparatively small amount of excavation at an exorbitant cost.

It was obvious [he writes] that the conditions of instability [in the dumps] would no longer apply if, instead of building spoil-banks parallel to the hillside they were built at right-angles to it. Of course the first railroad could no longer be laid simply by excavating a ledge along the horizontal slope of the hill: it would be necessary to build bridges perpendicular to the hillside, and to dump the soil from these bridges into the valley below. But once a dump was formed in this way it would be in contact with the hillside not by its length but by its width . . . seepage would be insignificant . . . This new idea led me to build a series of wooden bridges across the valleys chosen for dumping; and by using these bridges as the base from which to build spoil banks I was able to solve the problem which had hitherto caused such prolonged failure.

This claim is not substantiated by the facts. For Bunau-Varilla's scheme proved more ingenious than practical, and although it did indeed lead to increased excavation, it led also to the price of extraction per cubic metre rising from under one dollar to over twenty-two dollars! Nor when one looks at the cubage extracted is it all that impressive; for although Bunau-Varilla's company under-

Figure 8. French cableway at work in the Culebra Cut

took to remove twenty million cubic metres from the Cut and its environs, in fact they removed only 2,250,000.

The truth is that rearranging the excavated soil was no substitute for carrying it away. The French never looked as though they were succeeding at Culebra; and this, to quote Henry L. Abbot, "was because they failed to use the track of the Panama Railroad to transport their excavated spoil to the dumps."

This was a basic failure in planning which no subsequent hard work and ingenuity could rectify. At the start of Dingler's regime the significance of the mistake was little appreciated. But as the Cut deepened and the slides increased in size and frequency, those working at Culebra learned by bitter experience the truth of John F. Steven's dictum that a mistake made during the preparatory period is a basic mistake and can never be fully overcome.

Nor were slides Bunau-Varilla's only problem. For in the Culebra Cut, as in every other section of the canal, 1884 heralded an appalling increase in malaria and yellow fever.

Bunau-Varilla held the view—which was not uncommon a hundred years ago—that those who led a blameless life morally were less likely to succumb to illness than the self-indulgent. Here is his description of the epidemic which swept the isthmus that autumn:

> Death was constantly gathering its harvest all about me. Never had yellow fever been more deadly. Within a stone's-throw of my house in Colon, ships were anchored in the harbour without a single person aboard: their whole crew had died. I especially remember twelve English sailors, in full uniform, waiting to see the doctor: within the week every one of them was dead. I could not help noticing at this time how greatly a man's disdain of peril increased the strength of his resistance, and how swiftly the disease struck at the weak and the conscience-stricken. Soon after my arrival in Colon, I had an example of this. The head accountants of two divisions under my control were firm friends. They had come to the isthmus together, they lived in the same house and ate at the same table. One was a man of irreproachable character, but the reputation of the other was tarnished—rumour had it that he had been party to fraudulent payments made to a certain purveyor. An enquiry strengthened the case against him, and I ordered the incriminated man to appear before me on the following morning at seven o'clock. His heavily-burdened conscience, however, so troubled him that he fell ill during the night with fever, and was taken to hospital. Eight days later his body was laid to rest in the cemetery . . . I often went to meet the ships as they

arrived from Europe, full of Company employees. Although the men were all coming to us voluntarily, some of them, I could see, felt their hearts sink at the sight of the warm and misty shores of the dreaded isthmus. In some instances their faces bore the obvious mark of terror. I made a note of these men's names, and without exception every one of them was dead within three months.

Bunau-Varilla adds, in one of his more purple passages: "These constant dangers may have depressed the feeble-minded. But to those with a sincere love of our great task they were a challenge. For their irradiating influence made us conscious of the joy of the ultimate sacrifice which every one of us was prepared to make for the greatness of France."

Bearing in mind that Bunau-Varilla equated immunity to disease with the good life, one wonders how he accounted for the near-fatal attack of yellow fever to which he succumbed in the spring of 1886. One wonders too, how he accounted for the shattering series of bereavements suffered by Dingler.

Dingler, like de Lesseps, had the courage to bring his wife and children to the isthmus. But whereas de Lesseps confined his visits to the dry season, the chief engineer and his family stayed all the year round. A few days after his arrival Dingler told the press: "I intend to show the world that only the drunk and the dissipated will die here of yellow fever"; but for this boast Fate extracted the most appalling penalty. For although Dingler and his family were models of propriety, first his son, then his daughter and then his son-in-law died of fever. Nor was this the end of the tragedies that beset him. For on the first day of 1885, in the middle of the New Year celebrations, he was told of the death of the last and dearest surviving member of his family: his wife. "These trials," wrote Bunau-Varilla, "which might have driven a lesser man out of his mind, in no way made our hero swerve from the path of duty. The day after his wife's death he was at his office as usual at 7.30 in the morning." There is, however, a limit to the punishment that mind and body can take; and in the summer of 1885 Dingler was invalided back to France. He died soon afterwards, the epitome of a host of unsung engineers who sacrificed literally everything—health, family and eventually their lives—in a cause they thought of as noble.

The French suffered two other disasters in 1885, both of which retarded excavation just as it ought to have gathered pace: revolution in the spring and floods in the winter.

The cause of the revolution, which erupted at the end of February, was complex. Bunau-Varilla thought its origins were religious—

"this, like so many of the insurrections which disturb the Central American Republics was the visible expression of the conflict between the theocratic and democratic systems of government." Gerstle Mack, on the other hand, thought it symptomatic of the tendency of the various provinces to break away from the parent republic in order to achieve a greater degree of self-government. Whatever the cause, the effect was chaos, with loyalist and insurgent troops alternately capturing and recapturing key points on the isthmus. And in March the situation was further complicated by the intervention of a third party: Pedro Prestan, a Haitian mulatto who appeared on the Atlantic seaboard with a force of West Indian negroes. Prestan detested foreigners in general and Americans in particular; he seized Colon, and threatened to "shoot every prisoner and murder every American in the city", unless a contraband cargo of arms seized by the U.S. Navy was handed over. In the pitched battle which followed, Prestan was defeated, but not before he had set fire to Colon and reduced its wooden buildings quite literally to so many heaps of ash.

Throughout these disturbances the French preserved a commendable neutrality. One of their warships, the *Reine-Blanche*, was anchored off Colon, but her commander very properly refused to land his men unless all the consuls unanimously requested him to do so. The attitude of the Americans was more equivocal. Their behaviour towards Prestan was, at first, strictly non-committal; but for this their commanding officer was bitterly criticised and hauled in front of a court of enquiry. And this court was responsible for the highly dubious pronouncement that the American authorities had an obligation to prevent, *if necessary by force,* all conflict along the line of the Panama Railroad. This led, in April, to American troops occupying Panama and "persuading" the insurgent general, Rafael Aizpuru, to surrender.

This established a questionable precedent, and one which Bunau-Varilla, some twenty years later, seized on with relish. He is quite open about what he did. "The Colombians", he writes (referring to the events of 1903), "cherished the intention of getting hold of what remained of the French enterprise ... In this they could be thwarted only by force ... The isthmus was too weak at the time to foster a revolution of its own accord; but by reproducing artificially the conditions of 1885, I was able in 1903 (again) to force the United States to intervene."

It is a sobering thought that a man could be so obsessed with building a canal, that he admits to artificially sparking off a revolution to achieve his ends.

American intervention in the spring of 1885 came within a hairsbreadth of having another and far more beneficial result. While building the Panama Railroad in the 1850s, John Cresson Trautwine had written: "A veil over the face is a partial protection from miasmic vapours . . . Keep closed such doors and windows as are open to wind blowing in from the marshes; but if they must be open, have a screen of gauze or copper wire across them. *Mosquito nets are also good, not only against insects but miasma.*" And now again in 1885, Surgeon-General F. M. Gunnell, who was in charge of the U.S. troops put ashore at Panama, made much the same observation: "Our general health is good . . . and *mosquito netting for each man is a ready and efficient help against the effects of malaria.*" Gunnell in fact was on the brink of a momentous discovery: that of recognising the link between mosquitoes and malaria. But the implications of his own advice escaped him; he assumed that the nets prevented malaria not because they kept out mosquitoes, but because they absorbed the dampness of the air; and not for another eighteen years did doctors hit on the truth which was, at Panama, one of the prerequisites of success.

After the revolution came the flood.

Rainfall in the last half of November 1885 was unusually heavy, and on December 2nd the Atlantic seaboard was swept by a violent storm. The steam-ships in Limon Bay managed to escape, but the sailing vessels, unable to beat out against the wind, were trapped; eighteen were driven ashore; most of them became total wrecks, and over fifty seamen were drowned. Bunau-Varilla and a number of Company employees made valiant efforts to save what lives and property they could; then the chief-engineer was called inland, warned by urgent messages that the Chagres was in flood as never before. There wasn't much he could do, but he has left us a vivid account of the scene of desolation:

> The points where my locomotive passed on the previous day were now covered by fourteen feet of water, so I requisitioned three Indian canoes. We took these by train as far as we could, then embarked in them. As we paddled along through a channel apparently cut out of virgin forest all the workings were submerged and the tops of the telegraph poles were scarcely visible above the water. In places we had to drag the canoes over small hillocks, and in this way one canoe was damaged. We had, then, to crowd into the remaining boats, although the load was almost too much, and the freeboard was not more than an inch above water. One of the engineers, a M. Philippe, said that he couldn't

swim. I told him jokingly, "There is no danger. I could easily tow you to the nearest trees." It was only then that I noticed the strangest phenomenon: the tops of the trees were not their usual green, but a distinct and ever-shifting black; as we drew nearer, I saw they were covered with the most enormous and deadly spiders: tarantulas . . . As soon as we arrived at Panama, I wired all engineers to make recordings of this disastrous flood.

These recordings were later analysed by Abbot, who tells us that this was the first major flood during which an attempt was made to measure the discharge of the Chagres—"although," he adds, "a diligent search among documents has failed to discover the exact details as to methods of gauging, etc." It seems from this analysis that the highest point was reached at Gamboa at 8 p.m. on November 26th with a discharge of 64,488 cubic feet per second, as against the normal discharge of 3,000 cubic feet: that the second flood reached its peak between 4 and 6 p.m. on December 3rd, with a discharge of 44,923 cubic feet per second: and that the greatest average for forty-eight hours occurred between 5 a.m. of December 3rd and 5 a.m. of December 5th, when the rises at Bohio were 33.79 feet and 26.41 feet, indicating discharges of 74,800 and 47,466 cubic feet per second. In other words the river, at the height of the flood, was discharging twenty-five times its normal volume of water.

The year 1885 ended with the railroad out of use, the Chagres still in spate, and its waters ascour through the half-completed channel. It had been a disastrous year for the French. For at the very moment when excavation ought to have forged ahead, it had been pegged back: pegged back by flood, revolution, sickness and slides. The following table indicates the extent of the setback:

Year	Excavation in cubic yards
1882	under 500,000
1883	3,500,000
1884	9,847,556
1885	9,425,031

It was obvious even to the eternally optimistic de Lesseps, that things weren't going according to plan; and although now in his eighty-first year, he decided to make a personal tour of the workings.

5

DEATH OF A DREAM

The idea that de Lesseps should revisit the isthmus was first put forward at the Company's annual general meeting in July, 1885.

Shareholders, at this meeting, had every reason for anxiety—costs were soaring, disease was snowballing, there were sporadic labour troubles and the pace of excavation instead of gathering momentum had declined—but their fears were sponged away in the flood of de Lesseps' oratory. For at the end of what was not so much a speech as a *tour de force*, the redoubtable old man gave two promises: that he would himself visit the isthmus to inaugurate the "final stage of construction", and that he would organise a lottery (as he had done at Suez) to meet the increase in costs. It says much for his personal magnetism that in spite of the depressing statistics, he was able to charm an overwhelming vote of confidence out of his audience. *Figaro* waxed eloquent: "His clear, precise and lucid explanations convinced one and all. Here was a demonstration of the power of the honest word, hiding nothing, but disclosing with the same felicity those difficulties which still remained and those which had been successfully overcome." A cynic might point out that the press were being bribed at the time to give favourable publicity. But the fact remains that de Lesseps still had the power to convince tens of thousands of ordinary Frenchmen that Panama was another Suez, and that so long as they kept faith with him all would be well.

His tour of the isthmus was planned, once again, to coincide with the dry season. He was accompanied by a distinguished entourage—representatives of the French Chamber of Commerce, engineers from Germany and Holland, the Duke of Sutherland and Admiral Carpenter from Great Britain, and Nathan Appleton and John Bigelow from New York. On February 17th, 1886 he arrived in Colon to be received with all the pomp and circumstance traditionally reserved for a visiting monarch. It was the start of a triumphal fortnight. The days were filled with inspections of work-sites, barracks, machine-shops and hospitals, the nights with banquets, fireworks and balls; and everywhere de Lesseps went there were speeches, although most of the latter were remarkable for their verbosity rather than their practical value—"The day will come," trumpeted the eloquent Pablo Arosemena, "when from the summit

"A View through the Culebra Mountain"

Comte Ferdinand de Lesseps and some of his family

of an overpowered Culebra, the flags of all nations will announce to the world that you have crowned your glorious work, and the two oceans united will proclaim your victory and your greatness." The down-to-earth John Bigelow reported more prosaically that there appeared to be no insuperable difficulty in completing the work of construction, but that he feared that de Lesseps would be disappointed both as regards the time and the cost of it. Bigelow's warning, however, was lost in the flood of enthusiasm. "It seemed," wrote a correspondent in the *Bulletin*, "as if the whole isthmus had turned out to pay homage to the canal builder ... In the plaza a triumphal arch inscribed *Panama-Suez* rose above the solidly packed crowd. Flags were everywhere, and the windows were hidden behind a veritable barricade of flowers and palm branches." Few of those in the crowd can have suspected that the palms were symbolic: a harbinger of the Calvary to come.

De Lesseps spent fourteen days on the isthmus, taking in his stride a programme which exhausted his younger but less robust compatriots. For a man of eighty-one it was a remarkable achievement, and the stories told of it are legend: how on a snow-white horse he went galloping up a steep embankment "amid a roar of enthusiastic hurrahs from the workers who were astonished by so much ardour and youthfulness", and how he "rode everywhere like an eastern monarch clad in flowing robes of the most gorgeous colours." But what in fact did the visit achieve?

It is easy to make the point that fireworks and equestrian ability are no substitute for workable plans on the drawing-board. Yet it is worth bearing in mind that the gods of technology and statistics were not worshipped as devotedly a hundred years ago as they are today. The late nineteenth century was the age of the gifted amateur—of Brunel and Marconi, Edison and Eiffel—and of this distinguished company de Lesseps was the archetype. He was not and never pretended to be a professional engineer; he was an inspirational leader, and the proper place for such a leader is at the helm. So while it is perfectly true that his visit solved no technical problems, it did nonetheless achieve something of real value. For the sight of the father-figure himself clambering over the workings, sinking knee-deep in mud and standing bareheaded in the tropic rain, made the construction gangs feel that their problems were shared, understood and would soon be solved—witness Duval: "engineers and workers alike were inspired by de Lesseps' visit to greater efforts."

On the more practical side the visit led to an important change in the policy of awarding contracts.

In 1883, 1884 and 1885 the Company divided work among some

two hundred small subcontractors. In general this system worked well; but it had the disadvantage that the director-general found it impossible to control and co-ordinate so many small and virtually autonomous units. It was therefore agreed, early in 1886, to award fewer and larger contracts—to quote the report of the Chamber of Deputies, "from this moment the Canal Company reversed its policy and entrusted the entire project to six large firms, each of which had a specific task to perform." The firms in question were the American Contracting and Dredging Company; Jacob, a French syndicate based in Nantes; Artigue, Sonderegger and Company (Bunau-Varilla's corps of men "passionately devoted to the canal"); Vignaud, Barbaud, Blanleuil and Company; the *Société des Travaux Publics et Constructions;* and Baratoux, Letellier and Company. Their records make informative reading, and provide evidence of the fast-widening gap between expectation and fulfilment.

The American Contracting and Dredging Company undertook to excavate eighteen million cubic metres between the entrance to Limon Bay and Gatun. Of this they removed 16,991,797 metres—virtually the whole of their allotment, and almost as much as the other five contractors put together. For this work they were paid 70,812,896 francs, their profit being estimated by the French at over thirty million francs and by the company's accountants at under ten million. It has often been pointed out that this company had two basic advantages over its competitors. It started work earlier; and the soil it excavated was largely silt—easy to dredge and easy to dispose of (most of it being dumped far out to sea or on the earth platform at Colon). This is true. None the less the American Company provided its own first-class equipment, and did sterling work; if the other contractors had come as near to their targets, de Lesseps' canal would have been completed; and although the Slaven brothers' profits were undoubtedly enormous, so too were the services they rendered.

The Jacob company was allotted no specific target, for the cube they extracted was to be determined by the number of dredges and steam-shovels they hired from the *Compagnie Universelle*. In the event they removed 2,324,095 cubic metres, mostly from the valley of the Chagres, for which they were paid 16,540,684 francs. Their profit was estimated at 7,500,000 francs, which sounds excessive. Jacob, however, were exonerated by the investigating Committee of Deputies who declared, "this company executed its contracts faithfully and, unlike some of the others, made no attempt to extort successive price increases, or unanticipated advances and indemnities."

The contracts negotiated with Artigue, Sonderegger and Company were complex, devious and in many ways highly unsatisfactory. The original firm had started excavation in a strictly limited capacity in the upper reaches of the Chagres. When, however, it was clear that the adjacent Anglo-Dutch Company working in and around Culebra would never fulfil its contract, Artigue and Sonderegger (reconstituted as Artigue, Sonderegger and Company) stepped in and undertook to excavate twenty million cubic metres from Culebra and its environs. They would, they said, complete this vital section of the cutting to thirty feet below sea-level within three and a half years.

The guiding spirit of this ambitious enterprise was Bunau-Varilla, who in 1886 resigned his position with the *Compagnie Universelle* in order to take control of Artigue, Sonderegger and Company as a private individual. Bunau-Varilla explains at length in his book that his resignation was necessary because the Public Works Department forbade its employees to go into business as private contractors. He also explains that he made the move solely to help Charles de Lesseps, who said to him "this would be the greatest service you can render to the Panama undertaking". His detractors, however, infer that the change-over had a less altruistic motive: that his salary, as a consequence, more than quadrupled. Whatever the truth, Bunau-Varilla devoted himself heart and soul to the work at Culebra, and no one would have grudged him a fair financial reward. One can only wish that he hadn't claimed success when he achieved nothing of the sort. For the fact is that his account of the excavation carried out by Artigue and Sonderegger is pure sophistry. Here is what he says:

> During the two years my Culebra Company operated, the average level of the axis was lowered thirty feet, instead of six feet, which would have been the former average. It may be admitted that the deepening was ten feet in the first year and twenty in the second year, and that we had only reached an average level of 235 feet above the sea when the works were stopped. But the bad ground had by then been entirely removed. It is beyond doubt that the average level would have been lowered thirty feet in 1889 and fifty feet in 1890. Only fifteen feet would then have remained to be lowered in 1891. It is thus clear that, within two and a half years, the Cut through Culebra could have been made ... The increase of the amount of excavation made under these trying circumstances demonstrates our gradually increasing victory over Nature ... Every day the enemy was more and more completely conquered. The total excavation for the second year, compared

to that of the first would, thanks to the enormous improvement in the condition of the works, have given an average excavation of 200,000 cubic yards monthly and in the year following of at least 270,000.

Bunau-Varilla's argument is hard to follow let alone accept. In particular his claim that the bad ground had been entirely removed won't stand investigation. For the truth is that the deeper the Cut became, the greater was the danger of slides: the ground, in other words, got worse rather than better. Indeed the French never looked like conquering Culebra. Although Bunau-Varilla's company promised to excavate to a depth of 270 feet, they excavated in fact to a depth of only thirty; and although they promised to remove twenty million cubic metres of soil, they removed in fact only two and a quarter million. They achieved, in other words, barely a ninth of their target. For this work they were paid 32,646,479 francs of which the Deputies Committee estimated that 11,437,381 was pure profit—"far more than the circumstances warranted." Of these profits Bunau-Varilla received an undisclosed percentage through a private arrangement with one of the directors of Artigue and Sonderegger—his brother. Such an arrangement was not *per se* dishonest; but it was unfortunately typical of the way in which Company funds were all too frequently siphoned off to those who had no official status.

The fourth firm, Vignaud, Barbaud, Blanleuil and Company, undertook to remove twenty million cubic metres from the hills between Gorgona and Emperador; in fact they removed only 3,642,986, for which they were paid a shade over thirty million francs. The Deputies Committee singled out this firm as the solitary sheep in a herd of goats—"the only ones who made no profit out of their Panama contracts"—indeed when the *Compagnie Universelle* failed they too went into liquidation, their losses being assessed at almost three million francs. The Deputies accounted for this with a rare flash of humour: "Vignaud, Barbaud and Blanleuil appear simply to have been less shrewd than their competitors; we might say more honest, did we not fear to discourage probity."

Le Société des Travaux Publics et Constructions, on the other hand, incurred the wrath of the Deputies in no uncertain fashion. This company undertook to remove twenty-nine million cubic metres, eventually removed 3,421,870 and were paid the preposterous sum of 76,215,002 francs, of which nearly fifty million was pure profit. To quote Gerstle Mack: "The committee not only denounced these contractors for demanding exorbitant and quite unjustified increases with each new contract, but blamed the canal company for submitting tamely to the impositions—'when *Le Société* failed to observe its agreements, the company [merely] lavished more favours upon it'." The committee also disclosed that *Le Société* shared both offices and directors with another company (*Le Société des Dépôts et Comptes Courants*) which helped to float the Company's bonds; and these directors, it was insinuated, deliberately awarded lucrative contracts to their associates in order to line their own pockets.

The last of the contractors, Baratoux, Letellier and Company emerged with a better record. Their original contract called for the excavation of ten million cubic metres from Panama Bay and the lower reaches of the Rio Grande; this, however, was subsequently reduced by the transfer of some two million metres to Artigue and Sonderegger. Of the eight million cubic metres which remained, Baratoux, Letellier and Company removed a shade under seven million, quietly dredging away year after year with a commendable lack of publicity and acrimony. They received 37,627,656 francs for their work, of which approximately ten million was profit.

It is clear from these statistics that although progress in the coastal plains was not unsatisfactory, work in the central section among the hills was falling seriously behind schedule. By 1886 de Lesseps realised that to complete his canal he would need more money—hence his determination to run a lottery.

He decided on a lottery rather than a new issue of shares because the company had already floated one stock issue (bringing in 300 million francs) and three bond issues (bringing in 385 million), and he felt there was a limit to the amount of money which private individuals would pour into a private venture. Under French law a lottery could be run only with government approval, and by raising money in this way de Lesseps hoped to reap the benefits of government backing without incurring the incubus of its actual participation. The French government, however, very properly refused to allow a lottery until they had carried out an investigation of the company's affairs; they would, they said, send an official representative to tour the isthmus, and they would base their decision on his recommendations.

The man they entrusted with this important, and indeed vital mission was the fifty-one-year-old Armand Rousseau, a distinguished engineer, an ex-minister of public works and a former undersecretary. It says much for Rousseau's integrity that although his report was, in the years to come, the subject of bitter intrigue and acrimony, no one ever denied the scrupulous honesty with which it was compiled.

Rousseau arrived in the isthmus at the end of January and submitted his report at the end of April. It was a model of lucidity, clear-thinking and tact:

> I believe a cut through the isthmus to be a feasible undertaking, and that it has now progressed so far that abandonment would be a real disaster, not only for the shareholders but for French influence throughout America. [For] ... if the enterprise should fail in the hands of a French company it would at once be taken up by a foreign one ... The Panama Company therefore deserves exceptional consideration from the public authorities, [and] I believe that the government should assist it ... The extent of this assistance, however, must be clearly defined, so that the government can never be accused of becoming responsible or in any way improperly involved in the company's affairs.

(A *cri de coeur* which was later echoed by the Minister of the Interior, Charles Baihaut: "the government can assume no responsibility—not even a moral one—for an enterprise over which it has no supervision.")

> Since [Rousseau went on] the government has no control over plans, contracts or administration, and since the project evinces a number of serious technical defects, it should give the company no sort of guarantee or advice ... For although I believe the digging of a canal to be possible, its completion for the anticipated cost and within the estimated time appears to be more than doubtful, *unless the company will agree to radical modifications and simplifications.*

Rousseau goes on to say that it was not the government's job to suggest what these modifications ought to be, but that they should, before granting permission for a lottery, demand that the company make "a profound study" of the technical problems involved. It is obvious now, and it was even more obvious then, what modifications Rousseau was hinting ought to be made. He wanted de Lesseps' sea-level canal superseded by one with locks.

At the same time as Rousseau delivered his report to the government, two other eminent engineers, Jacquet and Boyer, also handed in reports to the *Compagnie Universelle*. They both said bluntly that within the limitations of the estimates and the allotted time a sea-level canal was impossible.

The ball was back in de Lesseps' court. It was a key moment in the history of the canal.

De Lesseps was disappointed by Rousseau's findings, for these led the government to postpone their decision on a lottery until the company had made its "profound study". Disappointed but far from defeated. "They have adjourned on me," he exclaimed. "But I am not the man to sit down under such treatment. When people try to stop me, I advance!" He withdrew his request for a lottery and went direct to the public, asking them to subscribe to yet another issue of bonds: "I am confident," he wrote in his circular to shareholders, "that together we will overcome all obstacles, and that you will march with me to a second victory by providing the 600 million francs I need."

It was a gesture more courageous than prudent. For the public, alarmed by rumours of the Company's instability and de Lesseps' ill health, subscribed only 354 million francs: a sum which represented a tremendous personal tribute to *le grand Français*, but was still insufficient to meet the company's ever-snowballing expenses—especially since bribery, extortion and costs whittled away more than a third of the money before it reached the company's books.

Looking back, it is easy to see what de Lesseps should, at this juncture, have done. He should have accepted the advice of well-qualified engineers that his sea-level canal was a pipe-dream, and have authorised the building of a canal with locks. If he had done this, there is little doubt but that the government would have allowed a lottery, the money would have been forthcoming, and a canal of sorts would have been completed in the early 1890s. As it was, the old man still refused to believe that the triumphs of Suez couldn't be repeated, at the eleventh hour, at Panama. He refused point-blank to consider "an inferior" canal with locks. Gerstle Mack puts the case very clearly.

> De Lesseps accepted without protest certain minor modifications ... He agreed willingly enough to the tidal lock at the Pacific end; to postpone the construction of a basin to enable ships to pass at the half-way point; to substitute an earth levee for the masonry dam at Gamboa, and if necessary to decrease temporarily the depth and breadth of the channel itself. What he was not ready to approve was the one modification which, had it been adopted soon enough, might even [now] have turned failure into success: the introduction of locks. Not until January, 1887 did he call upon the consulting committee to consider designs for a lock canal, and [even then] he still insisted that the substitution must be merely temporary: "Among the projects to be considered are some which would *permanently substitute* a lock canal for a sea-level canal. I will never consent to this."

Nevertheless de Lesseps was eventually forced, by shortage of funds, to consider a temporary lock canal; and it was such a project which was finally adopted in the autumn of 1887.

It was the irrepressible Bunau-Varilla who thought up the idea of a lock canal with a high-level central section which could be progressively transformed—with money received from tolls—into a sea-level channel. This idea was based on what he called his "two discoveries which unlocked the Secret of the Straits". The first discovery was a new technique of underwater rock excavation which he first experimented with in 1885; and the second was his revolutionary theory that by subdividing the cutting into a series of shallow pools it could be excavated by floating dredges.

These ideas he describes in his book with more enthusiasm than modesty:

> Soon after my arrival I found myself face to face with a great difficulty ... There has long been a saying among engineers that it was the dredge which made Suez a possibility; but at Panama, alas, the whole central mass is of rock, and dredges have long been considered powerless before rock ... But why, I asked myself, is rock deemed so impossible to dredge? Is it not because up to now no attempt has been made to render the rock dredgeable? If it were broken up in a homogeneous manner into pieces not larger than paving stones, then surely the dredges could excavate it? My thoughts reverted to an experiment I had made a couple of years before, when I was an officer of the military engineers at Arras. We were using a mining bar to bore a deep vertical hole $2\frac{1}{2}$ inches in diameter through a field of clay. Into this hole were introduced three continuous rows of dynamite cartridges. After the explosion the hole was found to be transformed into a perfectly regular vertical cylinder two feet in diameter, the constancy of its diameter being evidence of the homogeneous nature of the action of dynamite. "If I reproduce this experiment in rock," said I, "of course there will be no cylinder formed, the rock being incompressible; but there will be a regular fissuration of the rock all round the hole. So if I place and explode these holes at a yard apart, the whole mass of the rock will be regularly disintegrated and reduced homogeneously into pieces roughly the size of a man's head. The rock will then be dredgeable." I decided to carry out an experiment. I ordered rafts to be built; from these, miners, working with bars, made the necessary holes in the underwater rock; (these were filled with dynamite); and the rock was then pulverised by simultaneous explosion in the hundreds of

DEATH OF A DREAM 89

> symmetrically disposed holes. A dredge was brought quickly to the spot, and it worked unimpeded, not heeding whether it was attacking rock or soft ground. My new method had met with complete success. From that day onward, this particular difficulty was overcome. The presence of rock no longer prevented the use of dredges. I had given the dredge complete mastery in any field of action, and the consequences of this were of incalculable importance.

No one would deny that Bunau-Varilla's technique of underwater dredging achieved a breakthrough, since it was later adopted successfully by both French and Americans. It was, however, adopted in a strictly limited capacity—almost exclusively to deal with the soft and regular strata in Panama Bay—and whether the same technique could have been successfully applied to the far harder and more complex strata among the hills, is open to question. Bunau-Varilla's "discovery", therefore, although ingenious and useful, never had the far-reaching consequences that he claims.

His second "discovery" was a corollary of his first: the technique of building what was initially a lock canal and then transforming it to a sea-level canal by underwater dredging.

This conception he also explains in detail.

> One of the contractors boldly adopted my new method. He withdrew rails, trains and pumps from the cut in the Mindi hills, and began to excavate by dredge. This success demonstrated my new method to be not only equal to open-air excavation but more economical. What a magic transformation this meant. I resolved to concentrate all my efforts upon this triumph . . . and [accordingly] to begin right away excavating by dredges in the Culebra Cut itself. It was possible to do this by establishing artificial lagoons on either side of the saddle and at either extremity of the section. It sufficed to dig at each of these points a pool, and to bring water to it; it was then possible to float dredges and barges, and to excavate in the wet. To carry off the products of the dredging, an elevator was built at each lagoon . . . Thus I carried out for the first time the idea of attacking the cut by a floating dredge sixty feet above the level of the river . . . Some months later I judged the time was ripe for explaining fully my solution to the canal problem. I had not to say "I want a lock canal." The proposition had to be made quite differently: "See, we have reached at last the rational method of excavation: the dredging method. This makes us independent of rains and slides. I propose therefore to generalise my system. The isthmus

will be subdivided into a series of pools, in which we will float dredges, tugs and scows. If we unite these pools by locks, we shall have continuous water communication between the oceans. Make these locks sufficiently spacious for sea vessels. Conduct your work—and this will be easy—so as not to interfere with the passage of vessels. You will not then have built a lock canal: you will simply have utilised the work already carried out in order to open up transisthmian navigation. The company will be able to levy tolls and will have a future ahead of it of which it will be the master." This convincing argument overthrew all objections and decided the Company, in 1887, to adopt the so-called provisory lock canal. I had once more followed the example of the Greek philosopher who demonstrated movement by walking.

Bunau-Varilla's scheme was an ingenious compromise. It was acceptable to de Lesseps, it cut initial costs, and it presented no technical difficulties. It did, however, have serious disadvantages—or so at least the Americans concluded eighteen years later when he presented a similar scheme to their board of consulting engineers. These disadvantages were chiefly three: the delay and danger inherent in vessels using the canal while excavation was still in progress: the fact that a great deal of work (on the locks, for example) would be wasted, since these would be progressively destroyed; and the fact that no final date could be given for completion, since the canal would go on being improved *ad infinitum*.

It is hard to say whether these disadvantages were serious enough to rule out the possibility of success. Bunau-Varilla was certain they were not, and he claims it was only the premature and ill-advised liquidation of the *Compagnie Universelle* which robbed him of victory. Here is what he says:

> It was just when the canal enterprise deserved for the first time to be regarded as an absolute certainty that public confidence was withdrawn from it. On the 14th December, 1888, the Company failed. It was indeed a sinister day when the French abandoned, without the shadow of a reason, this glorious battlefield, after victory had been absolutely won over the quasi-insuperable obstacles of Nature . . . [so that] today we behold in foreign hands the great work our minds conceived, and which our gold and our blood brought forth from the domain of the Impossible.

Rhetoric and jingoism apart, the liquidation of de Lesseps' company was indeed a tragedy, and Bunau-Varilla's contention that it was a needless tragedy deserves looking into.

His argument is simple: that by the end of 1888 the Atlantic and Pacific extremities of the canal had been completed, and that in the central section among the hills his new technique of dredging was proving so successful that victory was within sight. It is certainly true that by the spring of 1888 the canal was open to traffic for a total of fifteen miles—eleven miles between the earth platform at Colon and Palo Horqueta in the Chagres valley, and four miles between La Boca wharf and Diablo Hill. It is also true that in the Culebra Cut, Artigue, Sonderegger and Company were making a supreme effort to boost excavation. Throughout that summer and autumn more than 2,900 men worked non-stop in the Cut, bludgeoned during the day by sadic sun and tropic rain, and toiling by night in the glare of more than 300 flood-lights; they used 800 dump-cars, fifty-four locomotives, twenty-three steam-shovels and four of Bunau-Varilla's floating dredges, all concentrated within a single mile, and the Panama *Star and Herald* has left us a vignette of their labours. "Enormously powerful dredges tear up the earth from the bed of the Cut and force it through seemingly impossible lengths of pipe to its destined resting place, whilst all along the sides of the Cut mighty excavators, moving slowly along the railroad-tracks tear away the bowels of the mountains with incredible rapidity, and deposit the debris in cars that bear it away." No one would deny the heroic scale of the effort. Unfortunately, however, the cubage removed was not commensurate with the energy expended. For although the French assault on Culebra was ingenious and dedicated, it was not based on an ideal plan as regards either excavation or transportation. If therefore one looks at hard facts—the cubage removed and the cubage which still remained—it is obvious that in spite of Bunau-Varilla's claim, success for the French was a chimera. For as the rains fell and the dumps slid in and the sides of the Cut had to be pushed farther and farther back, the end was always further away than it had seemed when work began.

What adds poignancy to this final phase of the French assault is the skill and enthusiasm with which the locks were built. This was due largely to the influence of Eiffel.

Alexander Gustave Eiffel was born in 1832, in Dijon, and his association with the canal dated back to the Paris Congress of 1879. He was a brilliant engineer, whose famous tower is the most spectacular but not the most technically-sophisticated of his achievements. On December 10, 1887 he signed a contract with the *Compagnie Universelle* for the creation of ten locks, five on the Atlantic slope of the divide (at Bohio, San Pablo, Matachin, Bas Obispo and Emperador) and five on the Pacific slope (at Cucuracha, Pedro

Miguel, Miraflores and a double flight at La Boca). These locks were carefully sited on solid rock and were adjacent to stations on the Panama Railroad; their gates were to be manufactured in Europe to a design patented by Eiffel himself.

A good deal of criticism has been levelled, and justly, at the terms of contract for this work, and some of the financial arrangements were indeed blatantly dishonest; this, however, should not blind us to the magnitude of Eiffel's achievements. For throughout the early months of 1888 he displayed remarkable energy and enthusiasm. On February 25th he wrote to de Lesseps: "My technical and administrative staffs have been busy on the isthmus since January 1st. Excavation of nine lock basins is now under way with a labour force of 3,500 men, and the work is proceeding more actively than I could have expected." This is corroborated by the Panama *Star and Herald*:

> At San Pablo [their reporter writes] I saw 600 men working on the 270 x 18 metre lock. Here, boring holes for the next blasting are 120 miners; here are men loading the large buckets which as soon as they are filled are lifted by cranes up to the level of the top cut and emptied onto the railroad track; at the end of the locks are still other gangs with wheelbarrows wheeling away the earth as fast as their barrows can be loaded.

The reporter goes on to add that many kinds of machinery and labour-saving devices were being installed—"rock crushers, machine shops and forges . . . At Paraiso and Miraflores the picture is the same, with great winches hauling the trains of Decauville dump-cars up the steep inclines, pumps draining water out of the sites: the whole appearance . . . [being] that of a gigantic undertaking well-handled."

In fact 1888 was a year of solid if unspectacular progress; and it is ironic that just as the French, were, for the first time, feeling their way towards a feasible target, de Lesseps ran out of funds.

The first crack in the Company's financial façade appeared in the spring of 1886. Prior to this, its various issues of stocks and bonds had always been oversubscribed; in April 1886, however (while the government was looking into the pros and cons of a lottery) de Lesseps tried to float an issue of 362,000 shares on the Bourse, and only 141,000 of them were taken up. There were two reasons for this. The year 1885 had been a bad one on the isthmus, a series of highly critical reports had appeared in the press, and these had sown doubts in the minds of the thousands of small investors who up to now had been the company's prop and stay. Even more damaging was the fact that the company had become involved in politics—an involvement which stemmed from de Lesseps' request for a lottery. So that at just the time the *Compagnie Universelle* needed money, it came under vociferous attack in both parliament and press.

It was to counter those attacks that the de Lesseps, father and son, resorted to bribery.

André Siegfried puts the case very clearly. "A dishonest press kept hounding the Company, and in particular a little rag called *La Panama* followed it like a wolf. De Lesseps gave way, too quickly perhaps. He got into the habit of paying for favourable publicity, and his monthly cheques were sometimes simply the price of silence." Edouard Drumont in *La Dernière Bataille* tells the same story:

> The top hats arrived first with enormous demands. Then came the smaller hats, and then the little ones—mere children's caps. Finally some vague reporter would appear, and he would get a little cheque for having inserted a single line mentioning The Great Frenchman or Tototte or Ismael or some other member of de Lesseps' family. Some didn't contribute anything, but got their cheques just the same. This was hush-money from a Company willing to pay simply to be left alone.

The rapaciousness of the press, however, was nothing to that of the financiers and politicians.

Reading de Lesseps' speeches one is struck again and again by the amount of time he spends denouncing "these enemies of our great enterprise". And with good reason; for the sums they extracted out of the *Compagnie Universelle* were astronomic. To give a single example: in 1886 the Company raised 354 million francs by the issue of bonds, a sum which, if it had been transferred *in toto* to the company's books, would have gone far to solving its financial difficulties; but before the money reached the company, the incredible sum of 146 million francs disappeared into the maw of syndicates, promoters, politicians, financiers and professional con-men.

"But this is an enormous sum," the President of the Court exclaimed subsequently at de Lesseps' trial. "Where on earth did it all go?"

"You must remember, Mr. President," Charles de Lesseps replied, "that we were lost in a financial jungle, having to cope with the customs and usages which were then common practice. When you wish to make an issue and have established an underwriting syndicate and organised the publicity, you are far from finished. For you then see arriving a crowd of people whom you have never heard of before. They seem to rise up from the gutter; and we had, somehow, to deal with their threats, their libels and their broken promises. We were ignorant of how to deal with them, so we turned for advice to people who knew about these things. We employed first M. Léug-Crémieux and then Baron de Reinach. We paid these persons handsomely for their services, and gave them enough not only for themselves but for all the others as well."

It is impossible not to sympathise with Charles and Ferdinand de Lesseps. A Puritan might condemn them with the judgment that "he who toucheth pitch shall be defiled therewith", a cynic might claim that their only crime was being found out; but the fact is that France in the 1880s was in the grip of postwar depression, the political atmosphere was tainted with cynicism and corruption, and it would have needed a Saint Joan to purge both parliament and Bourse. The de Lesseps were no saints—Ferdinand was too worldly, and Charles, except in his relationship with his father, lacked the divine spark. So they swam with the tide, until the tide backed up and engulfed them.

It was the failure of the lottery which gave the company its *coup de grâce*.

For two years the government had hesitated whether or not to come to de Lesseps' aid; at last, in the autumn of 1888 the longed-for permission came through; but due to what Bunau-Varilla describes as "an incredible error of judgment", the bonds were undersubscribed, and the lottery from which so much had been hoped turned out to be not a panacea but a fiasco.

The company and their financial adviser, Baron de Reinach, had intended to arrange for the lottery bonds to be issued in three separate instalments of fifty million dollars; French bankers, however, taking their lead from M. Germain, founder and president of *le Crédit Lyonnais*, insisted that in order to ensure sufficiently attractive prizes all the bonds (to the value of 144 million dollars) ought to be issued simultaneously. By agreeing, against their better judgment, to Germain's advice, the company put all their eggs in one basket. And the result was disastrous. For the effort asked of the market was too great. Also the day before the bonds were issued the enemies of the canal flooded the Bourse with shares, depressing their value from seventy-four dollars to fifty-seven; while on the actual morning of subscription the news that de Lesseps had died in his sleep was telegraphed throughout the world. De Lesseps himself describes the result: "Lying rumours and false telegrams announcing my death were circulated all over the world! The scoundrels had chosen their time well; for a denial could not be issued until too late . . . A complaint has been lodged with the public prosecutor, who has started an investigation into these criminal acts." The culprits, however, were never found, and the evil they perpetrated lived on long after the ink on their telegrams had dried. For the failure of the lottery sounded the death knell of de Lesseps' canal. "Such," writes Bunau-Varilla, "were the dire consequences of the error in financial strategy committed on the advice of a man [M. Germain] whose name had hitherto been a symbol of prudence, far-sightedness and business acumen."

De Lesseps, however, refused to admit defeat. Accompanied by his son, Charles, he embarked in the late autumn of 1888 on a whirl-wind tour of France; if only, he said, 500,000 Frenchmen would subscribe to just a couple of bonds apiece the greatest enterprise of the century could still, at the last minute, be saved.

His tour was, for a man of eighty-three, an almost incredible feat of endurance; for in less than six weeks he and Charles visited Periguex, Bergerac, Bordeaux, Roubaix, Tours, Blois, Chartres, Sens, Versailles, Le Mans, Rennes, Nancy, Dijon, Lyons, Vienne, Marseilles, Nîmes, Cette, Perpignan, Saint-Étienne, Clermont-Ferrand, Bourges, Brest, Lorient and Nantes, attending at each town a formal banquet, giving a two-hour lecture and answering as many questions as their audience cared to put. Nor would it be fair to describe the tour as nothing but a forlorn hope. For de Lesseps was still a magic figure, loved and revered by thousands of ordinary Frenchmen, and if only speculators and politicians had ceased to hound him he might, even at the eleventh hour, have raised the necessary funds. But, to quote André Siegfried, "one could now distinguish a very real hatred against the *Compagnie Universelle*. Some people took an unholy joy in pursuing it and trying to destroy it. 'The ruin is getting on fine,' announced Deputy Goirand from the floor of the Chamber, 'scarcely more than fifty per cent remains to be lost'." And attacks such as this did the company inestimable harm. For they induced the government to play the part of Pontius Pilate, to wash their hands of the whole affair and leave de Lesseps to fend for himself; they also induced thousands of small investors to withhold their support at the very moment the company needed it most.

At the end of his tour, on November 29th, de Lesseps placed the last of the lottery bonds on the market. It was his final throw, his company's *émission de l'agonie* or deathbed flotation; and on December 2nd he made a personal plea to the nation:

> I appeal to all Frenchmen. I appeal to all my associates whose fortunes are threatened.
> I have dedicated my life to two great works which have been

called impossible: Suez and Panama. Suez is completed and France has been enriched. Do you wish to complete Panama?

Your fate is in your hands. Decide!

The public decided—but in the negative. A minimum of 400,000 bonds had to be taken up to give the company even a temporary respite: less than 200,000 were sold.

Yet even now de Lesseps refused to admit defeat. He placed before the Chamber of Deputies a bill authorising the *Compagnie Universelle* to suspend payment of all debts and interest for three months, while he attempted to float a new company. On December 15th, however, the Chamber rejected his bill by 256 votes to 181. De Lesseps had played his last card and lost.

Ten minutes after the vote had been taken, a reporter called at his house with news of the bill's rejection and his company's impending liquidation. The old man turned pale: "*C'est impossible,*" he whispered. "*C'est indigne.*"

A legend has grown up that—like Mary Tudor after the loss of Calais—he never smiled again.

(*Above left*) Jules Dingler
(*Above*) Charles de Lesseps

Lucien N.-B. Wyse

Gatun

6

"IT IS NO CRIME TO GROW OLD"

The failure of the *Compagnie Universelle* was the prelude to a witch-hunt that rocked the nation. Before the tumult subsided hundreds of prominent names were besmirched, shares crashed, cabinets resigned, duels were fought, and the words *panamiste* and *chéquard* (meaning the recipient of a bribe) became written into the French language as synonyms of corruption.

On December 15th the *Tribunal Civil de la Seine* appointed three temporary receivers: Ms. Baudelot, Denormandie and Hue. These receivers ordered the immediate suspension of all payments by the Company except amortisation of the bond issues and lottery prizes which were guaranteed by special funds. They then turned their attention to the isthmus, where banks were refusing the Company's drafts, riots had broken out among the workers, and the contractors were threatening a shut-down. Realising that the abrupt cessation of work would ruin equipment and cause irreparable damage to the half-finished canal, the receivers arranged for warships to be despatched to Colon, and for the contractors to continue essential operations, being paid by ninety-day notes secured by shares of the Panama Railroad. The *Compagnie Universelle* was then officially dissolved, and Joseph Brunet (a former minister of education) was appointed as liquidator.

Brunet extended the agreement whereby essential work was continued while the number of employees on the Company payroll was progressively reduced. This reduction was carried out as sympathetically as possible, but it led nevertheless to a great deal of hardship. Within a year the working force was cut from 14,000 to 800; the bankrupt Company was unable to assist the large number of men thrown suddenly out of work, and many became squatters or took to the jungle. The Jamaican and American governments, however, repatriated their citizens free of charge. Brunet's next step was to appoint Wyse to negotiate an extension of the 1878 concession with Colombia; and as soon as this had been done, he set up a committee of prominent engineers to report on the possibility of completing the canal, either with locks or at sea-level. Liquidation, in other words, proceeded at first in an orderly manner under sympathetic public administration.

For several weeks de Lesseps co-operated with the liquidators, devoting the remnants of his once stupendous energy to salvaging what little he could from the wreck of his beloved enterprise. He tried to form a new corporation, the *Compagnie Universelle pour l'Achèvement du Canal Interocéanique;* but by early in February it was clear that sufficient funds would never be raised. For although *le grand Français* still commanded the love and affection of the men in the street (parents still sent him their children's savings and women in tears still tried to kiss his clothes) it was bankers and cartels who held the purse strings, and they made it plain that in their opinion only a fool would throw good money after bad into "the bottomless ditch of Panama".

A few weeks after his company was dissolved, Ferdinand de Lesseps retired to La Chesnaye, a small country estate about twenty miles from Issoudun. His spirit was utterly broken. In mid-December he had been a robust and inspiring leader, remarkable for both mental and physical virility. By mid-March he was a pathetic and feeble old man, sinking rapidly into senility. To quote Gerstle Mack:

> At first he was able to enjoy short strolls in the garden; then as he grew weaker he was pushed about in a wheelchair on sunny days. Most of the time he would sit quietly in front of the fire, too deaf to hear more than a few words of conversation but occasionally breaking into the talk with some anecdote of his own. Fortunately for his peace of mind his thoughts dwelt more often on the distant past than on the affairs of [the *Compagnie Universelle*] ... His strong body remained alive long after his mind had almost flickered out. And so he lived on [for almost five more years], tended like a child by his devoted wife, and humoured and protected by his children.

It would be pleasant to record that the man who had done so much for his country was allowed to end his days if not in honour at least in peace. On the contrary, he was hounded to his grave by a campaign whose virulence and calumny has few equals in history.

The storm broke in 1890 with the publication of *La Derniére Bataille* by Édouard Drumont, a scurrilous and sensational attack on the *Compagnie Universelle* in general and Ferdinand de Lesseps in particular. Drumont may have been actuated in part by a genuine desire to expose corruption in high places, but his book is wildly exaggerated and reads today like the composition of a hysterical schoolboy. Here is his account of mortality on the isthmus:

> The men died like flies at the rate of sixty per cent. The number of deaths can not have been less than 30,000. Sometimes the

[negro] workmen who died at their posts were merely tipped onto the embankments and covered with twenty inches of earth ... European workmen, on the other hand were interred with such zeal that they were frequently buried before they were even dead ... The isthmus has become one enormous boneyard.

Noteworthy too, are his bitter personal attacks on de Lesseps:

> This scoundrel is allowed to walk about like a triumphant hero. The poor devil who steals a loaf of bread is dragged before the judge of a criminal court. But no one has started an investigation into the swallowing up of almost a billion and a half francs: not once has this man been asked, "What have you done with our money?" The Panama undertaking is like the old-time witches' sabbath, the Mass read backwards, the sign of the Cross with the left hand; and the consecration of de Lesseps as *le grand Français* is a joke, and the antithesis of truth. For it can confidently be asserted that no contemporary Frenchman was ever more systematically hostile to French interests or did more harm to his country.

The judgment of history has refuted this. But at the time there were many who allowed themselves to be convinced of its truth—disgruntled shareholders, those whom the Company had bribed but hadn't bribed sufficiently, dismissed employees who bore a grudge, those to whom the canal had become no more than a football to be knocked around for political gain, and finally the great throng of ordinary men and women who joined the witch-hunt simply through fear of being labelled *chéquard* or *panamiste*. The latter was described with wry humour by Barrès in *Leurs Figures*:

> Everyone believed that if they gave the appearance of dreading exposure, they would at once be suspected of a multiplicity of crimes. It was cruel yet at the same time curiously satisfying to see all these cunning fellows—the innocent along with the guilty—marching along with blank faces and hunched shoulders, intoning in chorus: "We must see this thing through, and if there have been any grafters they indeed deserve to be punished."

In the last analysis, therefore, the witch-hunt was due to fear: fear and the age-old human foible of transferring guilt to a scapegoat.

Throughout the winter of 1890/91 mutterings of discontent were heard in parliament and press. A group of deputies, led by Delahaye, Gauthier and Le Provost de Launay, presented a sheaf of petitions to the Minister of Justice; a group of newspapers—led by *La*

Cocarde, La Libre Parole and *La Panama*—demanded a government investigation; and a group of security holders petitioned for an audit of the company's accounts. Eventually, in the summer of 1891, a reluctant government was goaded into action. On June 11th the public prosecutor, acting on instructions from Clément Fallières (Minister of Justice) preferred charges of fraud and breach of trust against Ferdinand, Charles and Victor de Lesseps, Marius Fontane (the company's secretary general) and Henri Cottu (one of the directors). It was the start of a veritable avalanche of prosecutions, testimonies, depositions, reports, charges, counter-charges, convictions and appeals which rocked France long after Ferdinand de Lesseps had been laid to rest.

Three separate sets of proceedings were brought against Company officials: the indictment of certain directors for fraud, breach of trust and maladministration; the indictment of directors and agents for the corruption of public officials, and a parliamentary enquiry which ran concurrently with the court cases and was conducted by a committee of the Chamber of Deputies. The proceedings dragged on for years. Before they were finished, a host of public figures had been dishonoured; there had been blackmail, extradition and attempted murder. Yet when all the sound and fury died away, less than half a dozen men were required to pay the penalty of imprisonment. Among these was one who deserved it less than any of his associates: Charles de Lesseps.

Charles had always doubted the practicability of building a canal through the isthmus. When, however, his warnings were disregarded he had agreed, against his better judgment, to join forces with his father, adding prophetically that whatever happened he would never complain. His fine words were now put to the test.

On June 22nd the public prosecutor expressed the wish to interrogate Ferdinand de Lesseps with regard to the Company's books. For the old man, now broken in health and spirit, the interview was a terrible ordeal; and Charles's account of it shows very clearly his wish to shield his father no matter what the cost to himself.

> On the day [my father] was to go to the counsellor's office, I called for him with Dr. Moissenet, who expressed the opinion that it would be very imprudent for my father to go out. I felt nevertheless that the meeting would have to take place sooner or later, and that it would be best for my father to get it over and done with; I felt, too that one meeting would suffice, and that thereafter the counsellor would accept me as my father's deputy . . . My father rose from his bed and said, "I shall go." He dressed carefully, and

by the time we reached M. Prinet's office he had apparently regained some of his former strength. He remained inside for three-quarters of an hour . . . and when he left his face was radiant with charm and energy—as was always the case in moments of crisis. By the time we got home, however, reaction had set in. It was frightful. For the next three weeks my father did not speak a single word, but lay quietly in his bed. We could see that he was troubled by something he couldn't express. Every day I tried to ease his depression, but in vain. At last, however, I thought of repeating a phrase I had often heard him use: "One thing is certain: in the end good will triumph over evil." At last my father spoke: "If that were not so," he whispered, "life would not be worth living." I embraced him, and said: "The words are yours: I shall always believe them: and I'm sure at your age that you won't want to change your philosophy." This seemed to comfort my father, and thenceforward his condition improved.

Charles's request to be accepted as his father's deputy was granted; and to quote Gerstle Mack: "The old man was not molested again. While he dreamed away his last years in front of the fire at La Chesnaye, serenely unaware of the sordid bedlam broken loose in Paris, the son shouldered his father's burden of disgrace as well as his own."

The trials which dragged on over the next eighteen months were travesties of justice; for the Advocate General was determined to obtain a conviction in order to satisfy the public clamour for a scapegoat. He described the attempt to build a canal as "the greatest fraud of modern times", and ended his summing up with the words: "You must not hesitate to punish these criminals who, in order to line their own pockets with millions, have had recourse to every manoeuvre, every fraud . . . I demand the most severe penalty."

Ferdinand and his son were sentenced to five years in prison and a fine of 3,000 francs, Cottu and Fontane to two years and 2,000 francs, and Eiffel to two years and 20,000 francs.

The severity of the sentences seems inexcusable today; and indeed even at the time they were partially rescinded on the grounds that the law of limitation had been exceeded: so mercy was found in the unlikely guise of red-tape. The old man was left in peace at La Chesnaye, but Charles served six months of his sentence before being released in the autumn of 1893 on the grounds of ill health. His tribulations, however, were far from over; for in January 1894 he was publicly humiliated by the erasure of his name from the Legion of Honour, and a couple of years later he was called on to pay a further 900,000 francs (the unfulfilled portion of a fine imposed on Baihaut and Blondin). He offered a smaller sum—quite literally everything he possessed—and when this was refused fled to London to avoid a further term of imprisonment.

In the middle of this ill-deserved persecution his father died.

For several years the old man had been virtually confined to his room in La Chesnaye, although sometimes on sunny days his family would wheel him up and down the terrace in a specially constructed chair. He died on December 7th, 1894, a few days after his eighty-ninth birthday, mercifully unaware of the scandal and disgrace which had followed the liquidation of his company.

He was buried in the cemetery of Père-Lachaise on December 15th; and there were still people who believed that his family amassed a considerable private fortune from their directorships of the *Compagnie Universelle*. In fact they were so poor that the funeral expenses had to be met by the board of directors of Suez.

It is perhaps fitting that the final word on de Lesseps should be left to the person who knew him best: his wife. In November 1892 a contributor to *Le Gaulois* suggested, not unkindly, that it might have been better if the old man had died before the collapse of the *Compagnie Universelle*, at the peak of his fame. To this Mme. de Lesseps made a moving reply:

> I read in your newspaper a few lines to the effect that M. de Lesseps has lived some weeks too long. I will not protest against this unchristian sentiment, except to say that its author can have given no thought to the wife and children who deeply love and revere this old man and to whom his life, however frail it may be, is more precious than anything in the world. It is no crime to grow old. It would be impossible to find another man who, having accomplished all that he did, would have retired from it with empty hands, making no provision for the future of his large family—a sacrifice in which I as well as my children take pride.

And when she spoke of sacrifice, this was no exaggeration. For de Lesseps, through whose hands had passed tens of millions of francs, died a poor man. If the Suez shareholders had not voted his family a pension, they would have been virtually destitute.

The judgment of history has endorsed Mme. de Lesseps' eulogy. For scandal and trials are forgotten today, and de Lesseps is remembered once again as *le grand Français*: the man who had the imagination to dream, and the courage to try to make his dream come true.

PART TWO

THE AMERICAN CANAL

7

"I TOOK THE CANAL ZONE AND LEFT CONGRESS TO DEBATE"
(President Theodore Roosevelt)

De Lesseps was dead. But his dream lingered on, kept alive along the line of the canal by a token force of workers, and in the lobbies of France and the United States by the machinations of two dedicated men—William Nelson Cromwell and Philippe Bunau-Varilla.

On the isthmus, the failure of the *Compagnie Universelle* left nearly 14,000 workers unemployed and destitute. Some were shipped back by the British consul to their homes in the West Indies. Others stayed where they were, sinking into easy-going poverty among the maroons and liberated slaves; they became squatters, each family with its tumble-down shack of wood and corrugated iron, and square of poorly cultivated ground. But some three or four hundred remained at work. For the liquidators had the good sense to realise that the half-finished canal and its machinery were assets worth preserving.

The Canal Zone at the turn of the century has often been described as a "graveyard"; and most writers have gone out of their way to stress the ruin and desolation—"the hundreds of tons of rusted and dilapidated machinery, the abandoned trains, the locomotives with trees sprouting out of their fireboxes, the great excavators wreathed in greenery, and the 2,000 ruined houses empty except for the termites which were steadily eating them away." This is picturesque but misleading. Some machinery, of course, was abandoned, and some buildings fell into disrepair. But by and large the French preserved their equipment with ingenuity and skill, oiling, greasing and mothballing their locomotives, dump-cars, steam-shovels and dredges so successfully that many of them were still being used twenty-five years later by the Americans. Also they kept up the work of excavation—albeit on a very limited scale—in the Culebra Cut.

The reason for this continued activity was simple. The French had hopes of selling their canal to the United States.

It must have seemed, in the years which immediately followed liquidation, a forlorn hope. For it would be idle to pretend that the French débâcle had not been viewed with considerable satisfaction in the New World, since much as the Americans admired de Lesseps as a man, they heartily disapproved of a canal through their continent being built by "a crowd of foreigners"—said President Hayes, "the policy of this country is for a canal under *American* control." When therefore the *Compagnie Universelle* went into liquidation there was widespread relief in the United States and people's thoughts began to turn again to the prospect of an American-built canal—but not through Panama, through Nicaragua.

Nicaragua had always been the favoured route of the American public. It lay further north than Panama, in a more civilised terrain and under a more stable government; also a canal through Nicaragua would reduce, even more drastically than a canal through Panama, the journey between Atlantic and Pacific ports. Within three months of French liquidation, a fleet of dredgers was shifting sandbars off the mouth of the Rio San Juan.

The Nicaraguan Canal Association was a private company with headquarters in New York. It cleared twenty miles of forest between Lake Nicaragua and the Caribbean, built eleven miles of railroad and dug a splendid canal 280 feet wide and seventeen feet deep—but, alas, only three quarters of a mile in length. Then it went bankrupt.

Its crash was less spectacular than that of de Lesseps' company but even more final. And for the time being the idea of a canal fell into abeyance; for its construction was proving a far tougher proposition than anyone had imagined. On the isthmus itself, Panama and Colon reverted to sleepy and not very sanitary tropical villages; the trains of the railroad, half-empty now, puffed peacefully to and fro, and the Cuna Indians in their dugout canoes came creeping back to the coral flats of the Chagres. Only in the Culebra Cut and the larger storage sheds were there indications that de Lesseps' dream was not dead but dormant.

The spark which brought it back to life was the Spanish-American War, and in particular the voyage of the U.S. *Oregon*.

The battleship *Oregon* left San Francisco on March 19th, 1898, a few weeks after the United States had declared war on Spain. She was needed, it was said urgently, in the Caribbean. Yet her transit via the Straits of Magellan involved a voyage of 13,000 miles and sixty-eight days. By the time she arrived at Key West the war was virtually over. Nothing could have brought home more clearly to the American public the need for an interoceanic canal. And early in 1899 Senator John T. Morgan introduced a bill providing for the "construction, operation and fortification of a canal by the United States government".

The proposed site of Morgan's waterway, however, was not

Panama but Nicaragua. And Nicaragua is where the canal would be today if it were not for Cromwell and Bunau-Varilla.

William Nelson Cromwell was a small and strikingly handsome man with aquiline features and, although he was not yet fifty, a great mane of snow-white hair. He was a New York attorney (co-founder of the famous partnership of Sullivan and Cromwell), and he counted among his friends a large number of influential politicians and businessmen.

In 1896 the *Compagnie Nouvelle* appointed him as its American counsel. It was a costly appointment, for Cromwell's fees were astronomic; but it was probably the wisest move that the company ever made. For Cromwell was an inspired lobbyist; and throughout the critical years 1897–1903 he advanced the interests of his clients with tireless energy and Machiavellian skill. It was he who blocked Morgan's bill through the House; it was he who organised a team of engineers to make a thorough survey of the Chagres basin and a team of journalists to make the results of their survey known; and it was largely due to his efforts that when in 1899 the U.S. government appointed a commission to survey possible routes through Central America, its terms of reference included the investigation not only of Nicaragua but also of Panama.

And while Cromwell campaigned for a canal through Panama as the accredited advocate of the *Compagnie Nouvelle*, Bunau-Varilla embarked on a private and intensely personal campaign of his own.

Philippe Bunau-Varilla, to quote his autobiography, had "consecrated [his] life to building the Panama canal". As a young man he had shown courage, enterprise and boundless energy in excavating the Culebra Cut, and now in his middle age he displayed the same qualities—plus, alas, a complete lack of moral scruples—in the field of amateur diplomacy: amateur because some of his antics were so preposterous that he was soon disowned not only by the French government but also by the *Compagnie Nouvelle*. To twentieth-century readers he appears in his latter role as a figure to be laughed at: flamboyantly moustached, absurdly vain, ludicrously self-opinionated and ever eager to spring to attention at the first note of the *Marseillaise*. But at the turn of the century flag-waving patriots were in fashion; Bunau-Varilla was obsessed with one idea—to vindicate French honour (and his own) by completing the canal—and men with an *idée fixe* have always been effective. In the early 1890s he tried to interest all and sundry in the idea of taking over de Lesseps' canal—the Colombian government, *Le Crédit Foncier*, even the Russian Ministry of Finance—but eventually he came to realise that there was only one possible purchaser: the government of the United States. So he joined forces with Cromwell.

They were an ill-matched pair, disapproving of each other's methods, suspecting each other's motives, and cordially disliking one another. Their virtues, however, were to some extent complementary; and they had one stroke of luck. On May 8th, 1902, only a few weeks before the Senate debate which was to decide on the respective merits of Nicaragua and Panama, Mont Pelée erupted with the loss of more than 30,000 lives. This made the public earthquake-conscious; and only a few days after the dust had settled on Pelée, Momotombo also burst into life. And Momotombo was on the shore of Lake Nicaragua.

Cromwell and Bunau-Varilla were quick to seize their chance. For years the advocates of Panama had been contrasting the absence of volcanoes on the isthmus with the conglomeration of volcanic craters in Nicaragua; and now, at just the right psychological moment, their point had been dramatically rammed home. Bunau-Varilla sent a copy of his pamphlet *Panama or Nicaragua?* to each of the ninety members of Senate, with the Nicaraguan craters conspicuously ringed in red; he also provided the New York *Sun* with data for a series on volcanic disasters. Here was something which the public could understand more easily than dry-as-dust statistics, and it wasn't long before lurid pictures began to be drawn of a Nicaraguan canal destroyed overnight by eruption. The Nicaraguan government did what it could to counter the adverse publicity by implying that all craters along the line of the proposed canal were extinct. But Bunau-Varilla rose magnificently to the challenge. He scoured the philatelists and bought ninety modern Nicaraguan postage stamps; these he mailed, a couple of days before the vital debate, to the ninety members of the Senate; and the evidence of the stamps was irrefutable; for there in lurid colour was the picture of a volcano overlooking Lake Nicaragua (less than twenty miles from the proposed route) in full eruption.

The Senate voted for Panama.

The whole business was distasteful to a good many Americans, who didn't like to think that an intention of Congress could be reversed by a French adventurer and an adroit lawyer. But in fact Cromwell and Bunau-Varilla, whatever their motives and methods, were pleading a just cause. Panama was a better route than Nicaragua. For although the latter's long, winding and many-locked canal might have coped with shipping in the early 1900s, it would have been altogether inadequate to handle the far larger vessels of the middle of the century. Bunau-Varilla, therefore, helped to save the United States from an expensive mistake; and if his contribution to building the Panama Canal had ended here he would be remembered today with affection. His machinations, however, were far from over.

The bill passed by the Senate on June 19th, 1902 authorised Roosevelt to acquire the effects of the French company for not more than forty million dollars, to acquire from the government of Colombia a strip of land six miles wide along the proposed route, and to draw up a treaty to authorise the building of a canal. But it also empowered him, in the event of French or Colombian recalcitrance, to reopen negotiations with Nicaragua.

The key, clearly, was the acquisition of land from Colombia; for once this had been effected the French would have an added incentive to sell their rights and equipment. A treaty was therefore quickly negotiated between John Hay, the American Secretary of State, and Thomas Herran, the Colombian Chargé d'Affaires in Washington. It was a good straightforward treaty, granting the United States administrative control over the land which it needed for a hundred years; in return Colombia was to be given an immediate payment of ten million dollars in gold, and an annual payment of 250,000 dollars from canal tolls. It was signed by the two negotiators, ratified by the Senate and passed to the Colombian government for their formal approval. Then there was trouble. Days dragged into weeks, weeks into months, and months into years: and still the Colombian Senate failed to ratify the treaty.

A multitude of articles, pamphlets and books have been written on what happened next. It is a complex story; but Gerstle Mack has neatly distilled the essence of it into a couple of sentences.

> Throughout negotiations the Bogota [Colombian] government, distracted by civil war, isolated in its remote mountain capital, and with its head figuratively as well as literally in the Andean clouds, displayed an exasperating ineptitude ... [Roosevelt lost patience], and having persuaded himself that the Colombians were bandits and blackmailers he proceeded to treat them as such.

To quote his own words, he took the isthmus, started the canal and left Congress to debate.

For this high-handed breach of international law he has been universally and justly condemned. But it is worth remembering that the Bogota government contributed in part to its own misfortune. Some Colombians, it is true, opposed the sale of territory to the United States through genuine patriotism—it was after all *their* country over which engineers and diplomats were haggling; but the majority simply felt that there had not been enough bargaining, and that a country which had willingly offered ten million dollars could, when it came to the crunch, be persuaded to offer a great deal more. So their Senate procrastinated.

These tactics appeared outrageous to those who wanted nothing more than to get on with building the canal. And in particular they appeared outrageous to the citizens of Panama, who had long regarded a canal through their territory as a guarantee of prosperity. Discontent in the isthmus started to snowball.

The links which bound Panama to Colombia had never been strong. Geographically Panama was out on a limb, cut off by jungle from the main body of the country (even in 1900 the journey from isthmus to capital took three weeks); and the republics of South and Central America have a traditional penchant for revolution. It wasn't long before both Bogota and Washington were inundated with a spate of warnings: if the Hay–Herran treaty wasn't ratified, Panama would secede.

These warnings were given little credence at first; but as month followed month, it began to seem to those who wanted the canal that a revolution was their best if not their only hope: if the Colombian government refused to sell them the land they needed, why shouldn't they help to set up a government in Panama who would?

It has been said—although without conclusive proof—that the revolution was touched off by members of the Panama Railroad. Certainly the revolutionary junta which forced on the isthmus in the summer of 1903 included a fair number of Railroad officials; and certainly they chose as their spokesman Dr. Manuel Amador, the railway's medical officer. And it was Amador who, that August, was sent as an emissary to the United States: his mission, to find out if a *coup d'état* would be greeted by prompt recognition, money and military aid.

Amador was a sound physician and a delightful man; but he was no revolutionary. His portrait gives us the clue to his character: a thin neck rising out of a too-large collar, puzzled eyes, a sad moustache (very different from the waxed and aggressive extravaganzas of Bunau-Varilla!) and an awry pince-nez; he looked exactly what he was: a dear old family doctor, rather past his prime, who found himself plunged suddenly into a maelstrom of intrigue which he neither approved of nor understood. If he had been dealing only with Cromwell he might have been able to cope. But after a first meeting full of *bonhomie* and promises, Cromwell departed post-haste for Europe—for the very good reason that the Colombian government had served him with formal notice that if members of the *Compagnie Nouvelle*, were caught trying to instigate a revolution, the French charter would be rescinded. So for a couple of weeks the unfortunate Amador wandered the streets of New York, rebuffed by members of the *Compagnie Nouvelle*, ignored by American officials and tailed by Colombian detectives. Then on September 22nd he met Bunau-Varilla.

The events of the next few weeks were a compound of tragedy and comic opera.

It seemed as if fate had suddenly dealt Bunau-Varilla every trump in the pack. Cromwell was away, the Americans wanted a revolution but didn't dare to forment one openly, and the spokesman of the revolutionaries was a meek little man in desperate need of a friend. Bunau-Varilla befriended him.

Having found out precisely what the revolutionaries wanted, he engineered a meeting between himself and the President. The two men understood one another perfectly. As Roosevelt wrote later: "Bunau-Varilla never had any assurance either from Hay or myself or anyone authorised to speak for us. However, he is an able fellow; he made it his business to find out what he thought our government would do, and he was able to advise his people accordingly." Whatever was or was not said at their meeting, Bunau-Varilla came away well satisfied; and his next step was to call on Hay.

"Mr. Secretary," he said, "a revolution on the isthmus appears to be imminent."

"Ah yes," Hay answered, "but we shan't be caught napping. Orders have been given to our naval forces to be ready to sail toward the isthmus."

Rightly or wrongly Bunau-Varilla chose to interpret this as a promise that if and when Panama seceded, the U.S. Navy would protect it.

Back in the Waldorf Astoria he presented Amador with an ultimatum. The revolution needed recognition: he had the President's word, he said, that it would be given promptly. The revolution needed military aid: he had the Secretary's word, he said, that warships would be forthcoming. The revolution needed money; he, Bunau-Varilla, would provide it himself—he dangled in front of Amador a cheque for a 100,000 dollars. There was, the little Frenchman added, only one stipulation: the new republic must appoint him (Bunau-Varilla) as its ambassador-extraordinary in Washington, giving him full powers to negotiate a treaty for completing the canal.

Amador didn't like it—nobody likes being blackmailed—but realising he was in no position to bargain he promised to try and persuade his colleagues to agree. And the smugly satisfied Bunau-Varilla proceeded that night to draft a declaration, of independence to invent a revolutionary code, to write out in full the telegram announcing his appointment as ambassador, and to get his wife to design and sew together a flag for the embryo republic.

Back on the isthmus the revolutionaries were in a quandary. Not unnaturally they wanted to know on what authority Bunau-Varilla was dispensing American dollars, promises and warships; and Amador advanced the plausible but wildly mistaken theory that he might perhaps be a member of the American secret service, acting as a go-between. And within forty-eight hours this theory appeared to be confirmed. For hearing that Colombian troops were advancing on the canal, the revolutionaries sent an urgent message to Bunau-Varilla begging him to have warships despatched at once. Bunau-Varilla, reading in the press that the cruiser *Nashville* had just left Jamaica under sealed orders, made an inspired guess and cabled in reply that a ship would arrive within two and a half days.

Two and a half days later the Colombian troops and the *Nashville* appeared simultaneously off Limon Bay.

And the junta, thinking the warship's presence was concrete evidence of American support, triggered off the revolution.

Along the line of the canal hardly a shot was fired in anger. The Colombian troops landed, and their generals demanded transport to Panama. The railroad staff, however, had prudently sent all their coaches except one to the opposite side of the isthmus. They ushered the unsuspecting generals into the one remaining coach, coupled it up and set off at high speed. Arriving in Panama, the generals were arrested; the Colombian officer in charge of the troops left behind in Limon Bay was bribed to take them away, and a revolution was officially declared. Within forty-eight hours the United States had given *de facto* recognition to the new republic.

The slickness with which the revolution had apparently been engineered and protected, and the indecent haste with which the new regime was recognised, left a nasty taste in the mouths of those with a sense of justice and international law—as the editor of *Out West* wrote in a leading article: "There was never precedent nor parallel for this Caesarian recognition of a 'republic' before it was delivered. We did not recognise even our own Texas *quite* so precipitately." Colombia, in short, had been robbed of a vital part of her territory.

An even greater injustice was to follow.

The revolution sparked off an exchange of telegrams between Amador and Bunau-Varilla, Amador demanding his 100,000 dollars and Bunau-Varilla demanding his appointment as minister-extraordinary. The revolutionaries disliked the idea of appointing a Frenchman as their country's first ambassador: not unnaturally it offended their sense of national pride, and they did their best to palm Bunau-Varilla off with a sinecure. But he simply held back the money which the revolution needed to pay its troops, and in the end Amador was obliged to give way. After a Gilbertian interlude in which their code broke down (one cable apparently reading: "Enthusiasm cable ships Atlantic help need rabbish thousand dollars Pacific little coal took flight Padilla pursues rest department!") Bunau-Varilla's appointment came through. He at once had himself photographed in diplomatic dress, presented his credentials to Roosevelt, and set to work to rush through a treaty to ensure the completion of his beloved canal.

The rush was a tragedy; and if Bunau-Varilla had not been so eaten up with his obsession, the subsequent history of the isthmus, and indeed of the whole of Central and South America, might have been a great deal happier. He was in a rush because he knew that a Panamanian delegation (consisting of Amador, Boyd and Arosemena) was en route to Washington, intent on having a hand in drafting the canal treaty; and he was terrified that his co-revolutionaries might insist on provisions which would hold up negotiations and jeopardise the project so dear to his heart. So he decided to go it alone: to draft, draw-up and sign the treaty himself.

He had less than three days before the delegation arrived; and it speaks volumes for his energy and ingenuity—if not for his moral scruples—that he achieved his goal with a couple of hours to spare.

He impressed Hay with the need for urgency. "I told the Secretary, 'so long as the delegation has not arrived in Washington, I am free to deal with you alone, armed with complete and absolute powers. When they arrive, I shall no longer be alone; in fact I may not be here at all!'" Hay took the hint, and immediately provided Bunau-Varilla with a draft treaty: the old Hay-Herran treaty, reworded to apply to the new republic. Bunau-Varilla took this treaty back to his room in the Waldorf Astoria. And here, to his everlasting shame, he altered it, making it so favourable to the United States that he knew they would be unable to resist signing it at once. He had never written a treaty in his life. He knew nothing of international law. He couldn't even write decent English. But none of this deterred him. He worked all night, and at dawn sent for a lawyer to correct his English and insert a flourish of legal embellishments. He then handed the treaty back to Hay, who, when he read the proposed alterations, could hardly believe his eyes.

Writing a few weeks later the Secretary admitted: "We have here a treaty very advantageous to the United States and, we must admit with what face we can muster, not so advantageous to Panama." While a senator in the ensuing debate remarked with even greater candour: "This treaty is more liberal in its concessions to us than anyone would ever have dreamed of. In fact it sounds very much as if we wrote it ourselves." Hay checked Bunau-Varilla's credentials, found (rather to his surprise) they were in order, and said he was willing to sign at once. At 6.40 p.m. on November 18th, 1903 the two men affixed their names to the treaty.

Two hours later—and two hours too late—Amador and his delegation arrived in Washington. Bunau-Varilla met them at the station and told them they might as well go home because the treaty had already been sealed and signed. "Amador," the little Frenchman wrote with repulsive glee, "nearly swooned . . . it gave me no little amusement."

The people of the United States have every reason to be proud of their role in building and administering the canal. They have less cause for pride in the method of its acquisition. For Roosevelt's lack of patience and Bunau-Varilla's lack of scruple left a legacy of ill-feeling, bitterness and bloodshed which has lasted seventy years and still hangs like a dark cloud over North-South American relations.

As for Bunau-Varilla himself: with the ratification on February 25th, 1904, of his treaty, he retired from active participation in the affairs of the canal. He shook hands with Hay, saying, not without dignity, "it seems to me that together we have fashioned something great"; then he retired to France to start work on his monumental apologia *Panama: the Creation, Destruction and Resurrection*. An extract from the latter, describing the events of 25th February, sums up his feelings. "[After I had signed the treaty] I walked away, having at last unburned my heart of the load which had so long weighed on it. I had fulfilled my mission, the mission I had taken on myself. I had safeguarded the work of French genius; I had avenged its honour; I had served France."

Once the Hay-Bunau-Varilla treaty had been signed it was inevitable that the Americans should purchase the assets of the *Compagnie Nouvelle*.

This is not to say that the purchase proceeded smoothly or without incident. On the contrary, the Colombian government and the French company both raised a whole series of moral, fiscal and legal issues. But the Americans held the ace of trumps. They had both legal and physical possession of the canal—"the Republic of

Panama" (to quote Bunau-Varilla's iniquitous document) "grants to the United States all the rights, power and authority within this zone which the United States would possess if it were the sovereign of the territory." It was obvious, therefore, that although for sentimental and ethical reasons the canal's past lay with France and Colombia, its future for practical purposes lay with the United States.

The transfer of assets would have been far more protracted if it hadn't been for the energy and acumen of Cromwell. For in the five months of legal cut and thrust which spanned the signing of the treaty and the signing of the transfer of deeds with the *Compagnie Nouvelle*, the New York attorney was in his element, refuting his opponents on points of law and skilfully by-passing the pitfalls of appeal, arbitration and writ. It has been pointed out that he and his associates made a vast sum of money out of handling the Company's affairs. This is true. But Cromwell's fees were no more astronomic than his services: and by mid-April his preparations were complete.

It would be hard to picture a more delightful setting than Paris in April, with the chestnut trees along the Avenue Kléber in bud. But it was a far from happy moment for France when, on the morning of April 16th, 1904, the assets of the *Compagnie Nouvelle* were formally assigned to the United States in exchange for forty million dollars. For with the flourish of the attorneys' pens France lost more than stock, property, railroad and rights; she lost more than the half-completed canal on which so many of her best and bravest engineers had worked and died; she lost forever the chance of fulfilling de Lesseps' dream.

8

CHAOS

The first of the U.S. construction gangs arrived on the isthmus in the early summer of 1904.

It was a daunting land to which they came: a graveyard of reputations and dreams, with the jungle, wet and wild as when Balboa first set foot in it, reasserting its hold on the abandoned diggings; Colon had degenerated to a shanty town, Panama was a "cesspit", some 25,000 workers lay buried along the line of the canal, and the ghosts of de Lesseps' failure were ubiquitous as the fever-carrying mosquitoes.

Yet it was not only a legacy of failure which the Americans inherited from the French. They inherited also a number of concrete and very substantial assets.

Most important of these was a canal already more than two-fifths completed: 78,146,960 cubic yards of excavation valued at more than twenty-five million dollars. It has been claimed that only about forty per cent of this French excavation was of use to the Americans. This, however, is not altogether true. For even those parts of de Lesseps' canal which were subsequently resited or submerged beneath Gatun Lake were used for many years to transport material—nearly all the rock, sand and cement for Gatun spillway and dam was transported along the old French cutting from Cristobal to Bohio. Also the Americans had the priceless advantage of being able to see the problems facing them along the whole line of the canal. While a list of ancillary assets bequeathed by the French makes impressive reading.

Perhaps the most important of these was the Panama Railroad—fifty miles of five-foot track (which a generation earlier had been one of the engineering wonders of the day), a hundred and fifty items of heavy rolling-stock, more than a hundred buildings in Panama, Colon and La Boca. The track was in tolerable repair; it was, however, only a single track, and it lacked sidings, signals and repair yards, while the rolling-stock was light in weight and old in years. Nevertheless an American—and hence presumably a conservative—valuation estimated the railroad to be worth more than nine million dollars.

An asset not so easy to value was the vast conglomeration of abandoned machinery: "enough to cover a 500 acre farm three foot deep and then to build a six foot fence around it." The book value of this equipment was twenty-nine million dollars; but some of it was in poor condition, much of it was obsolete, and in the final analysis its value was set at no more than two million dollars—a figure which seems far too low in view of the fact that more than 500 of de Lesseps' dump cars together with seventeen of his locomotives and nearly a dozen of his dredges worked for the Americans right through to the canal's completion. As evidence of this we have Goethals' order of February 1914: "much French equipment is still in use; no French scrap is to be loaded, and no French parts are to be used for repairing other equipment": a statement which refutes the misconception that the machinery handed over by the French was "little more than junk".

Last but by no means least the Americans inherited a veritable thesaurus of maps, plans, surveys and records. These had been compiled with skill and care: witness again Goethals' comment, "whenever I wanted information on a specific point I consulted the French records; they were first rate."

Apart from these tangible assets the Americans, when they started work, had two other incalculable advantages. Between 1881 and 1904 machinery for excavation had improved almost beyond recognition. Also doctors had acquired the necessary knowledge, at least in theory, to combat malaria and yellow fever.

Starting with these advantages it might have been thought that the Americans would make short work of the canal.

They did not. Indeed at the end of fifteen months, with virtually nothing accomplished, their effort was on the brink of petering out in panic and confusion. For they, like the French a generation before them, underestimated the isthmus. They placed construction work in the hands of an unwieldy Commission; they then demanded that the Commission "make the dirt fly" before the foundations which were a prerequisite of success had been properly laid.

Looking back, it is easy to see what ought to have been done. The Commission ought first to have eradicated disease, built up an efficient transport system, and organised accommodation and a commissariat; not until these essentials had been attended to should the actual work of construction have been put under way. And yet it is easy, too, to see why the public was so vociferous in demanding quick results. For twelve years Americans had endured the sight of a "crowd of foreigners" failing to cut a forty-mile ditch through the neck of "their" continent; then for another twelve they had suffered the procrastinations of the Colombian government. Small wonder that when at last Roosevelt won control of the Zone, the average citizen heaved a sigh of relief and felt that "now the dirt will be made to fly and the mountains to yield".

But it was not to be. The first step on the road to chaos was Roosevelt's appointment of the Army and Navy Commission in March 1904. This consisted of Admiral John G. Walker (chairman), General George W. Davis (governor), Colonel Frank J. Hecker and Messrs. Burr, Grunsky, Harrod and Parsons. However competent the members of this Commission may have been as individuals, they proved *in toto* inept and querulous, "unable to agree with one another or with anyone else". Part of the trouble rose from the fact that their duties were never clearly defined, and as a result each member of the Commission demanded a say in each and every minor decision; the result was that it became impossible to order a plank of wood, a bag of cement or a dose of quinine without first obtaining seven signatures. More fatal, however, than the Commission's cumbersome procedure and its residence in Washington far from the scene of operations, was the personality of its chairman.

Admiral Walker had in the past served his country with distinction, but when he took up his duties as chairman of the Commission he was well past his prime. His portrait indicates his character—a quarterdeck bearing and the "mutton-chop" whiskers of a bygone age—and his main preoccupation turned out to be not building the canal, but safeguarding the Commission's reputation against the sort of charges of waste which had been levelled at the French. His parsimony and ignorance are epitomised in the treatment he meted out to his senior medical officer, Major Gorgas, who spent long hours in the admiral's office pleading for the supplies of sulphur, wire-mesh, pyrethrum and oil which would, he knew, safeguard the isthmus from disease. Walker, however, only laughed at him, put his requisitions in a pigeonhole and said pointedly: "We must economise, Gorgas. And one thing is certain. Whether we build the canal or not, we will leave things so fixed that those fellows up on the hill can't find anything after us in the shape of graft." Such eventually came the old admiral's horror of spending money, that when at last he was forced to retire, more than a hundred and sixty vital requisitions, some of them five months old, were found in his desk unopened.

The failings of the Commission might have been partially offset by the appointment of a strong character as Chief Engineer. On May 6th, however, this important position was offered to John Wallace, a first-rate engineer but a man who was to prove sadly lacking in the qualities of leadership.

John Findley Wallace had risen from chainman to president of the American Society of Civil Engineers; he had rebuilt the Illinois Central Railroad, organised public transport for the Chicago World Fair, and was highly thought of both as an engineer and an administrator. He arrived in Colon on June 29th, and after a lightning tour of the diggings declared himself appalled—"I found nothing but jungle and chaos," he wrote, "from one end of the isthmus to the other, with a great deal of unrest among the labourers." In a fatal effort to achieve quick results, he trebled the working force in the Culebra Cut, setting new arrivals to dig piecemeal without proper plans, proper accommodation or proper equipment. This was the shortest road to chaos. For the antiquated railroad couldn't carry away even the small quantity of soil which was excavated; the men suffered from insanitary and overcrowded quarters, inadequate food, impure water and lack of medical services; and when new equipment did at last begin to arrive, it piled up in the docks because there was neither transport, storage nor plan to put it to use. In fairness to Wallace it must be pointed out that he was hampered rather than helped by the Commission. For his seven parsimonious bosses delayed or pigeonholed his vital requisitions, and when he cabled his complaints all they did was reprimand him for not appreciating that telegrams were expensive. A tougher character would have resented this. But Wallace was not by nature a rebel, and his successor John F. Stevens hit the nail on the head when he wrote: "Wallace was not an aggressive man, [and] a more strenuous attitude toward his superiors would have tended to a more active state of affairs."

So throughout the summer of 1904, unfulfilled requisitions piled up in Washington, dissatisfaction in the isthmus spread, goods stockpiled unopened along the quays, and the cost of food and accommodation soared—by October eggs were treble and rooms quadruple their price in the United States. A few examples give the picture all too clearly. On 2nd August, 1904, Wallace placed an order for urgently needed sewage pipes, which under normal circumstances these should have been obtainable in three to four weeks. After two months' deliberation the Commission replied by letter that they were unable to agree among themselves on the pipes' specification; on 7th October Wallace cabled in despair that he wanted *any* pipes, regardless of specification, and thus galvanised to action, the Commission placed an order toward the end of December. Unfortunately, however, they chose a small inland manufacturer who had no experience of expediting deliveries by sea; the result was that the pipes were shipped in dribs and drabs, the final consignment not arriving in Colon until 21st April, 1905—nine months after they had been asked for; by which time the trenches dug to house them had not surprisingly caved-in.

In the case of door-hinges the Commission went to the opposite extreme. An architect in Colon estimated that 15,000 new doorways would eventually be needed; he therefore ordered 15,000 frames, 15,000 doors and 15,000 pairs of hinges (i.e. the correct number of hinges, one pair for each door). The Commission, for reasons best known to themselves, reduced the order for doors to 12,000 but increased the order for door-hinges to 60,000. A couple of months later the order was duplicated by mistake; and this time the Commission deleted the doors altogether but further increased the order for hinges to 104,000, to which they subsequently added another unsolicited 84,000. The result was that there eventually arrived on the isthmus 12,000 doors and 248,000 pairs of door-hinges.

In September there were 1,800 labourers on the Commission's books; their fortnightly payment took six and a half hours to complete, and involved the filling in of 7,500 individual sheets of paper weighing more than 102 pounds.

If an engineer in the course of his work needed the loan of some simple piece of equipment (such as a hand-cart) even for half an hour, he had to fill in and sign six separate vouchers emanating from five different departments.

But there is little point in detailing the Commission's shortcomings *ad nauseam*. Enough has been said to underline the weighty opinion of Gerstle Mack that "the first year of American administration was a year of bungling, bickering and incompetence".

Yet in the middle of so much that was depressing was a glimmer of light. For in the spring of 1904 there arrived on the isthmus a man who had both the skill and the dedication of his calling to sweep away what was probably the greatest obstacle of all to the construction of the canal.

William Crawford Gorgas was born in Mobile in 1854, son of the Confederate Chief of Ordnance. He followed his father into the army, but throughout his life he was a doctor first and an army officer second. From 1898 to 1902 he served in Havana, working initially on the experimental work which established the connection between fever and mosquitoes, and then on the preventive measures which in a few short months eliminated malaria and yellow fever from what for centuries had been an endemic centre. In March 1904 he was appointed Chief Sanitary Officer to the Isthmian Commission —probably the wisest appointment that Roosevelt ever made. He at once set up his headquarters in Ancon hospital, determined in his own words "to do what I could to prevent the enormous loss of life which had attended the efforts of the French". The Army and Navy Commission, however, lacked the wit to recognise an expert when they saw one. In spite of the evidence of what had happened in Havana, they regarded Gorgas's theories as a lot of new-fangled nonsense: *vide* chairman Walker, "the whole idea of mosquitoes carrying fever is the veriest balderdash." Witness too, governor Davis, "I'm trying to set you right, Gorgas. On the mosquito you are simply wild. Get the idea out of your head. Everyone knows that yellow fever is caused by filth." One has to remember in the Commission's defence that people in 1904 didn't accept medical breakthroughs with the unquestioning faith which they accord them today, and ninety-nine per cent of those on the isthmus undoubtedly agreed with Walker and Davis that the idea of a doctor chasing after and killing mosquitoes was risible. Initially therefore Gorgas was frustrated, and his requisitions for sulphur, oil and larvacides were tossed impatiently aside. But to his everlasting credit he didn't quit. He stayed in Ancon, a quiet kindly figure of unshakable integrity, waiting patiently for the time when he would be allowed to carry out the programme of sanitation which would, he knew, transform the isthmus within months from a plague-centre to a zone as healthy as any mid-west town.

And while Gorgas was fighting a losing battle with the forces of bureaucracy and ignorance, discontent spread cancer-like along the line of the canal.

Most of the men would have tolerated hardship and confusion initially if there had been the promise of better things to come, or if the authorities had produced an overall plan which they could understand. But there was no promise and no plan. For even by the summer of 1905 the Commission had not yet agreed on the fundamental question of whether to build their canal at sea-level or with locks. Wallace favoured a canal at sea-level. But never once during his thirteen months of office did he produce any sort of plan. He said portentiously that, "I had such a plan outlined in my head . . . [but] of course my subordinates did not know what the plan was—" a statement hardly calculated to fill his subordinates with confidence. Engineers who had come to the isthmus with high hopes, began that winter to book their passage home.

Typical of the thousands who left the Zone in disillusion was Charles L. Carroll, a graduate of Pittsburgh. He arrived in the isthmus in August 1904, a young man of twenty-two with plenty of common sense and a genuine desire to serve under Wallace (whose reputation was as yet untarnished). He was unimpressed with Colon and surprised by the general air of cynicism and the complaints of bad food, bad accommodation and bad management; he consoled himself, however, with the thought that a seaport at the end of the line probably attracted malcontents and that things would be different in Culebra. He was equally unimpressed with the railroad, having to wait a day and a half for a train, and finally being packed sardine-like into a rickety and overcrowded compartment for a journey of nearly six hours. At last the train pulled up at a semi-derelict platform ankle-deep in mud: Culebra: the Mecca of so many apprentice engineers. Carroll asked the station-master the way to his "hotel", and the station-master laughed and pointed to a group of tumble-down huts. It was then that Carroll's dream of a Panamanian paradise vanished. And never returned. He lugged his bags up a path knee-deep in clay in search of his quarters. In Pittsburgh he had been promised "a room of his own, equipped with a single bed, a mattress, lamp, two chairs, a dresser, table, washstand, bowl and a pitcher". What he found was a leaking, unscreened shack which he shared with five others; he had his own bunk, but nothing more. The dining-room stank, and the reading room was empty except for a great humming of mosquitoes aswarm round the single kerosene lamp.

A month later Carroll wrote to his mother:

> I am thoroughly sick of this country and everything to do with the canal . . . Everyone is afflicted with running sores. We are compelled to sleep in an old shed, six to a room. Rain water is drunk rather than the river water, because it is purer. The meals would sicken a dog . . . Tell the boys at home to stay there, even if they get no more than a dollar a day.

One thing only was needed to escalate the discontent to panic. And this came about in the last months of 1904: an outbreak of yellow fever.

Gorgas had seen it coming. "The work here," he wrote in September, "is great work, and very attractive to me. [But] the Commission have their own ideas of sanitation, and do not seem much impressed by mine! I fear an epidemic is inevitable. If only we could convince them! If only they knew!" In October he submitted a requisition for vital medical supplies which he marked "most urgent"; but by the following April not a single item on it had been supplied. His wife tells us in her biography: "to those who knew him well, there was one unmistakable sign when Gorgas was worried; he would go about his work softly whistling. This whistling now became a familiar sound."

The first case of yellow fever was reported on November 24th, the first death on November 29th, and early in December the disease spread to the administration buildings in Colon. The Sanitary Inspector, Joseph Le Prince, pointed out to the authorities that the buildings were unscreened and that the bowls of water used to dampen the architects' copying brushes were ideal places for mosquitoes to breed in. The young architect in charge of the buildings was incredulous: "Le Prince," he said, "you're off in the upper storey!"

"But suppose," the inspector argued, "we have twenty deaths here. Who'll be responsible?"

The architect laughed, "I'll stand the responsibility," he said.

Within three weeks he was dead: the first of many victims to be bitten by mosquitoes which flew in through the windows he laughingly neglected to screen.

From Christmas onward cases began to break out in Panama, Colon, and the villages along the line of the canal: a few this week, a few more the next: until by the end of January it was clear that a fair-sized epidemic was under way. Mercifully the dry season had just started, the mosquitoes lacked their usual abundance of water in which to breed, and the epidemic failed to gather momentum. But the threat was enough. The construction workers remembered the 20,000 graves of the French. And the exodus of the discontent increased to a stampede. To quote Mrs. Gorgas (who was on the spot and knew what she was talking about): "The rush to get away quickly assumed the proportions of a panic. The canal force—labourers, engineers and office men alike—seemed to be possessed of one single view: 'Let's get out of this hell hole,' ... and men arriving one day would take their departure the next, on the same boat if they could afford it."

There were in fact no more than 246 cases of fever, that winter, and no more than eighty-four deaths. But the consequences were out of all proportion to the casualties. And with a pinch-penny Commission in Washington withholding supplies, and men leaving the isthmus at the rate of several hundred a week, work in the spring of 1905 came virtually to a halt.

It wasn't long before adverse reports percolated through to the President.

When he first appointed the Army and Navy Commission Roosevelt had told them bluntly: "What this nation will insist upon is that results be achieved." Now, ten months later, it was all too obvious that results were *not* being achieved, and that a canal in Panama would never be dug by a committee in Washington. Roosevelt therefore asked the Army and Navy Commission to resign, and appointed in its place the Second Isthmian Commission: Theodore P. Shonts (chairman), Charles E. Magoon (governor), John F. Wallace (chief engineer), Admiral Endicott, General Haines, Colonel Ernst and Mr. B. J. Harrod (committee). Executive power was to be concentrated in the hands of three men: the chairman in Washington, and the governor and chief engineer on the isthmus. Wallace was delighted; for this, he thought, would surely mark the end of the procrastinations and ineptitude which for so long had tied his hands. "Plan excellent," he cabled Secretary Taft. "*Gracias*."

Yet within ten weeks he had resigned, following what has been described as "the most regrettable incident in the history of the canal".

Why did he do it? Why at the moment when greatness was within his grasp, did Wallace turn his back on Panama and sink unremembered into the limbo of those who failed? There would seem to be three reasons. Firstly, he was no frontiersman; all his life he had worked in civilised surroundings (Illinois, Chicago and New Orleans), and he regarded Panama's riot of mountain and jungle as a nightmare rather than a challenge—"this God-forsaken country" he called it, cursing what at heart he feared. Secondly, he had a morbid, almost pathological terror of yellow fever. Practically every book written on the canal contains the story that when he and his wife arrived in Colon they brought with them "two handsome metal caskets"—coffins for shipping their bodies back to the States. And thirdly he had the misfortune to fall foul, at a critical moment, of the influential William Cromwell. There is plenty of evidence that the two men cordially disliked one another, and in the final analysis it was Cromwell who was to goad the chief engineer into a position from which there could be no return.

On June 4th Wallace wrote to Secretary Taft that "certain complications" in his personal affairs necessitated a return to the States; he would be glad, he said, of an interview. Taft was not pleased. He was about to sail for the Philippines; and he thought that the appointment of the Second Commission should have solved Wallace's problems and that the chief engineer ought to be in the isthmus getting on with his job. On June 11th Taft received a cable from governor Magoon. Wallace, the governor confided, was demanding a period of recuperation in the States; he was also hinting that he had received the offer from back home of a job worth 60,000 dollars a year (more than double his present salary). Taft's displeasure hardened to anger. And when Wallace arrived in New York for his interview he found that the Secretary was accompanied by his attorney—Cromwell.

"Now Wallace," the Secretary said, "go ahead and tell us what you came up for."

The chief engineer was trapped. There seems little doubt as to what he *really* wanted. He wanted Taft to dismiss him, so that he could take up safer and more lucrative employment in the States. But the Secretary wasn't playing. He wanted his chief engineer, he said, back on the isthmus. Wallace, goaded by Cromwell's probing questions, lost his temper and refused point-blank to go; he would rather, he said, resign. It was what Taft had been waiting for. "Well," he said, "I won't stoop to bicker with you. For mere lucre you change your position overnight, without thought of the embarrassing position in which you place the government . . . If you are going to resign, you might as well resign now."

And resign Wallace did. A few days later, in spite of his protests, the circumstances were made known to the press, and the unfortunate engineer suffered a public castigation the like of which has seldom been equalled for severity and aspersion.

Looking back, it is amazing to see how little was achieved during the first year of the American regime. Wallace inherited a working force of 700; he left, it is true, a working force of over 7,000, but they, almost without exception, were discontented and anxious to leave. He inherited fifty miles of railroad; he left no more than fifty-six miles. He inherited 2,265 buildings in poor repair; by the time he left only 350 had been restored. He inherited a mass of potentially useful equipment; but at the end of a year less than five per cent of it had been repaired, and very little new machinery had been ordered. The number of steam-shovels at work in the Culebra Cut had, it is true, trebled; but the machines were idle seven hours out of ten because the debris they excavated couldn't be carried away. Wallace in fact, in spite of his determination to make the dirt fly, excavated in a year less soil than de Lesseps had excavated in a month (279,778 cubic yards as against 282,528). To modern eyes it seems strangely un-American.

Back on the isthmus the resignation of the chief engineer sparked off a fresh wave of panic—for if the captain deserts his ship, the construction workers argued, why should the crew remain? The rainy season had started; the jungle was sombre and depressing, and rumours of disease were magnified hysterically so that men each morning examined themselves for symptoms of fever and at the first indication of sickness gave themselves up for lost. Lacking the patriotic and idealistic fervour which had inspired the French, they fled.

By midsummer the American effort had ground to a halt; yellow fever was escalating, work was at a stand-still, and it looked as if the isthmus was going to triumph again. And triumph it would have, if it had not been for the efforts of two men: William Gorgas and John F. Stevens.

9

THE FOUNDATIONS OF SUCCESS

In the midsummer of 1905 the future of the Panama canal lay in the hands of one man: Wallace's successor. Another failure in the key position of chief engineer, and the project would have folded up.

As had happened before, and was to happen again, it was Cromwell, working behind the scenes, who at a critical moment came to the aid of what he had come to call "his" canal. He knew that Taft and Shonts, after examining the records of more than twenty men, had offered the position of chief engineer to John F. Stevens; but he knew too that Stevens had turned it down. The attorney called on him, and after "a couple of hours of silver-tongued argument" persuaded him to change his mind. It was not the least of Cromwell's services to the canal.

For Stevens turned out to be an inspired choice, a forthright leader of men who brought to the office of chief engineer a new vigour, courage and clarity of mind. He accepted the job only on certain conditions: conditions which he made known to the President with characteristic bluntness: "that I was to have a free hand: that I was not to be hampered or handicapped by anyone high or low . . . and that I was to stay on the isthmus only until success had been assured." Roosevelt agreed, summing up his feelings by telling Stevens the story of the *nouveau riche* who engaged a butler and set him to work with the words, "I don't know in the least what you are to do—but one thing I *do* know, you get busy and buttle like hell!"

The new chief engineer arrived in Colon on July 25th, 1905 and at once made a tour of the diggings. In the Culebra Cut he saw seven steam-shovels every one of them idle, and seven work-trains every one of them derailed; he saw hungry men foraging the swamps for sugar cane and the jungle for bananas, and in the face of officeworkers and labourers alike he saw disillusion and fear.

Roosevelt had warned him that Panama was "in a hell of a mess"; this he could now see for himself had been no exaggeration. But the challenge didn't dismay him, for he was a man of very different calibre from Wallace.

John Frank Stevens was born in Maine in 1853. He was a man of commanding presence and considerable physical courage. And he was a pioneer, a man accustomed to facing the challenge of the frontier, a man to whom mountain and flood were adversaries whom he had tamed before and had every intention of taming again. Two stories epitomise his character. In the 1870s, while working on the Arizona Railroad, a construction gang were cut off by marauding Apache; someone had to get through with a message, and the foreman offered a reward of 500 dollars to anyone who would try. Stevens was the only volunteer. He made the journey of more than a hundred miles through Apache territory on foot, and when he eventually returned to the railroad declined the reward. A decade later, he set out from Montana with two Indian guides and a mule to try and find a route for the Great Northern Railroad across the Rockies. The mule died and the Indians deserted, but Stevens, though weak with hunger and exposure, pushed on alone to discover and survey the vital pass—Stevens Pass the railmen and mapmakers wanted to call it, but again he turned the offer down.

To a man accustomed to dealing with Apache and semi-Arctic blizzards Panama held few terrors, and Stevens was quick to let the construction workers know what he thought of their panic. He loaded a freight car with food, went down the line distributing it at cost and told the men bluntly, "There are three diseases on the isthmus: yellow fever, malaria and cold feet. The worst of these is cold feet. And that's what's ailing you." It was straight talk in language the men could understand. And Stevens's actions were as eloquent as his words. He waved aside the imposing mansion being built for him overlooking Panama Bay, and moved into a knocked-up iron-roofed bungalow in the Culebra Cut; he relegated the railroad's executive coach to storage and rode like everyone else by freight train: he set aside a time each day when any labourer could see him, air his grievance and be sure of a fair hearing; he wore overalls and a slouch hat; a drunken worker who threatened him with violence he threw bodily out of his office; he was, a contemporary magazine stresses, "not an office engineer but a mixer; he would drop in for an unexpected meal at a mess where the men were grumbling, and afterwards express his opinion either of the men or the manager in language forceful and not at all polite." And the boost to morale was miraculous—witness *The Independent*: "By his democratic manner Stevens has quickly done wonders in heartening the men."

Stevens in fact had the common touch. He also had common sense, that all too rare capacity of grasping essentials and dealing with things in their proper order. He was, for example, the first man (either French or American) to realise that the canal would never be built at all unless certain fundamental preliminaries had been attended to. And on August 1st, exactly a week after his arrival, he brought construction work to a halt, dismissed a host of now-redundant workers and set about laying the foundations of success. "I am determined," he wrote to the Secretary of War, "to prepare well before [I embark on] construction. And I shall continue to prepare, regardless of clamour and criticism . . . so long as I am in charge. For I am confident that if this policy is adhered to, the future will show its wisdom."

The Commission were dismayed; the press were sceptical; even Roosevelt had his doubts. But history in no uncertain manner has vindicated Stevens's judgment.

His work of preparation fell into four categories: sanitation, housing and feeding, transport and equipment. He felt confident of handling transport and equipment himself. In the other fields he sought the advice of experts, found the best man for the job, put him in charge and gave him a free hand. And the best man to be in charge of sanitation, he decided, was Gorgas.

Up to this moment Gorgas had been frustrated and laughed at. The first Commission had described his mosquito-theory as "balderdash". The second Commission under Shonts had gone farther: they had recommended that he "be replaced by a man of more practical views". Roosevelt, however, had insisted that Gorgas was retained; and Stevens now gave him, for the first time, official backing. On August 2nd he told the patiently waiting doctor that he could have all the money, supplies, equipment and men that he needed.

It was the chance which Gorgas had been praying for for eighteen months; and within hours of Stevens's directive, sanitary squads along the line of the canal had started the battle on the outcome of which all other battles depended: the battle against disease.

(a) *Reorganisation of Public Health.*
As chief sanitary officer Gorgas's task was to eliminate two distinct and entirely separate diseases: yellow fever and malaria. To the achievement of this goal all other aspects of his work were subordinate.

Yellow fever, the dreaded *vomito negro*, is a disease endemic in the West Indies, Central America, parts of Africa and Brazil. Its symptoms are peculiarly nauseating, the climax being reached on the third or fourth day by which time the skin is yellow, and vomit dark with blood is being almost continuously discharged; more than half of those infected die. Already tens of thousands of labourers had succumbed to yellow fever while working on railroad and canal.

Another fourteen to fifteen thousand, it was estimated, would succumb before the canal was finished—unless the disease was stamped out.

Throughout the nineteenth century it was believed that yellow fever had its origin either in "noxious vapours" (the mist which in the tropics often forms by night over low-lying rivers and swamps) or else in "filth" (the sewage which in towns like Panama and Colon was frequently seen floating to the surface from inadequate cesspits and drains). But the truth, it was discovered in the early 1900s, was stranger and more complex. Yellow fever was caused, under certain specific conditions, by the bite of the *Stegomyiae* (*Aëdes Calopus*) mosquito.

It was the brilliant Carlos Finlay, a doctor of Franco-Scottish extraction living in Cuba, who as early as 1881 first put forward the theory of a link between yellow fever and the mosquito. But for years no one listened to him. Nor was this altogether surprising, because although Finlay kept a veritable menagerie of mosquitoes which he encouraged to bite all and sundry who visited his house, no one was apparently infected. It needed the influx of an American garrison and the appointment of a special medical commission to prove that Finlay was right.

In 1898 the U.S. Army occupied Havana, and a health department was brought into being to clean the city up. Sanitary squads methodically removed the beggars, the dead bodies, the vultures and the garbage and trash piles, and the general health of Havana quickly improved. The incidence of yellow fever, however increased; and in 1899 a trio of doctors (Carter, Lazear and Reed) clutching at any straw in their efforts to stem the epidemic, began to look more carefully into Finlay's theories. Lazear, as part of their experiments, allowed himself to be bitten by a *Stegomyiae*—the mosquito which Finlay had been insisting for years was the carrier. Within a week he was dead.

Among those who sat by his bedside was a doctor who had hitherto been sceptical of the mosquito theory, but who from this moment became its most famous protagonist: Gorgas.

The experiments which followed were directed by Gorgas and Read with a thoroughness which within the year transformed Finlay's inspired guess to a proven fact. Volunteers, some soldiers, some civilians, were put through a series of macabre and terrifying tests: being bitten by fever-carrying mosquitoes, injected with parasites and toxins, and made to sleep in vomit-covered bedding surrounded by bowls of excreta. Many of these martyrs to the cause of humanity contracted fever. Some of them died. But they didn't die unrecognised or in vain. For early in 1901 the Army Medical Board was able to publish its findings:

1. Yellow fever is transmitted by the bite of the *Aëdes (Stegomyiae) Calopus* mosquito.

2. This mosquito must previously have fed on the blood of an individual sick with fever, within the first three days of the disease.

3. An interval of at least twelve days after feeding on the blood of a yellow fever victim is needed before the infected mosquito can pass on the disease.

4. The period of incubation after a bite is between forty-one and 137 hours.

5. "Fomites"—such as clothes, bedding or vomit—can not pass on the infection.

It was clear to those who had eyes to see that the eradication of yellow fever (in Havana, Panama or anywhere else) depended on two factors: the destruction of the *Aëdes Calopus* mosquitoes, and the screening of already infected victims.

Aëdes Calopus, it was discovered after patient research, fly by day, frequent houses, and breed in household water: i.e. in jars, cisterns, water butts and gutters, etc. To quote Le Prince, the Commission's Chief Sanitary Inspector:

> [Both] Panama and Colon, in 1905, were infected with this particular breed of mosquito, conditions for their propagation being exceedingly favourable . . . For the inhabitants of these cities depend very much on rain water which is peddled by watermen and kept in numerous vessels in the house. These vessels, together with cisterns, eave-troughs, butts and barrels etc. are not protected in any way, but are a favourite place for the ovipositing mosquitoes.

In the late summer of 1905 Gorgas launched an all-out attack on the breeding grounds.

Within a hundred yards of a piped supply, the use of water containers was prohibited; ponds, cisterns and cesspools were coated in oil once a week; and where water barrels had to be used they were screened (see Figure 9 on page 132).

It was made a punishable offence to harbour mosquito larvae.

> Ordinance No. 6, decree No. 25: Breeding of larvae is prohibited within the limits of the city, and the occupants of premises will be held accountable for violation of this regulation. All cisterns, water barrels and deposits of fresh water must be made mosquito-proof.

Panama was divided into eleven districts, Colon into four, and in each district inspectors made a house-to-house search for the telltale larvae. An adverse report was quickly followed by a visit from the department's carpenters, who repaired sagging gutters, screened cisterns and water butts with eighteen-mesh copper-and-wire, and emptied out the infected *tinajars* (the open stoneware jugs used for storing the peddlers' water). The inhabitants submitted with bewildered but good-humoured resignation. They were less good-humoured, however, when Gorgas embarked on the second phase of his campaign: fumigation.

Figure 9. A mosquito-proof water-barrel

At first the only houses to be fumigated were those in which a case of yellow fever had been confirmed. But when it was seen how effectively fumigation destroyed the mosquitoes it was decided to extend operations to *all* houses, and by the summer of 1906 every building in Panama and Colon had been meticulously sterilised. The procedure was simple. The inhabitants were given both verbal and written notice to quit, and at a specified time their premises were handed over to the fumigation brigade. Doors and windows were closed, cracks and crevices were pasted over; and while the whole building was made airtight an inspector calculated the cubic capacity of each room. Pans of sulphur or pyrethrum were then placed in the rooms, the right quantity of powder was weighed out (two pounds per thousand cubic feet), and the pans were sprinkled with wood-alcohol and set alight. The inspector stayed long enough to be sure that the powder was burning correctly, then left, and the building remained sealed up for between three and a half and four hours. At the end of this time the brigade returned, unsealed the windows and doors, removed the paste and the pans, swept up the dead and anaesthetised mosquitoes, and obtained a signed certificate from the residents to say that nothing was missing. In spite of the obvious hazards there was not, in Panama, a single case of fire during three years of fumigation, and only four cases of theft. At first the fumigation brigade were none too popular; but such was the improvement in health that by the end of the year even their most vehement critics had been silenced.

Gorgas's final weapon was the careful screening of those who had already contracted fever. His department knew that unless a mosquito was able to feed on the blood of an already infected patient, it couldn't act as a carrier. The most elaborate precautions were therefore taken to ensure that every fever victim was immediately and effectively screened. As soon as a possible case was reported, the quarantine division of Ancon Hospital visited the suspect and at once erected round him a portable fever-cage (see Figure 10 below). After a diagnosis every effort was made to persuade the patient to

Figure 10. A portable fever-cage

move voluntarily to Ancon, and over ninety per cent of those infected agreed. Once in hospital the victim, still in his cage, was isolated in a special fever wing, where the windows were double-screened and the doors treble-screened, non-immunes were denied access, and pans of pyrethrum were kept continuously alight. To quote Le Prince: "These precautions made it necessary for a mosquito to pass through a cloud of smoke and four screened doors before it could reach a patient, and then escape into a ward where it must survive a twelve-day search before biting a non-immune. It was almost impossible for such a combination to happen." And happen it never did.

In twelve months Gorgas's sanitary squads used 1,000 tons of timber and 200 tons of wire-and-copper mesh; they burned 300 tons of sulphur and 120 tons of pyrethrum (the entire output of the United States); and at the height of the campaign, 4,500 men were screening, oiling, ditching and fumigating ten hours a day, seven days a week. Small wonder that under an assault of such sustained efficiency the majority of the *Aëdes Calopus* were exterminated, while the few which remained were rendered harmless because they couldn't find an already infected victim to bite.

By January 1906 yellow fever had been eradicated from the isthmus. And it never returned.

Gorgas's campaign, it has been estimated, saved something like 14,000 lives*; and his achievements have been extolled in speeches, pamphlets, treatises and books. He himself, however, would wish for no other panegyric than a simple statement of fact:

Year:	1903	1904	1905	1906	1907	1908	1909–1914
Cases of yellow fever:	51	40	206	1	nil	nil	nil

Gorgas's second task, the eradication of malaria, posed a different and in some ways a more difficult problem.

The "ague fit", as it was termed in the nineteenth century, is an intermittent and recurrent fever brought about by micro-parasites in the blood. Its symptoms are initial coldness, with the face turning pale and the nails blue, subsequent fever with the skin dry and flushed, and finally profuse and often drenching sweat; less than five per cent of those infected, die. Malaria, in other words, is a less terrifying disease than yellow fever. Its effects, however, are more

---

*Le Prince bases this figure on the very reasonable assumption that if it hadn't been for the efforts of Gorgas, American losses from yellow fever would have been in the same ratio at the French: i.e. four per cent per annum; or, with a working force of between 35,000 and 40,000, roughly 1,400 a year, or 14,000 over the ten-year period of construction.

pernicious. For whereas a yellow fever patient either dies or recovers and is subsequently immune, a malaria patient retains the parasites in his blood and is for many years prone to further and cumulatively weakening attacks—witness the informed opinion of Gorgas: "Malaria in the tropics is by far the most important disease on account of the tremendous disability caused by it. While the percentage of fatalities is not especially high, the incapacity caused is very much greater than that due to all other tropical diseases combined." A glance at Figure 11 (page 136), discloses the startling fact that in 1905, before Gorgas's campaign got under way, more than eighty-three per cent of the canal working force were suffering from malaria.

It was a French doctor, Laveran, who in 1880 first isolated malaria parasites in the blood; and an Italian doctor, Marchiafara, who first discovered that these parasites could be transmitted by mosquito. The real breakthrough, however, didn't occur until 1895 when Major Ross of the Indian Army discovered the bizarre truth that whereas malaria parasites reproduce only asexually and slowly in human blood, in the stomach of the female of one particular species of mosquito they reproduce sexually and fast, and that their multitudinous offspring with a horrifying semblance of intelligence, migrate to the mosquito's salivary glands, ready the moment the insect makes its bite to be passed on to a host. By the turn of the century it had been proved that the one and only propagator of malaria was the female *Anopheles*: a mosquito which flies by night and breeds in open country, in swamps, marshes, ditches and lakes.

Once this had been established, it was clear that the eradication of malaria depended on two factors: the destruction of the female *Anopheles*, and the widespread use by night of mosquito nets and screens.

In his campaign against malaria Gorgas used five lines of attack: eliminating the *Anopheles*' breeding grounds, destroying their larvae, killing the full-grown mosquitoes, screening the labour force by night, and immunising the working force with doses of quinine.

The most satisfactory and permanent method of eliminating the mosquitoes' breeding grounds was to fill them in: i.e. to transfer excavated soil from canal prism to swamp. There were two ways of doing this. Either the soil was loaded onto Lidgerwood dump-cars, conveyed to a suitable site by rail and tipped direct into the marshland; or alternatively muddy liquid was excavated by dredge and pumped away hydraulically by pipeline over distances of anything up to a couple of miles. By these methods more than sixty square

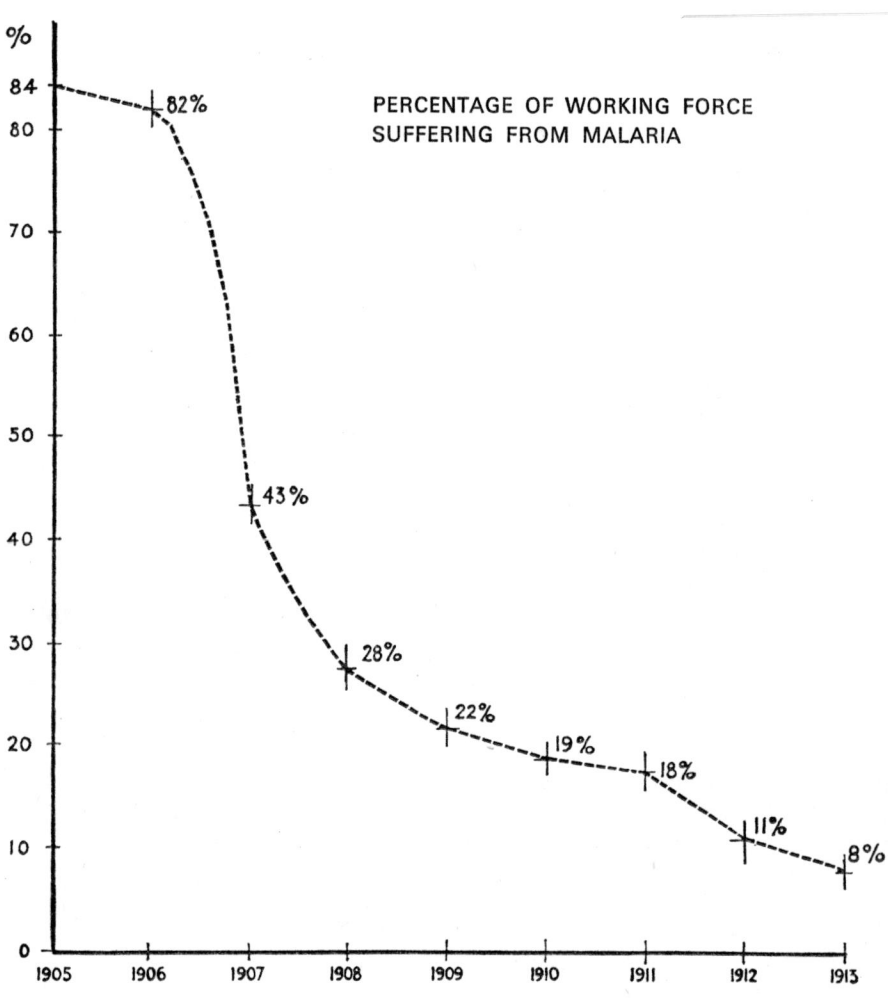

Figure 11. Decline of malaria among employees, 1905–13

miles of swamp were reclaimed—both Balboa and the new district of Colon, for example, were built on a foundation of mud laid by hydraulic-fill.

Filling, however, was slow and expensive, and a far larger area of swamp land was denied to the *Anopheles* by draining—witness Le Prince: "Without doubt, proper drainage is the all-important and most effective method of eliminating malaria." Gorgas appreciated this. And in his campaign against the *Anopheles* his sanitary squads laid 987 miles of ditch, 307 miles of concrete ditch, and over 200 miles of tiled drain. Within eighteen months they had drained 170 square miles of marsh. It is hard to wax eloquent over drains. But the fact remains that if these ditches had not been dug—and dug correctly and maintained meticulously—the mosquitoes would have continued to breed, the incidence of malaria would have snowballed, and the working force would have been seriously debilitated.

Some areas, however, couldn't be drained; some *Anopheles*, inevitably, managed to deposit their larvae; and on this larvae the sanitary squads waged a protracted non-stop war.

Their principal weapon was oil: 600,000 gallons of it every year. The oil (twenty-five degrees Baumé) was shipped from California, stored at the Pacific terminal of Balboa, and piped the width of the isthmus. The pipeline was tapped at intervals, and subsidiary tanks were established at more than thirty points along the line of the cutting. From these subsidiary tanks oil was carried to the various lakes, streams and ditches, etc. where it was needed. It was then applied either by continuous drip-barrel or by intermittent spray.

The drip-barrel most frequently used was a standard thirty-gallon garbage can, with a spout soldered onto it about five inches from the bottom; a lamp-wick was inserted into the spout which was then compressed until the oil dripped out at the required number of drops per minute. The barrel was filled with ninety-five per cent oil and five per cent larvacide (a mixture of resin, soda and carbolic acid); it was then carried to the ditch or stream where larvae were forming, and suspended roughly three feet above the water (see Figure 12 on page 139). Here it hung, dripping at regular intervals until the surface of the water became coated with a thin but permanent film of oil. This oil reduced the ability of the larvae to cling to the water, killing them in an hour; it also discouraged ovipositing. These drip-barrels were cheap and easy to make; easy too to maintain—all they needed was inspecting and topping up once a week. And by the autumn of 1906 every stream, ditch and waterway leading down to the settlements along the canal had been equipped with its barrel.

In cases where a permanent film of oil couldn't be created—perhaps the stream was too fast, or the ditch too choked with vegetation—an intermittent type of spray had to be used. Where the stream or ditch in question ran parallel to a road, horse-drawn oil-carts (see Figure 12) were effective. The oil was carried in a 250-gallon drum at the back of the cart, and fed out through a ten-foot pipe, the end of which was perforated by holes out of which the oil dripped freely and evenly. In remote areas, on the other hand, the spray most commonly used was the knapsack pump (see Figure 12). This consisted of a five-gallon drum equipped with a small but powerful pump which forced out a spray of oil-cum-larvacide to a distance of twenty feet. Throughout the decade of construction work, a force of more than a hundred and fifty West Indian knapsack-sprayers were continually at work along the line of the canal.

Other methods used to eliminate larvae were the cutting of grass and foliage, the letting in wherever possible of sea water, the breeding of surface-feeding fish and the introduction of spiders, small lizards and ants.

Efforts to kill the fully grown *Anopheles* in the open—by fumigation for example—were not successful; and Gorgas soon concentrated his efforts on destroying those few mosquitoes which managed to find a way into the screened houses. His main weapons here were the fixed trap (designed by Inspectors Bath and Proctor), and the employment of paid mosquito-catchers. The latter were surprisingly effective; and after the spring of 1906 several hundred workers, paid at ten cents an hour and equipped with slapper, lamp and chloroform-tube, made a daily inspection of the labourers' quarters. And they caught between them several thousand mosquitoes, any one of which might several times have passed on its parasites. Swatting mosquitoes with a wire-mesh slapper may not sound the most scientific way of combating malaria, but there is no doubting its effectiveness. As evidence of this, in June 1908 a force of marines were stationed on the upper slopes of Diablo Hill; they lived in the same type of quarters as a group of workmen on the lower slopes; screening arrangements in both barracks were identical; but the workmen's were visited each day by mosquito-catchers whereas the marines' were not. And the malaria incidence among the marines was fourteen per cent per week, while that among the workmen was 0.3 per cent. It was this sort of attention to detail which made Gorgas's campaign such an outstanding success.

The fourth remedy was screening. In 1900 Doctors Sambon and Low of the London School of Tropical Medicine spent four months in the Roman Campagna, then one of the most unhealthy malarial

Figure 12. Three methods of destroying mosquito larvae: (a) by oil-drip barrel; (b) by horse-drawn oil-cart; (c) by knapsack spray

plains in the world; they escaped infection simply by staying each night, from sunset to sunrise, in a mosquito-proof tent. This lesson was not lost on Gorgas, who knew that if he could deny the *Anopheles* access by night to the working force's quarters, malaria would be virtually eliminated. After careful experiment his department perfected a method of screening which was cheap, simple and effective. In the tropics every house has its verandah, and it was these which were screened rather than individual windows and doors. Eighteen-mesh pure copper gauze was stretched taut over wooden frames eight feet high and three feet wide, and these were meticulously fitted round the outside of every verandah (see Figure 13 opposite). The one door—always on the windward side of the house—was then screened, made to open outwards, and equipped with a rapid-action self-closing spring. In large buildings, where there was much coming and going, a vestibule with twin doors was specially built; and in the relatively few cases where men had to sleep in tents or railway cars, these too were sedulously screened. To quote Le Prince:

> The crucial point about screening is the thoroughness with which the work is done, and the constant vigilance and care that must be exercised in detecting and remedying defects. Mosquitoes, and particularly *Anopheles*, will readily find a very small aperture in their endeavour to enter a house, but once within they seldom if ever try to find their way out. A screened house with rents in the mesh, cracks in the floor, knot-holes in the wood and openings between plate and roof is therefore a veritable death trap . . . To maintain efficiently the mosquito-proofing of the men's quarters, a weekly inspection was made of every house, and the needed repairs noted and seen to at once.

This work was originally carried out by Gorgas's Sanitation Department; but when Stevens was superseded as chief engineer by Goethals, the work was relegated to the Quartermaster's Department. This was a retrogressive step. As Le Prince wrote sadly in 1911: "After experience of both systems it is earnestly recommended that all questions of mosquito-proofing should be entrusted to the sanitary authorities, who are more competent to judge the importance of defects often deemed unworthy of attention by the average layman or builder." To this very sensible plea, however, Goethals (who had no love of the Sanitary Department) turned a blind eye.

Gorgas's final weapon was quinine. Between Cristobal and Balboa he set up a chain of more than twenty dispensaries, where free medical treatment was available to all. These dispensaries handed out, among other things, an enormous quantity of quinine—

THE FOUNDATIONS OF SUCCESS

2,874 pounds in a single year. The quinine was taken as a prophylactic in doses of 0.15 grams twice a day. White Americans were quick to appreciate its value; but negroes and West Indians had a peculiar aversion, to start with, to its bitter taste. However, when Gorgas hit on the happy idea of dissolving the quinine in the "extra-sweet pink lemonade" which was served each day in the canteens, its use became universal. The effect of quinine prophylaxis is difficult to judge; but it was generally agreed by doctors in the zone that it helped both to prevent infection and to lessen the severity of attacks.

By these measures Gorgas was able to win and maintain a stranglehold on malaria. But, to his lasting regret, he was never able to eliminate it as he had eliminated yellow fever. Perhaps in the conditions, elimination was an impossible ideal; perhaps he would have succeeded if it hadn't been for the animosity of Goethals. Be that as it may, Gorgas's campaign has been described as "the greatest sanitary achievement the world has ever seen . . . It was perfect work; no greater has ever been done." Nor did his labours go unrewarded. He was congratulated by Roosevelt, showered with honours and awards from almost every country in the world, and in 1908 elected president of the American Medical Association. But as had been the case with yellow fever, facts meant more to him than panegyrics.

Year:	1906	1907	1908	1909	1910	1911	1912	1913
Percentage of working force to suffer from malaria:	82%	43%	28%	22%	19%	18%	11%	under 8%

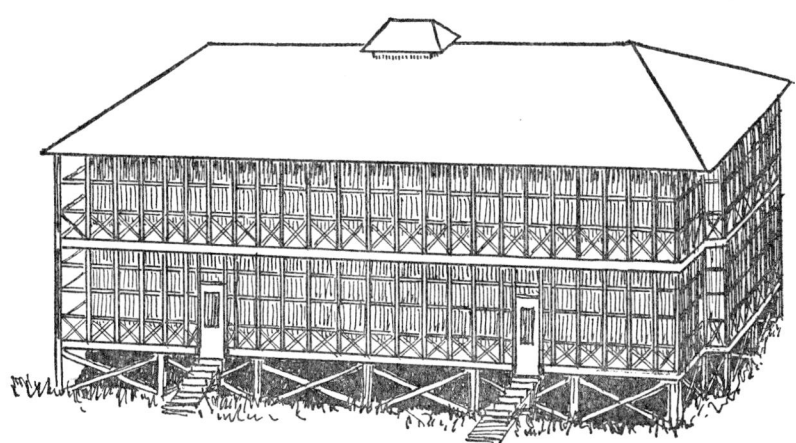

Figure 13. Mosquito-screened verandahs

The cost of this intensive and protracted campaign can be looked at in two ways. To Goethals, who saw the canal only as a great impersonal undertaking, the cost was 400,000 dollars a year; and this was exorbitant. To Gorgas, who saw the canal in terms of the men and women who were building it, the cost was less than a cent per person per day; and this he felt (and who today would disagree with him) was a small enough payment to make for the blessing of good health.

By the autumn of 1906 yellow fever had been eliminated, malaria had been brought under control, and the first and most important of Stevens's preliminary goals had been achieved. The good health of the construction workers was assured.

(b) *Reorganisation of Living Quarters and the Commissariat.*
Stevens's second goal was to ensure that the working force was adequately housed and fed. This was no easy task, for there were soon at work on the canal more than 42,000 labourers drawn from ninety-seven countries—according to Stevens "the largest number of men ever employed in modern times on a peaceful enterprise". It was fortunate that their well-being was placed in the hands of an outstanding administrator, "Square-foot" Jackson Smith.

Jackson Smith has never been given the recognition he deserves— several full-length books on the canal fail even to mention his name— yet at a critical moment it was he who brought order out of chaos by establishing a system of recruiting, housing and feeding which was both efficient and eminently fair.

The recruiting of skilled labour took place exclusively in the United States. In the early years, the isthmus had so evil a reputation for discomfort and disease that men could only be tempted there by the promise of exceptional wages. Four recruiting officers, one in New York, one in New Orleans and two with roving commissions, interviewed each applicant personally and offered him anything up to double his current wages in the States; and yet to quote Major Wood (who served in the Quartermaster's Department from 1905 to 1915):

> The type of man secured at first was rather discouraging. Most of them were men who, for one reason or another, were unable to retain positions in the States, and were equally unable to give good results on the Isthmus. For the reputation of the Canal Zone deterred the better class of applicants . . . By degrees, however, fair treatment and improved living conditions had their influence, and toward the middle of 1906 men began coming to work on the canal of their own accord.

By 1908 the recruiting officers were declared redundant, for there were now too many applicants for too few jobs. And it was not long before the construction gangs became imbued with the pride and *esprit de corps* which a generation earlier had inspired the French.

The recruiting of unskilled workers followed a similar pattern. The West Indies were a natural reservoir of labour; but the authorities, remembering the decimation of the railroad workers and the French, were loath at first to grant exit permits. Barbados, where there was a great deal of poverty and unemployment, was the first to relax its ruling, closely followed by Martinique and Guadeloupe; and in the autumn of 1905 several thousand workers left these islands for the Zone. The reports they sent home were encouraging (wages of ten cents an hour, free quarters, free medical attention and cut-price food) and the trickle of immigrants soon built up to a flood. By 1908 recruiting agencies were withdrawn from the Indies; for once again there were too many men applying for too few jobs.

Agencies in Europe, on the other hand, were retained. For one of the first groups of immigrants to reach the Zone had been a party of Spaniards from Cuba, and they worked so effectively that after consultation with the Spanish government a recruiting agency was established in Madrid. Agencies in Rome and Athens followed; and between 1907 and 1909 more than 10,000 Spanish, Italian and Greek workers arrived in the Zone. They did sterling service. For although they were paid only double the wages of the West Indians, it was estimated they did three times the work.

The following table gives a rough idea of the working force's composition:

Country of Origin of those working on the Canal (March 1908)

Barbados	5,625	Saint Lucia	452
United States	4,655	Guadeloupe	394
Jamaica	3,835	Granada	344
Spain	3,800	Greece	316
Martinique	1,676	Colombia	296
Italy	762	United Kingdom	296
Panama	535	Trinidad	246
Antigua	533	Portugal	106

Housing so large and polyglot a working force would not have been easy in the States. In a remote corner of the tropics, where rainfall was heavy and food and building materials scarce, it was a job to tax the wisdom of Solomon. Smith, however, rose to the occasion. He had served before on large-scale construction projects in Mexico and Ecuador; he had Stevens's clear-sighted grasp of essentials; and in the late summer of 1905, having obtained from the chief engineer a promise that housing would be given a top priority, he put forward a solution both practicable and fair.

"Silver roll" (or unskilled) workers were to be housed in standard barracks, equipped with either twenty-four or forty-eight bunks. The foundation of these barracks were laid at once on sites selected by the Sanitary Department, special attention was paid to screening, draining, ventilation and the provision of sewers and rooms for drying clothes; and a bunk was allocated free to everyone on the Commission's pay roll. Although austere and bleak by modern standards, the barracks were considered luxurious by the majority of West Indian labourers, and were kept shipshape by daily inspection.

"Gold roll" (or skilled) workers, Smith decided, should be housed in accommodation determined by their salary—one square foot of floor space for every dollar of their annual pay: hence the sobriquet "Square-foot". This, according to Stevens, "gave very satisfactory results . . . It did away with favouritism, and established a standard that was easily understood by all. It also proved a strong incentive to individual ambition. For a promotion in rank meant not only a better wage, but more commodious living accommodation, and a corresponding rise in the social scale." Smith's gold roll houses were of different sizes, but were all built to the same basic specification. Footings were of cement, two foot square and one foot deep; on top of the footings were placed a series of concrete cubes, which carried the wooden floor and provided ventilation. Walls and ceilings were of frame construction and were made entirely of wood (either Gulf timber or north-west Pacific pine); there was no plastering or papering because of the humidity, but the woodwork was painted or stained. All houses had verandahs on at least two and usually three sides; these were carefully screened, together with any extraneous windows and doors. Roofs were of corrugated iron. Plumbing and lighting were provided free, and so was a minimum of furniture.

In spite of its obvious fairness, Smith's scheme of allocating these houses according to salary earned him the hatred of a number of tenants. For "Square-foot" made concessions to no one, high nor low. Only a few days before he was due to leave the isthmus, for example, he was approached by a fellow Commissioner.

"There's a house next door to mine," the Commissioner said, "that I'd like a friend to apply for. His salary isn't all that high, but in his case you can stretch the rules a bit, I'm sure."

"Mr. Commissioner," was the reply, "I leave my department on Tuesday. If your friend is wise he won't apply for that house before Wednesday morning!"

Smith, in fact, was a prickly pear. But it was due to his uncompromising fairness that tens of thousands of unknown labourers lived in comfort rather than squalor. And the facts of his achievement speak for themselves. In a year under Wallace 360 men were employed on the building programme; they renovated 336 houses, built 150 new ones, and used rather less than a million feet board-measure of timber. In a year under Jackson Smith 4,600 men were employed on building; they renovated 1,200 houses, built 1,250 new ones, and used rather more than forty-three million feet board-measure of lumber and pine.

In October 1905, with his housing programme well under way, Smith turned his attention to the Commissariat.

The task of feeding some 40,000 employees and their dependents was complex, for the isthmus raised little food of its own and lay far from the chief producing centres of meat, grain and rice. Under the Army and Navy Commission little effort had been made to solve the problem, and employees had been expected to buy their own food from local shops, most of which were one-man businesses run by Chinese; the result was that prices had soared, supplies had run short, and the working force had gone hungry. In the summer of 1905 the Panama Railroad stepped in and signed an agreement with Jacob Markel of Omaha under the terms of which Markel contracted to supply the Commission's employees with meals at the rate of thirty-six dollars per head per month. However, when Stevens and Smith looked into Markel's prices they found he was budgeting to make a profit of more than a million dollars a year! The contract was annulled; and acting on the time-honoured principle that if you want a job well done you must do it yourself, the Commission assumed responsibility for feeding its employees.

Smith's first step was to build a subsistence depot at Cristobal. Judged by modern standards this depot would be considered no more than large; but in its day it was gargantuan—by far the most advanced of its kind in the world. Sited by No. 11 deep-water pier—so that ships of the Panama Steamship Company could unload direct from hold to storage—the buildings were manned by a staff of more than 400 and were subdivided into cold storage plant, ice-cream factory, bakery, coffee roaster and laundry. The cold storage depot had a capacity for refrigerated food of 94,000 cubic feet, with an additional storage space of 102,000 cubic feet for food kept at forty degrees Farenheit; the ice-cream factory had a daily output of 400 gallons of pasteurised fruit-flavoured cream; the bakery had a daily output of 20,000 loaves, 500 pounds of cake and 500 pies, while the coffee roaster ground and blended in a day anything up to

3,000 pounds of coffee. The greatest volume of work, however, was achieved by the laundry which handled on an average more than 6,500 individual articles of clothing a day.

The output of the depot was distributed by rail. Each morning in the brief tropic dawn a train of eight cold storage cars and five freight cars pulled out of Cristobal station; it stopped at every wayside halt along the line of the canal, distributing supplies, and arrived in Panama soon after nine-thirty. A further eight supply cars left the depot later in the morning, and all twenty-one cars returned empty to Cristobal between midnight and two a.m., at the hour when railroad traffic was at a minimum. In this way an average of 186,000 pounds of provisions were delivered each day along the line of the canal; and to quote Stevens, "so perfect were these arrangements that from the time perishable goods were loaded at New York they never came into contact with the outside air until [they were] delivered to the consumer."

By ten o'clock supplies had been delivered to the various hotels, restaurants and mess-halls along the canal. There were seventy-six of these: twenty gold roll hotels providing top quality American food at ninety cents a day; twenty-five mess-halls for the Europeans, providing continental-type food (including wine on holidays) at forty cents a day; and thirty-one mess-halls for the West Indians providing food at thirty cents a day. The Commission made no attempt to show a profit, and bulk purchases on an enormous scale assured a high standard of food at the minimum price. Indeed, as the following table shows, food on the isthmus frequently cost less than in the shops of New York:

Comparison of Food Prices: October, 1907

		New York Price	Commissary Price
Sirloin beef	(cents per lb.)	20	22
Sirloin steak	,,	22	22
Stewing veal	,,	16	8
Lamb	,,	14	11
Butter	,,	39	38
Cheese	,,	44	32
Onions	,,	3	2
Sausages	(cents per pack)	25	16
Oranges	(cents per dozen)	60	12
Apples	,,	35	8
Eggs	,,	35	34

But to this roseate picture there was an initial blemish. A large number of West Indians didn't, to start with, avail themselves of the cut-price meals. Accustomed to a near-starvation diet of bananas and yams, they failed for some time to appreciate that they needed nourishing food when engaged on continuous manual labour. The problem was eventually solved by providing them with free meals twice a day: and as soon as this was done the efficiency of the working force increased out of all recognition. Indolence, it was discovered, had been synonymous with malnutrition.

By the winter of 1907 Quartermaster Wood was able to write complacently but with truth: "Every effort is made to ensure good and proper food; and although this was an uphill task in the beginning, the problems have now been worked out, and no large body of men have ever been housed and fed under such favourable conditions as the employees in the Panama canal."

It would be pleasant to record that Smith was given the credit for this which he so richly deserved. On the contrary. In the winter of 1908 he quarrelled with Stevens's successor, Goethals, and was summarily dismissed.

"With respect to Mr. Smith," Goethals wrote to the Secretary of War, "I am convinced of two things: first, of his ability . . . and second, that his unpopularity is so pronounced as to interfere with the efficiency of his department." The truth, after all these years, is not easy to unravel. Smith undoubtedly had a caustic tongue, he didn't suffer fools gladly, and he made enemies in high places; yet his administrative flair was beyond question, and he had worked harmoniously with Stevens for several years. It therefore seems likely that his quarrel with Goethals stemmed from a clash of personalities—neither man being conspicuous for his humility. Smith was king of his department. But Goethals was Tsar over all. So Smith had to go.

He served the canal too well to merit either his summary dismissal, or posterity's lack of appreciation of his very considerable services.

(c) *Reorganisation of Transport.*
Stevens was perhaps the greatest authority of his day on railways. He had laid track in Texas, New Mexico and Arizona; he had pioneered trial routes in Wyoming, Idaho and Montana; he had risen from chainman to president of one of the largest companies in the United States; and in the summer of 1905 he had taken one look at the Panama Railroad and been appalled. On his first day in the isthmus (the story goes) he was shown over the track by a railroad official who said to him with pride, "We've a fine record this year. No collisions on the main line."

"A collision," grunted Stevens, "has its good points. It shows something is moving!"

In the case of health and housing and feeding the chief engineer had delegated preparatory work to an expert. But on transport *he* was the expert: he would, he decided, deal with the railroad himself.

It was a complex problem that faced him. As ports, neither Panama nor Cristobal had been laid out with a view to handling heavy traffic; unloading facilities were primitive in the extreme—goods often having to be manhandled from ship to lighter to shore—and the quays lacked facilities for storage. This would not have mattered so greatly if the goods, once ashore, could have been shifted quickly to their destination; but roads on the isthmus were virtually non-existent, and the ancient single-track railway was utterly inadequate to deal with the vast quantities of food, equipment and supplies which soon began to pile up at the terminals; it was utterly inadequate too to cope with the millions of tons of soil which were excavated from the bed of the embryo canal. The result, under the first Commission, had been chaos.

Stevens realised that three things were needed: to improve facilities at the terminals, to double-track and modernise the railroad, and to create a system of branch lines and sidings which would quickly dispose of the excavated soil.

At Cristobal the old half-rotten wharves were dismantled and replaced by two concrete deep-water piers at which ships could unload at any state of the tide. Warehouses were built alongside the piers, and railway sidings alongside the warehouses. A modern coal-hoist was installed; and within the year cargo ships which had previously taken three weeks to discharge and refuel, were achieving a turnaround in three days. At Panama the transformation was even more spectacular; for Stevens's reconstruction of the dock area coincided with the improvements which Wallace had initiated in the town. New sewers, water mains and street-paving were laid side by side with new docks, warehouses and railway sidings; and once again the transformation was radical. Goods which under Wallace had accumulated undispatched for fifteen months, were soon under Stevens being disposed of in fifteen hours.

And the instrument of their disposal was the railroad.

Completed in 1855 at a cost of eight million dollars and, according to legend, "a dead man for every tie in the track," the Panama Railroad, when new, had been one of the engineering wonders of the day. It was still, when Stevens took over, a magnificent piece of construction work; forty-seven miles of five-foot track, spanning river, swamp and ravine, its bed ballasted in gravel and rock, and its fifty-six-pound rails in good repair. But it was old. Its rails were too light to carry the more sophisticated locomotives and rolling-stock of the twentieth century; its signalling system was archaic (a single worn-out telegraph line and hand-operated points); it had few stations, marshalling yards or repair sheds; it had no more than twenty-six miles of sidings; and, most serious defect of all, it was single rather than double track. Built to cope with the gold-rush passenger-traffic of the 1890s, it had no hope two generations later of coping with the enormous volume of freight engendered by work on the canal.

Under the Army and Navy Commission little had been done to improve it (in the eighteen months of the Wallace regime less than seven and a half miles of new track had been laid), but in the summer of 1905 Stevens set to work in no uncertain manner. For he was the first man to realise that this antiquated ribbon of track was the key to constructing the canal.

In his own words:

> The work of rejuvenation was begun in the summer of 1905 and pressed vigorously through 1905 and 1906. Embankments and cuts were widened; bridges and culverts were renewed and rebuilt to the proper width for double track; an entire new telegraph line was erected; enormous new sidings and assembly yards were laid out . . . the old fifty-six-pound rails of iron were replaced by ninety-pound rails of steel; more than a hundred miles of track was carefully graded and ballasted; new stations were installed, and new and modern machine shops were constructed.

While over its entire length the railroad was double-tracked. This double-tracking was the cornerstone of success. For it meant that, given efficient management and sufficient rolling-stock, trains could be run virtually non-stop, in either direction, the width of the isthmus.

Management, to start with, was a problem; for the Panama Railroad, over the years, had declined into a sleepy branch line. Stevens introduced new blood. He recruited experienced men from the States, and introduced up-to-date systems of accounting and store-keeping. He also established a remarkable rapport between those who worked on the railway and those who worked on the canal. Railroad personnel, it ought to be remembered, were never an official part of the canal working force; they were affiliated rather than integrated. If things had not worked smoothly, this arrangement could have led to friction. But in fact Stevens was able to write years later: "The operating of the railroad and the construction of the canal were virtually interlocked; and the deep interest which railroad officials took in the building of the canal led to perfect teamwork and very satisfactory results."

Rolling-stock was ordered in vast quantities. And figures here speak more eloquently than words. Stevens inherited in working order some thirty-five locomotives, twenty-four coaches and 560 flat-cars. At the end of eighteen months he bequeathed to his successor 293 locomotives, fifty-two coaches, sixteen cold storage cars, and the incredible (but still insufficient!) number of 3,915 flat-cars. He inherited seventy-three miles of light-weight track; he bequeathed more than 350 miles of heavy relaid track. Whereas the old railway had been hard put to it to run twenty trains a day, the new railway ran anything up to 570. And the journey from Panama to Colon was cut from five and a half hours to less than two.

In addition to this work of rejuvenation on the main line, Stevens also planned a track layout for disposing of the excavated soil.

This was a labour of Hercules. The Americans dug out from the bed of the canal more than 232 million cubic yards (or 388 million tons) of soil. It had to go somewhere. And more than eighty per cent of it was loaded in dump-cars, hauled onto the Panama Railroad, and taken to a tip five, ten or even fifteen miles from the spot where it was excavated. The quantities involved were fantastic: an average of 200 trains a day, hauling 3,000 trucks, loaded with 71,000 cubic yards of soil. If the arrangements for loading, hauling away, tipping, and returning the empty trucks had not worked like clockwork there would have been chaos.

In this enormous redistribution of soil the nub of the problem was the Culebra Cut, out of which over seventy per cent of the excavated debris was removed. Stevens's plan had the virtue of simplicity. He took as his starting point the watershed of the divide, a spot midway between Empire and Culebra which was the highest level in the cut. From here he laid anything up to fourteen parallel lines of track along the bed of the embryo canal: tracks which ran down at a gradient of thirty-six feet in the mile until they reached either Bas Obispo to the north of the divide or Paraiso to the south. Here, at either end of the cut, the tracks branched out to intersect with the main line of the Panama Railroad (see Figure 14 opposite). Excavated soil was loaded direct from shovels to trucks; the trucks when full were hauled on a down gradient out of the Cut and onto the main line of the railroad; they were then taken to one of the dumps or tips, the soil was swept off by Lidgerwood ploughs and the empty trucks were finally hauled back to the Cut. The process was then repeated. To quote Stevens:

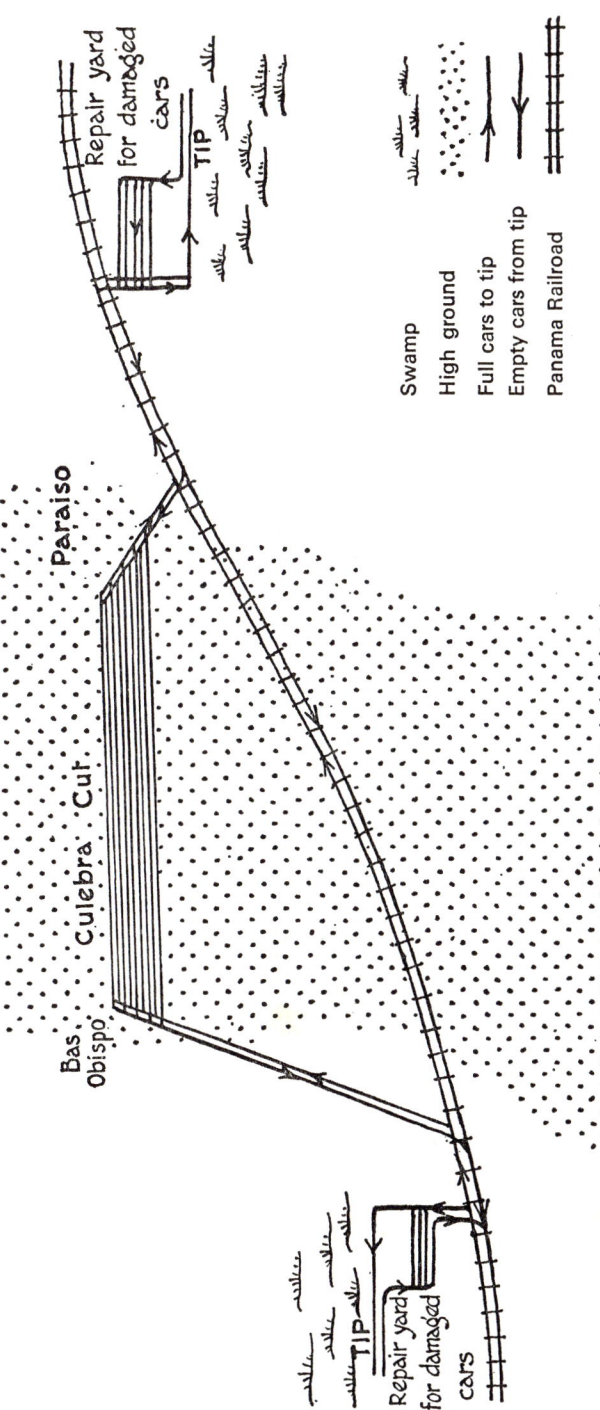

Figure 14. Track layout for disposal of soil from the Culebra Cut

All material in the Cut was waste and had to be disposed of, and this was the limiting factor in completing the canal. A simple but extensive and flexible system of trackage was designed by myself personally and was installed according to my plans. It proved a success, and was in use until the last yard of material had been removed from the Cut. This [system of trackage] was probably the greatest single factor, in the nature of a machine that contributed to the successful building of the canal.

It was said at the time that the Panama Railroad was the busiest in the world—a claim which the tables below help to substantiate:

Maximum movement of trains per day through Miraflores

Loaded spoil-trains south	97
(approximately 2,000 trucks carrying 36,000 cu. yds. of soil)	
Empty spoil-trains north	97
Isthmian work-trains south	15
Isthmian work-trains north	15
P.R. passenger and freight-trains south	6
P.R. passenger and freight-trains north	6
Total in eight-hour working day	236
Balance of P.R. night and miscellaneous trains	16
Grand total in 24 hours	252 trains

Maximum movement of trains per day through Bas Obispo

Loaded spoil-trains north	78
(approximately 1,500 trucks carrying 27,000 cu. yds. of soil)	
Empty spoil-trains south	78
Isthmian work-trains north	18
Isthmian work-trains south	18
P.R. passenger and freight-trains north	6
P.R. passenger and freight-trains south	6
Total in eight-hour working day	204
Balance of P.R. night and miscellaneous trains	16
Grand total in 24 hours	220 trains

Maximum movement of trains per day through Gatun

Loaded spoil-trains south	30
(approximately 600 trucks carrying 8,800 cu. yds. of soil)	
Empty spoil-trains north	30
Isthmian work-trains south	7
Isthmian work-trains north	7
P.R. passenger and freight-trains south	6
P.R. passenger and freight-trains north	6
Total in eight-hour working day	86
Balance of P.R. night and miscellaneous trains	16
Grand total in 24 hours	102 trains

It will be seen from these tables that on one of its busier days the Panama Railroad handled anything up to 579 trains, two-thirds of which would be engaged in carrying from cutting to tip over 70,000 cubic yards of rock, sandstone, breccia and clay.

And here in a nutshell is the explanation for French failure and American success. For neither Dingler nor Bunau-Varilla ever solved the problem of what to do with the soil they so laboriously excavated. Not until Stevens thought of using the Panama Railroad as a conveyor-belt did soil flow freely out of the cutting; and the enormous quantities which were subsequently shifted bear witness to the soundness of his plans and the efficiency with which they were carried out.

By the winter of 1906 the railroad had been reconstituted. 165 miles of double main-line track, and 187 miles of tracks for the disposal of soil. "I don't mind trying to make the dirt fly," Stevens said, "now we have somewhere to put it!"

(d) *Reorganisation of Equipment.*
When Stevens arrived on the isthmus he saw at once that the procedure for purchasing equipment had broken down; he saw too that he would need to steer a course midway between the extravagances of the French and the parsimony of the First Commission.

His first step was to create a special Department of Machinery whose job was to ensure that every item ordered was well suited to the work it would be expected to do. On the recommendations of this Department he wrote out the necessary requisitions and passed them to the Chairman for approval; Shonts then signed them and mailed them to the Purchasing Office of the Commission in Washington, whose instructions were to fulfil all orders promptly and with the minimum of red-tape. This procedure worked well so long as Stevens and Shonts saw eye to eye. Unfortunately the latter, working in Washington, was subject to a great deal of political pressure, and this eventually brought about a rift over the awarding of contracts. It would, nevertheless, be true to say that for two years Stevens was able to order pretty well what he liked; and the success or failure of a decade of construction work hung largely on the orders he placed.

He could easily have made a mistake. His predecessor had ordered practically nothing, saying cautiously that he "needed a preparatory period of at least a year for experiment". Stevens might well have played safe and said the same; or he might have plumped for bigger and better dredges, or bigger and better explosive charges, or, now that the health of the working force was assured, simply an increase in labour by hand. Instead, he plumped for two things; steam-shovels to excavate, and railroad accessories to carry the excavated debris away. It is easy in retrospect to see that this decision was right, but it can not have been so obvious at the time.

The equipment he ordered fell by and large into one of seven categories: steam-shovels, track, locomotives, cars, unloaders, spreaders and track-shifters.

Steam shovels did ninety per cent of the dry excavation. They broke the back of the continental divide, and without them the canal would never have been completed. Stevens ordered more than 100, including enormous 105-ton monsters (see Figure 15 opposite) which bit out at a single mouthful $5\frac{1}{2}$ cubic yards of soil. The shovels were made by Marion or Bucyrus, the latter enjoying a virtual monopoly until Taft for political reasons awarded a contract to Marion*. The most satisfactory machines turned out to be the ninety-five-ton Bucyruses, one of which held the record for monthly excavation (70,290 cubic yards, or 121,600 tons) and another for daily excavation (4,465 cubic yards or 7,720 tons). Their method of operation was simple. First the area to be excavated was drilled and blasted with gunpowder; next, two lines of parallel railway track were laid alongside the debris; steam-shovels were then hauled into

---

*The authors of *Designed for Digging* (Williamson and Myers) put the case very clearly. Bucyrus shovels had been particularly asked for by the Department of Machinery, and the Bucyrus management were much chagrined by Taft's decision and asked for an explanation. "The Secretary seems to have been most reluctant to commit himself in writing, for it took him nearly a year to compose a reply. This excused his action on the grounds that the government's interest required an 'on the site' comparison of competitive machines, and that the Government ought not to be dependent upon only one source of supply. Both are plausible explanations, but the rumour has persisted that political pressure played an important part in Taft's intercession on behalf of Marion." It is interesting to note that Marion's foundry was in the Secretary's home state of Ohio.

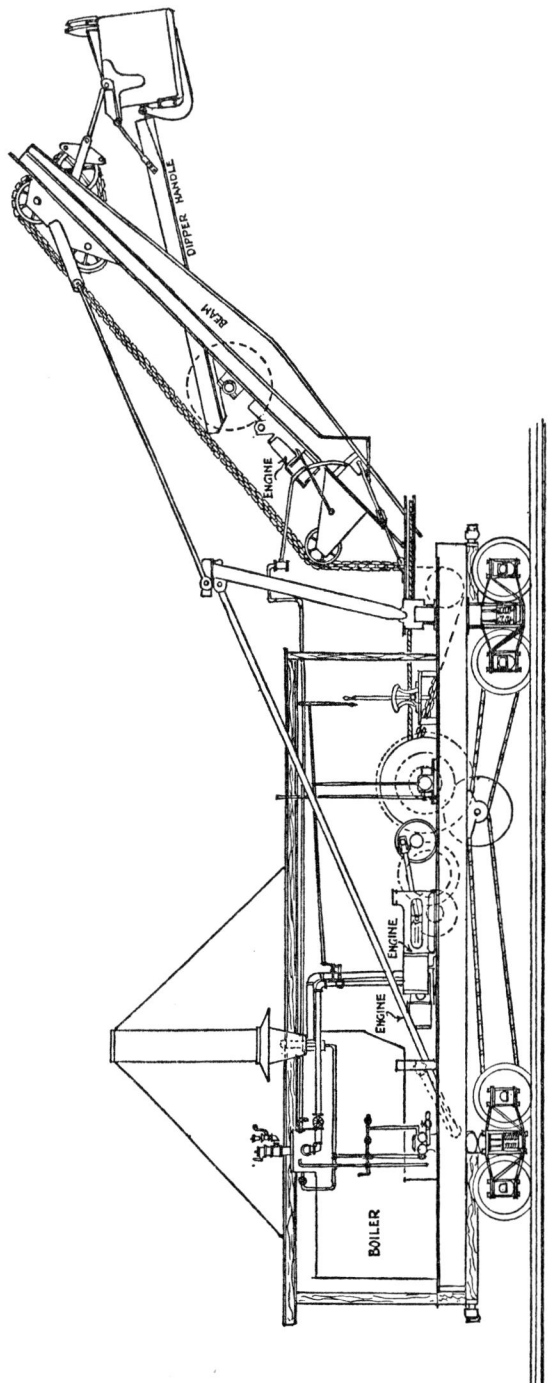

Figure 15. Bucyrus steam-shovel

position along the lower track and dump-cars along the upper. The shovels would grub up debris and swing it directly into the dump-cars; and as soon as a trainload of the latter was full it would be hauled away and replaced by another. In this way the steam-shovels could be worked virtually non-stop until the debris was cleared. It was heavy work, a large proportion of the excavated material being rock or rock-cum-clay; and booms, circles, lips, teeth and shaft pinions had to be frequently renewed. Ninety-five per cent of this repair work, however, was done on the spot at night by a roving working party equipped with forge, drills and lathes. The shovels were therefore able to stay in the Cut month after month, slowly widening and lowering the bed of the canal foot by hard-won foot.

French subcontractors had used many different gauges of lightweight track. This they had often laid on soft wood with neither tie-plates nor ballasting. The result had been a lack of liaison between the various sections of the line, trouble with spares, and no overall plan for the disposal of soil. When Stevens took over he insisted that all rails, even the temporary ones in the Cut, should be ninety pounds in weight and five foot in gauge, properly ballasted and tied. For he never forgot his first impression of Culebra, with every one of the work-trains derailed. By the time he left, the trackage had increased from seventy-three miles of light-weight rail to 350 miles of heavy well-ballasted rail; it was a common sight to see anything up to fifty trains at work in the Cut and its environs, while derailments were virtually unknown.

Locomotives were dealt with in the same way; they were standardised and increased in both number and size. In place of the thirty-five lightweight engines with an average hauling capacity of under 2,000 tons which he inherited from Wallace, Stevens passed on to his successor some three hundred magnificent machines (principally Cookes, Baldwins and Brooks) none of which had a hauling capacity of under 3,300 tons. These locomotives were hostled each night for minor repairs, and kept in first-class condition by periodic overhauls in the yards at Gorgona, Empire and Paraiso.

The French used many different types of car, varying in capacity from $5\frac{1}{2}$ to $8\frac{3}{4}$ cubic yards, and in gauge from 4 feet 6 inches to 5 feet $1\frac{1}{2}$ inches; some were unloaded from one side and some from the other, most were of wood, and almost all were too light for carrying rock and clay. Wallace was well aware of their limitations. "I found," he wrote, "that the gauge varied with almost every car, so that in a train hardly any two were the same; we even found cars where the two pairs of wheels were of different gauges. Derailments

THE FOUNDATIONS OF SUCCESS 157

were therefore frequent, it was impossible to keep the excavators supplied with trains, and a large proportion of the time lost was due to 'waiting for cars'." Stevens's Department of Machinery standardised their requirements. They concentrated on two types only: wooden Lidgerwood flat-cars with a capacity of eleven cubic yards, and steel dumps with a capacity of either twelve or eighteen cubic yards. 4,300 were ordered, and this wasn't one too many.

Unloaders were an innovation undreamed of by the French: $3\frac{1}{2}$-ton steel ploughs which, when drawn from one end of a train of flat-cars to the other, swept off the excavated soil. The flat-cars had one high side and one open side, and were joined by steel aprons which turned their floor-boards into a smooth and continuous surface. Over this surface the unloading plough was drawn by a cable wound round the drum of a steam-driven winch. The plough itself was shaped like a tick ($\sqrt{}$) with its longer surface sloping backward from the open side of the cars, and as it was drawn forward by the winch it forced debris over the side in a continuous stream. Twenty flat-cars carrying 600 tons could be unloaded by this method in twelve minutes—a job which by hand would have taken a hundred men more than an hour. Stevens ordered twenty-eight of these machines, twenty-six of which were in service by the end of his term of office.

Spreaders were used in conjunction with the unloaders. The latter invariably left debris piled up in a ridge along the edge of the track; this ridge had to be flattened out, and the flattening was done by a soil-spreader—a car operated by compressed air and equipped with an enormous twelve-foot wing of pressed steel. This wing jutted out over the side of the car and could be raised and lowered by its operator; it was used to level the debris off to the same height as the track. Stevens ordered thirteen soil-spreaders; and his Department of Machinery estimated that each did the work of more than 350 men.

Track-shifters were sophisticated, highly complex machines invented by William G. Bierd, manager of the Panama Railroad. They consisted of a flat-car equipped with two steel booms, one reaching thirty feet in front of the car and one thirty feet to the side. A system of grapples and pulleys levered up a section of track on the forward boom, transferred it to the lateral boom and swung it into position parallel to the original track. Each shifter was manned by a crew of nine, and was able to relay a mile of track in eight hours—a job which six hundred men would have been hard pressed to finish in the same time.

In addition to these standard items, the Department of Machinery ordered a vast quantity of miscellaneous equipment—pile-drivers, dredges, cranes, rock-breakers, derricks, clapets (steel-built barges), tugs and lighters, etc.: not to mention 180,000 feet of piping and 45,000 feet of lateral drop pipes. The table below shows the principal items; and it is interesting to note how sharply the quantity of equipment rises during the regime of Stevens—the number of items increasing fivefold within a couple of years. And this equipment was remarkable not only for its quantity but also for its quality and suitability. Writing twenty-five years later Stevens was able to claim with perfect truth:

> The Department of Machinery was of the utmost importance. A quantity of construction plant, tools and machinery such as never before had been gotten together in the history of the world was planned, specified, requisitioned, purchased and delivered to the site in record time. This equipment consisted of almost every mechanical device which judgment and experience indicated was best adapted to do quickly and economically the vast work which lay ahead of the engineers. Detailed specifications for individual classes of machinery such as locomotives, cars, steam-shovels, etc. were drawn up by the department. Cast steel was substituted for iron, copper boiler tubes for ones of iron and a like standard of excellence was insisted on for the entire list. The numbers involved were enormous. I remember, for example, purchasing on a single

Equipment used in construction work

	1905	*1907*	*1911*
Steam-shovels			
Bucyrus	8	63	88
Marion	—	—	23
Cars			
French	248	622	650
Lidgerwood flats	560	2,000	2,300
Steel dumps	—	350	2,000
Miscellaneous	60	81	51
Locomotives	35	293	369
Coaches	24	68	78
Unloaders	—	26	30
Spreaders	—	13	26
Trackshifters	—	3	9
Pile-drivers	—	6	14
Drills	390	484	553
Dredges	7	9	20
Boats, barges, tugs, lighters, etc.	48	71	126
	1,380	4,089	6,337

order 125 locomotives and seventy-five steam-shovels, and on another 900 Lidgerwood dump-cars . . . Some French cars, locomotives and dredges were, it is true, reconditioned and put into service; but ninety-nine per cent of the equipment used in building the canal was new; and of the immense amount ordered during my time as Chief Engineer, every single item, I am told, was well-adapted to its job. Nothing was wasted.

The Americans have always been proud of the excellence of their equipment. Never has this pride been better justified than in the case of the vast and complex range of machinery which was brought together for building the Panama Canal.

Freedom from disease, adequate living conditions, efficient transport, suitable equipment: these were the cornerstones of success. And by the spring of 1907 they had been laid with such thoroughness that the building of the canal was virtually assured. "Virtually" rather than "inevitably" because there was still one pitfall which the Americans had to avoid—the pitfall which had brought about the downfall of the French—that of trying to build their canal at sea-level.

Before preparation gave way to construction, Stevens was naturally anxious to know precisely what type of canal he was expected to build; and it was the last and perhaps the greatest of his achievements that he was able to persuade the President, Congress and the Senate to forgo the obvious attractions of a canal at sea-level in favour of the very real but not so obvious advantages of a canal with locks.

(e) *The Final Plan.*
On June 24th, 1905, Roosevelt appointed a board of consulting engineers to finalise the details of construction—"I expect you to recommend," he told them, "not what you think I *want* to hear but what I *ought* to hear." There were thirteen members of the board, five Europeans and eight Americans, the most knowledgeable of the latter being Henry L. Abbot who had served on *Le Comité Technique* and had made a detailed study of the hydrography of the Chagres. They did their work conscientiously and well, visiting the isthmus, studying the great mass of recommendations and reports which had accumulated over the years, and sifting through a large number of individual proposals. Among the latter was a scheme by the irrepressible Bunau-Varilla for a temporary high-level canal with locks which was to be completed in four years and then (while still

in use) lowered stage by stage; but in spite of Bunau-Varilla's wealth of statistics his scheme was rejected, and the board was eventually left with two clear-cut but diametrically opposed proposals: the first for a canal with locks at an eighty-five-foot level, to be completed in nine years at a cost of 150 million dollars; and the second for a canal without locks at sea-level, to be completed in twelve years at a cost of 405 million dollars. The board couldn't agree among themselves, eight members (the five Europeans and the Americans Burr, Davis and Parsons) voting for a canal at sea-level, and five members (the Americans Abbot, Noble, Randolph, Ripley and Stearns) voting for a canal with locks. A majority and a minority report were therefore both submitted to the President.

There followed a six months' battle in Congress and the Senate.

The sea-level canal had powerful advocates. It appealed to the layman, even Stevens admitting that when he first arrived in Panama he had "visions of a wide expanse of blue water, with great ships ploughing through it, like the Straits of Magellan minus the current"; it was supported by influential figures such as Davis and Wallace; it had been the desideratum of de Lesseps—and why, people asked, should America draw back where France had dared? A canal-with-locks, on the other hand, *sounded* inferior. It would, it is true, be cheaper and quicker to build, but to a lot of people the corollary of this appeared to be that it was second-best; its advocates were principally men who had lived on the isthmus and were not therefore in the public eye; and it resurrected ghosts—"if we are going to have a canal with locks," a senator remarked testily, "we might as well have built it in Nicaragua." No one therefore was altogether surprised when in May 1906 a sub-committee of Congress recommended by six votes to five that the canal be built at sea-level.

It was fortunate that two men had the courage and foresight not to accept the sub-committee's decision as final. Roosevelt suspected misjudgment; he called Stevens to Oyster Bay; and Stevens (to quote his own words) "talked to Teddy like a Dutch uncle . . . and soon convinced him that a canal with locks was the only possible answer."

The Senate, however, were not convinced so easily, and Stevens was obliged that summer to desert the isthmus and argue his case on the floor of the House. He became a lobbyist. It was a role he abhorred; for he was a straightforward man of action, impatient of the subtleties and petty dishonesties which are part and parcel of political life. Perhaps for this very reason he was an outstanding success. His answers, forthright and simple, swept like a sea breeze through the Hearings of the Senate.

"I suggest you are too positive in your opinions, Mr. Stevens."

"Well, I am a positive man."

"I suggest to you that this dam [at Gatun] ought to be made stronger."

"The dam is strong enough. This is like killing a duck; when you kill him he is dead; there is no use trying to kill him deader."

Stevens spent nearly two months in Washington, collecting data and helping senators to prepare their speeches; and before he left he summarised his views in a brief statement.

My conclusion is that the lock or high-level canal is preferable to the sea-level canal for the following reasons:

1. It will provide a safer and quicker passage for ships.

2. It will, beyond question, provide the best solution to the vital problem of how to care for the flood waters of the Chagres.

3. Provisions can be made more easily for enlarging it.

4. The time and cost of its construction will be only half that of a sea-level canal.

To this he added: "If I had to build the canal with my own money, I would choose the high-level plan, even if I expected that my family after me would have to operate it for generations."

This was plain speaking; it was also plain common sense; and sentiment that summer began to swing gradually towards a canal with locks.

The vital debate was on June 20th and 21st. Senator Philander C. Knox was the principal speaker, and Stevens supplied him with a large-scale map of the isthmus, with the sea-level canal depicted in red and the lock canal in blue: this was projected onto a wall of the Chamber. In his speech Knox compared the rival schemes with a wealth of statistics (briefly summarised below).

SEA-LEVEL CANAL v. LOCK CANAL: COMPARATIVE DATA

	Sea-level canal	Lock canal
Bottom width:	Over 750': none 300'–750': 5 miles 150'–300': 23 „ under 150': 21 „	Over 750': 19 miles 300'–750': 16 „ 150'–300': 14 „ under 150': none
Depth:	40' throughout	41'–45'
Volume of Water:	100,000,000 cu. yds.	303,000,000 cu. yds.
Chagres floods:	Held back by a dam at Gamboa to form a lake of 30 sq. miles, the flood waters of which would be discharged through sluices into the canal.	Held back by a dam at Gatun to form a lake of 170 sq. miles, the flood waters of which would be discharged through a spillway into the open sea.

	Sea-level canal	Lock canal
Flow of current:	Up to 3 knots	Nil
Excavation required:	110,000,000 cu. yds.	230,000,000 cu. yds.
Time of transit:	14 hours	10½ hours
Time of completion:	12 years	9 years.
Cost:	405,000,000 dollars	150,000,000 dollars

He was scrupulously fair in his comparisons, but in his peroration he came down heavily in favour of a canal with locks. Amid mounting tension a vote was taken, and by thirty-six votes to thirty-one the lock canal was approved.

It was a decisive moment.

For looking back at the difficulties which the French had experienced with the Chagres, and looking forward to the difficulties which the Americans were soon to experience in the Culebra Cut, it seems probable that in 1910 as in 1880 a sea-level canal simply could not have been built. The floods would have been too catastrophic, the geology too recalcitrant; the isthmus would have triumphed again. Stevens realised this; and years later in the Journal of the Society of Civil Engineers he wrote: "I have been privileged to be of some little service to my country, and the greatest service I ever gave it was, I am sure, the part I took in preventing foreign votes from foisting a useless thing—namely a sea-level canal as proposed by the majority of the Consulting Board—upon a too credulous American people."

On June 29th, 1906 Roosevelt signed the bill which authorised by law the implementing of the minority report.

At last, after twenty-seven years of trial and error, hardship and mortality, false start and false alarm, the isthmus was about to be challenged by an organised assault force working to a feasible plan.

The essence of this plan has been neatly summarised by Stevens's successor, Goethals:

> It is not so much a canal we are hoping to build as a bridge of water, consisting of lakes, locks and sea-approaches. The rivers which flow into the Atlantic and Pacific are to be dammed back so that they form lakes eighty-five feet above the sea, and these lakes will then be connected through the lowest point in the mountains by a deep cut . . . At the point where each river is to be dammed, locks will be built into the retaining walls, so that ships can be raised or lowered to the eighty-five foot level. And finally, approach channels will be dug from either ocean to the foot of the dams [see Figure 16 opposite].

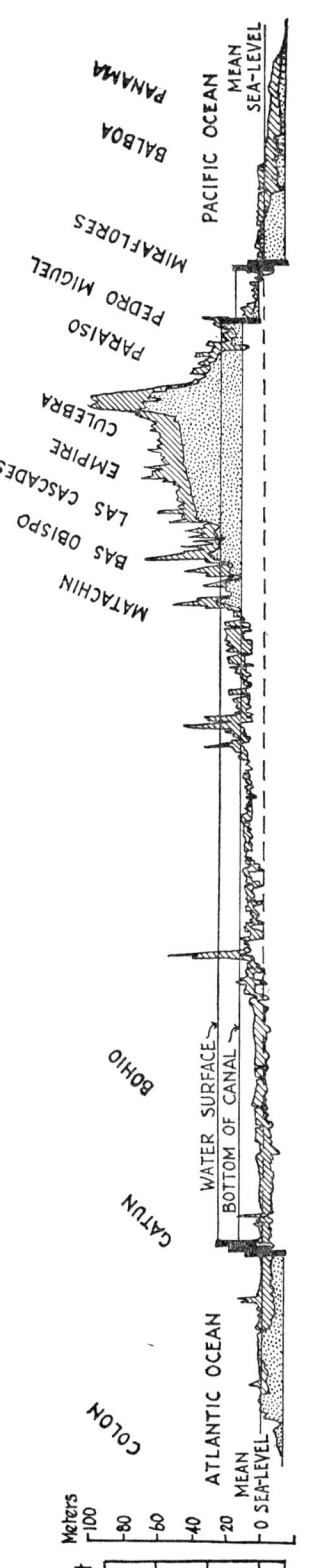

Figure 16. "Not so much a canal as a bridge of water" (longitudinal section of the Panama Canal)

This plan was a sensible combination of technical expertise and the knowledge which comes from analysing other peoples' mistakes. It was not, however, original. It was, in every essential detail, the same scheme as had been championed with such eloquence twenty-seven years earlier at the *Congrès International d'Études du Canal Interocéanique* by Godin de Lèpinay. How many lives and how many millions of francs and dollars would have been saved if the advice of this far-sighted Frenchman had been adhered to.

At the beginning of 1907 it seemed that at long last the canal's vicissitudes were over. A final plan had been agreed, a working force was assembled, good health was assured, equipment was at hand, and construction proper was due any moment to get under way. The years of preparation, it seemed were about to bring forth fruit. But it was now that the bombshell burst: a bombshell as tragic as it was unexpected.

The architect of victory, John F. Stevens, resigned.

10

THE TRANSFER OF POWER

Why did he do it? Why at the very moment when victory was assured did Stevens turn his back on Panama and drift like Wallace into the ranks of those whose names are little remembered and whose accomplishments seldom sung? Three factors influenced him: the terms under which he originally came to the isthmus, his personality, and the muddle which took place in spring 1907 over the awarding of contracts.

The first point is soon disposed of. Stevens had never sought the position of chief engineer. He had been persuaded into it against his better judgment, and had accepted it on the clear understanding that he "was to stay on the isthmus only until success had been assured". Success, by the spring of 1907, *was* assured. Therefore, he resigned. In one respect it was as simple as that.

It would, however, be naïve to imagine that this was the whole story. For almost two years Stevens had been in charge of the greatest construction project the world has ever seen; his common sense, experience and technical expertise had been unsparingly devoted to getting this project under way, and other things being equal he would naturally have wished to remain in charge to supervise the reaping of the seed he had with such proficiency sown. Other things, however, were not equal. Stevens's path was strewn with as many thorns as roses. And in the spring of 1907 he found himself faced with opposition on a major point of policy. A lesser man would have trimmed his sails to the winds of expedience; but Stevens held out for the things he knew to be right; and eventually (to quote Miles P. Duval) he was forced into resigning as "a voluntary sacrifice on the altar of political expedience".

Perhaps, in view of the sort of man he was, it was inevitable. For Stevens was essentially a frontiersman, a man who was more at home in the cabins of his railroad workers than the corridors of the Senate, and he had a fine contempt for politicians: "If I have," he wrote, "to mix and mingle with every politician in the United States, the sooner I drop [this project] the better I will be satisfied." The trouble was that in an undertaking of this magnitude, mixing and mingling with politicians was exactly what had to be done. It was Stevens's strength, and his weakness, that he would have no truck with patronage, artifice or expediency; and when in 1907 he saw these evils—against his every advice—being allowed to extend their tentacles over the construction of the canal, he resigned.

It was the question of contracts which brought matters to a head: whether the canal should be built by the Commission, by a series of small contractors, or by a single large contractor.

Stevens's attitude was reasonable and consistent. He wanted the canal to be built by a number of small contractors working under the general supervision of the Commission. He was, he wrote as early as November 1906, "strongly opposed to endeavouring, by advertisement or otherwise, to let the entire work to any one firm . . . since this would take too much power from the Commission." Roosevelt agreed. Secretary Taft, however, expressed his desire to advertise, "in order to achieve an element of competition". Taft's intervention was nothing short of a disaster; and it is indeed remarkable that as regards the canal, the Secretary seems to have had a positive genius for making unfortunate decisions—*vide* the Marion steam-shovels and the Miraflores locks. Advertising resulted in a conglomeration of bids, many of them from firms who were quite unsuited to carry out the required works. Shonts, disgusted with Washington red-tape and Washington political interference, resigned. And a few weeks later Stevens was informed without consultation, that a contract for the entire work was about to be awarded to William J. Oliver and Anson M. Bangs of New York. He was incredulous. The idea of *any* single contractor was abhorrent to him; and Oliver in particular were intensely unpopular among the canal workers, and were not in his opinion "qualified by nature, experience or achievement to perform the necessary work"; also they included on their board men such as Parsons who were known to be bitterly opposed to a canal with locks.

There followed a spate of letters and telegrams between Taft and Stevens. The latter tore Oliver's contract plans to shreds, proving (in the words of Duval) "that no man familiar with the problems of the isthmus could have made so many errors as this ambitious contractor". Taft, however, either could not or would not see the foolishness of awarding Oliver the contract; he procrastinated, prevaricated, and appeared to put more trust in the advice of speculators in New York than of well-qualified engineers on the isthmus. And eventually Stevens lost both heart and patience. Fearing that all he had worked for for the past eighteen months was about to be thrown away, he offered Roosevelt his resignation. It was the one way left to him, he felt, of publicly dissociating himself from a course of action which he knew would be disastrous to the canal.

His resignation, coming so soon after Shonts', was a bitter blow to Roosevelt, who considered the building of the canal to be the achievement by which he would be remembered by posterity: a feat of even greater importance than the Louisiana Purchase. Heartily sick of engineers who were for ever throwing in their hands, the President wrote: "I propose now to put the works in charge of men who will stay on the job until I get tired of having them there, or until I say they may abandon it. I shall turn it over to the Army."

Oliver and Bangs had been defeated: but at the price of the chief engineer's head.

It is pleasant to record that Stevens's resignation was attended by none of the bitterness and acerbity which had made Wallace's a *cause célèbre*. He wrote an unusually frank letter to the President— "I have been obliged to engage in a continuous battle with enemies in the rear ... and have been attacked by people I would not wipe my boots on in the United States." But he did on the other hand, express his gratitude to Roosevelt for his personal approval and support. And he indulged in no post-mortems. At the time, with the isthmus alive with rumours, he said simply, "Don't talk, dig." And years later he was equally reticent: "The reasons," he wrote, "for my resignation were purely personal. I have never declared them, and I never will." He had, perhaps, qualms which might be considered old-fashioned today about washing dirty linen in public.

His resignation left Washington with the difficult task of choosing a successor; and here Roosevelt and Taft made a wise decision. Acting on the advice of General Mackenzie, Chief of Engineers, the President offered the position to Major Goethals—a man virtually unknown except in Army circles where he was recognised as a sound engineer and a highly efficient administrator.

George Washington Goethals was born in Brooklyn in 1858; and his character and appearance have been astutely delineated by Mrs. Gorgas.

> His name in the original Dutch was "goet-hals", meaning "stiff-neck", and his friends have always regarded this as a happy description ... He was an impressive figure, and walked with a decisive stride, his whole bearing indicating self-confidence and industry. His round head surmounted by crisp white hair, his weather-beaten handsome face, his penetrating violet-blue eyes— all these features suggested poise and determination; here certainly was a man who would suffer no equal in authority and would not avoid responsibility. In a few months this somewhat grim self-sufficing and silent figure became one of the familiar

sights on the isthmus. Clad in a spotless white suit and invariably smoking a cigarette, the impression conveyed to the onlooker—and perhaps intended to be conveyed—was that the Panama Canal, after many vicissitudes, had at last found its master . . . About his whole personality was an air of boss-ship . . . he was a man who loved power.

It ought perhaps to be borne in mind that Goethals and Gorgas cordially disliked one another; Mrs. Gorgas, therefore, was not likely to be over-charitable in her judgment; and the new chief engineer had in fact virtues to which her description does less than justice. For he was a brilliant organiser and a masterful leader of men; and like Stevens he had courage, the sort of mental resilience which enabled him to take disaster after disaster in his stride and never lose heart. (The story goes that in 1913, with the canal virtually completed, he was woken one morning, and told that the Cucaracha slide had collapsed, spewing some five million cubic yards of debris across the cutting. Gaillard—who was in charge of excavation among the central hills—was beside himself with despair. "What on earth," he whispered, as the two men stood looking down on the scene of desolation, "are we to do?" Goethals lit a cigarette. "Hell," he said quietly, "we'll just have to dig it out.") And the new chief engineer had one other quality which became evident the moment he set foot on the isthmus. He was essentially fair-minded; he gave credit where credit was due; for then and throughout the rest of his life he was unstinting in the praise he accorded Stevens.

> People talk [he said] about the success of the army at Panama, but it was fortunate that Mr. Stevens preceded us. The real problem in digging the canal has been the disposal of soil, and no army engineer in America could have laid out the transportation scheme as Mr. Stevens did. We are building on the foundations he laid, and the world can not give him too much credit.

It was as well for Goethals that he was willing to state these views in public. For Stevens's resignation was greeted in the isthmus with an upsurge of amazement, anger and very genuine regret. "Culebra's cut to the heart," an old steam-shovel operator lamented. "We are all of us cut through and through." The Panama *Star and Herald* was equally vehement: "We, here on the ground, speak for every worker on the isthmus when we say that the credit [for building the canal] will justly belong to John F. Stevens." A petition was circulated, begging him to withdraw his resignation—"please remain in charge," it read, "and we will show our loyalty by working for you even harder than we have up to now"; and within a couple of days the petition had more than 10,000 signatures—including those of virtually every American in the Zone.

Stevens, however, was not the sort of man to change his mind. Goethals arrived in Cristobal on March 12th, and within three weeks the transfer of power had taken place, the smoothness with which it was effected being a tribute to the tact and level-headedness of both.

For the new chief engineer had a problem. Stevens was so popular and his work so successful that almost everyone on the isthmus regretted his going and looked askance at his successor. Goethals realised this; and from the moment he arrived he went out of his way to stress both his indebtedness to Stevens and his determination to work on exactly the same lines. After talking to men in the Culebra Cut, for example, he told the Panama *Star and Herald:* "I have never seen so much affection displayed for any one man, and if I can carry on so as to build up a similar feeling it will be the proudest work of my life." And again: "The magnitude of the work grows and grows on me; it seems to get bigger all the time, but Mr. Stevens has perfected such an organisation that there is nothing left [for me] to do but just allow it to continue."

He had been in the Zone only four days when his qualities of leadership were put to the test. On the night of Saturday, March 16th a meeting was held at the Corozal Club in front of a vast and none too orderly audience. In speeches made by the toastmaster and visiting congressmen, Stevens's name was invariably greeted with cheers whereas his successor's met with a pointed silence. Goethals was the last speaker. If he was nervous he gave no sign of it. Relaxed and confident, he began by comparing the chaos of 1905 with the efficiency of 1907: "I fully realise," he told his audience, "that in the past eighteen months Mr. Stevens has perfected an organisation which will carry the canal through to completion . . . And I say here and now that it is my intention to keep this organisation as he has established it." This brought him his first applause. He went on to deal with militarism. The men, he knew, didn't fancy the prospect of an army regime; and there had been a spate of speculation, letters and editorials about the adverse effects of Army discipline—epitomised in a cartoon showing canal workers standing at the salute while the Chagres in flood swept through the workings. But on this point Goethals was unequivocal.

> I want to state right from the start that I don't expect a salute from any man on the job . . . I consider myself no longer a

commander in the United States Army. I now consider myself commander of the Army of Panama, and that the enemy we are going to combat is the Culebra Cut and the locks and dams at both ends of the canal, and any man on the work who does his duty will never have cause to complain of militarism.

It was by speeches such as this, repeated along the line of the canal, that Goethals gradually won the respect of the construction gangs. Their affection he never sought. And he was never accorded it; for he lacked the warmth of personality of his predecessor.

On March 27th Stevens formally placed his resignation in the hands of the Commission; and ten days later he left the isthmus, never in official capacity to return.

His departure sparked off a mass demonstration of regard and affection the like of which had not been seen on the isthmus since the days of de Lesseps. To quote the Panama *Star and Herald*:

> The reception in honour of John F. Stevens brought together every American in Cristobal and as many as could be conveyed there from the rest of the Zone in a series of special trains . . . [By nine thirty p.m.] the crowd on the wharf was the largest that has ever waved *adieu* to a ship leaving Colon; . . . flags, lights and palms were in profusion, and while the band played *Here The Conquering Hero Comes* the assembled guests made an aisle through which Mr. Stevens and his party passed to the stand. His entry was the signal for a burst of prolonged applause which continued until Mr. Bierd rose to say good-bye in the name of the men at work on the canal. With a great deal of feeling Mr. Bierd said it was unnecessary for him to announce the reason for the gathering, that its common and inspiring cause was so deeply impressed in the heart of everyone present that he could only hope to make Mr. Stevens understand the full measure of the regard and affection in which he was held by the men who served under him. [He went on to review briefly] the work of the past two years, and said that Mr. Stevens had won the respect and even the love of his employees because he had convinced them that he was a man able to overcome the problems involved, and whose decisions were made for what he believed to be right . . . It was to bid such a chief Godspeed that they had assembled.
>
> [In reply] Mr. Stevens said that two years ago he was almost overawed by the amount of preparation and construction work required; but that conditions were now such that he felt absolutely assured the canal would be opened by January 1915. He asked the men, as their sincere friend, to take any little differences and

complaints direct to Colonel Goethals, for whom he asked the same loyalty as heretofore had been shown to himself. [And finally he paid tribute to the work of the Sanitary Department] . . . Until Colonel Gorgas lifted the dark cloud which unsanitary conditions placed over the work, he was, he said, in doubt as to success. But when this doubt had been removed he knew that the canal would be pushed to completion.

[The final ceremony was the most moving.] Mr. Stevens was told that the men had subscribed for some tokens of their regard: a silver service, a watch and a gold ring. Three gifts had been selected because the men had wanted Mr. Stevens to have from them something he could pass on to each of his three sons . . . [The gift of the ring moved him very deeply]—for years he had worn a plain gold ring of which he was particularly fond. This had been stolen . . . and the men wanted their ring to be made as like as possible to the one he had lost. Just before leaving he was also presented with the petitions signed by more than 10,000 workers the moment his resignation had become known. This was in two volumes, one containing signatures of men on the Commission and the other signatures of men on the Railroad, and together they made a souvenir which appealed to and affected Mr. Stevens deeply.

It was midnight before the former chief engineer and his family were able to embark in the S.S. *Panama* as she lay at anchor in Limon Bay. The *Panama* wasn't due to sail till the following morning; but the crowd refused to disperse; they thronged the waterfront, singing, clapping and cheering throughout the night; and when early on April 10th the ship at last stood north into the Caribbean, she was given an inspiring send-off to the tune of 'Auld Lang Syne' and the cheering of men who felt they were saying goodbye not to an employer but to a friend.

The departure of John F. Stevens marks the end of an era dominated by personalities: the ebullient de Lesseps, the self-opinionated Bunau-Varilla, the vacillating old men of the First Commission, and the quietly dedicated Gorgas. By 1907 these key figures had acted out their roles, and the isthmus, as a result, was vulnerable. All that remained to be done was the actual digging—about 220 million cubic yards of it.

From now on, to quote the *Saturday Evening Post*, "Yardage was king".

It was Goethals himself who said, years later, somewhat cavalierly that "the construction of the Panama Canal involved no great technical problem". What it *did* involve was the excavation of difficult soil on a scale hitherto undreamed of in the history of the world. And the diagram below (Figure 17) shows just how much of this soil still remained to be excavated in the summer of 1907.

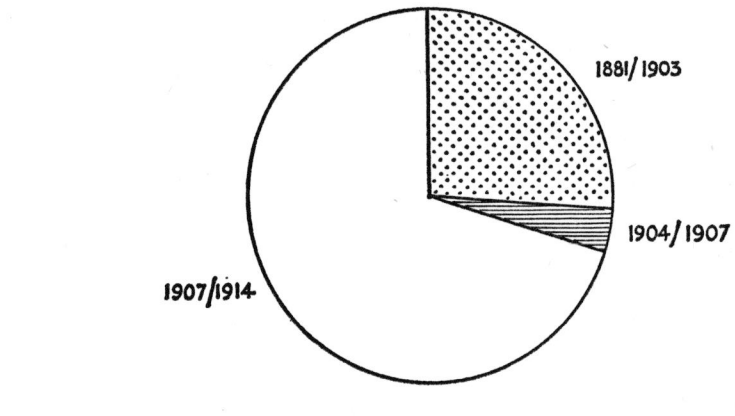

	1881/1903	Excavated by French	78,000,000 cubic yards
	1904/1907	Excavated by Americans	14,000,000 cubic yards
	1907/1914	Excavated by Americans	219,000,000 cubic yards

Figure 17. Annual excavation in the Culebra Cut

From the moment Goethals took over he concentrated on excavation, sometimes moving in a single day more than his predecessors had moved in a month. All credit to him. But it should never be forgotten that he was reaping where others—Gorgas and Stevens in particular—had sowed. Gorgas has long been recognised as one of the master-builders of the canal; but Stevens has drifted into an ill-deserved obscurity. One man, as early as 1907, recognised what was likely to happen. "Mr. Stevens," wrote Joseph G. Cannon, Speaker of the House of Representatives, "will never get credit for the work he has done; or if he does, he will never get enough."

11

THE ATLANTIC DIVISION

Goethals divided the work of construction into three regions. The Atlantic Division (from the entrance to Limon Bay up to and including Gatun Dam) he placed in the hands of the army under Major William Sibert: the Central Division (Gatun Lake and the Culebra Cut) he handed over to a composite force of army-cum-civilians controlled by Major David Gaillard: and the Pacific Division (from the end of the Culebra Cut to the forty-five-foot mean tide contour in Panama Bay) he gave to a purely civilian force under Sydney B. Williamson. This arrangement led in effect to the setting up of three chief engineers each with his clearly defined kingdom, while Goethals was left free to concentrate on overall administration. Each kingdom had its own problems, its own key force of technicians, and after a while its own *esprit de corps*.

The Atlantic Division was the smallest and in many ways—apart from the weather—the most pleasant in which to work: 7.7 miles stretching from Toro Point at the entrance to Limon Bay to the old Indian village of Gatun three and a half miles inland on the banks of the Chagres. The task in this division was twofold: to dredge an approach channel through Limon Bay and its immediate hinterland, and to construct a dam and locks at Gatun.

(1) *Excavation of the Atlantic approach-channel.*
Limon Bay is a shallow, unprotected anchorage. It used to be vulnerable to the storms known as "northers" which once or twice a year would sweep with great force into the exposed harbour. De Lesseps had tried to minimise the effect of the "northers" by building his canal in the shelter of the east or Cristobal shore. The American canal, however, was sited to pass through the centre of the bay; and Goethals realised at once that breakwaters would be essential, to quote his own words, "to create a safe anchorage within the limits of the canal, to ensure that vessels should enter the channel through quiet water, and to prevent the approaches from silting up". A committee (Sibert, Maltby, Jadwin, Chester Harding and Judson) was therefore appointed to draw up plans for protecting the harbour,

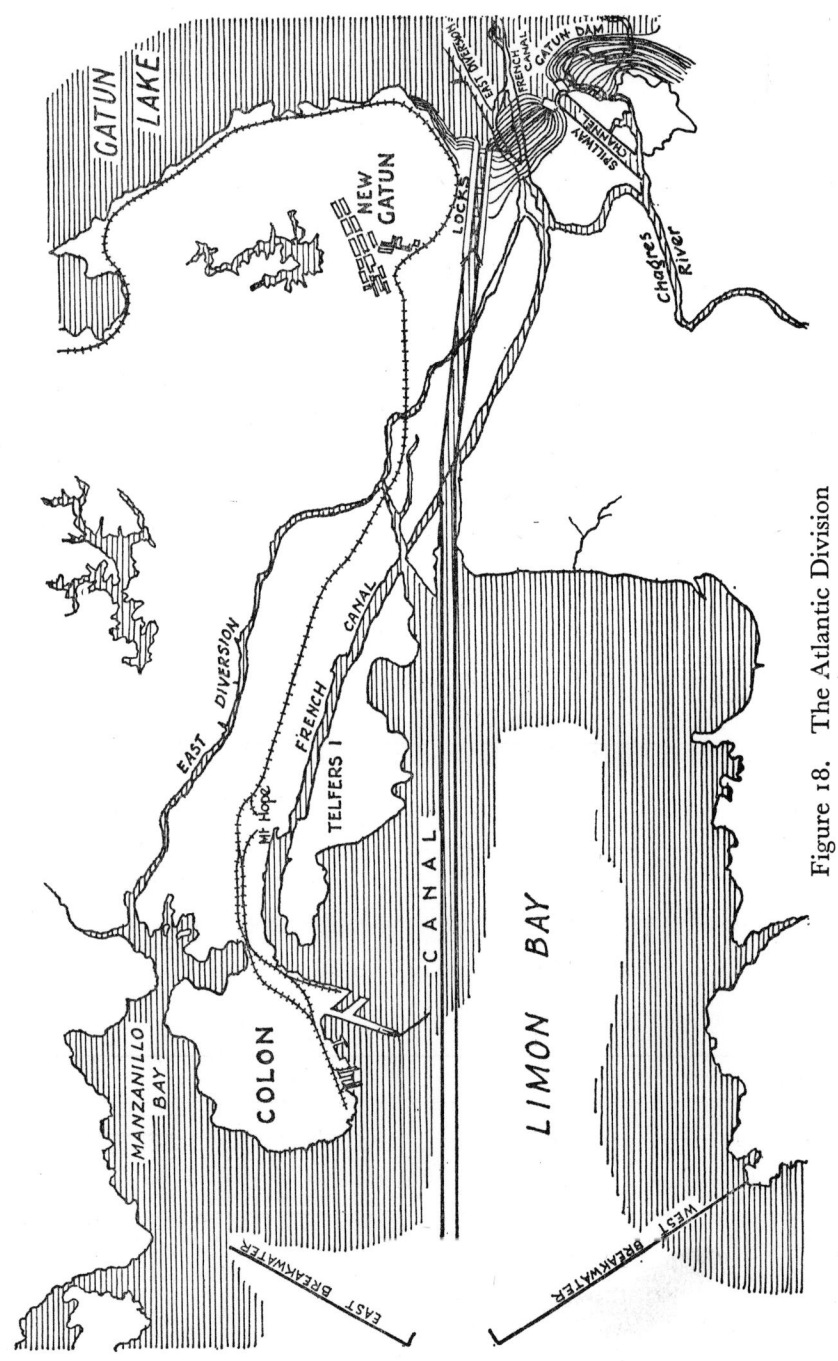

Figure 18. The Atlantic Division

and they quickly prepared drawings and specifications. It was not, however, until early in 1910 that work got under way.

Two breakwaters were planned: the longer from Toro Point in the west, and the shorter from Manzanillo Bay in the east.

The Toro Point barrier was started first. Like so much work connected with the canal, it was conceived on what for those days was a gargantuan scale: 11,600 feet in length, five million tons in weight and more than seven million dollars in cost. The main difficulty was one of transportation: how to assemble cheaply and handle expeditiously the vast quantities of rock and stone which were the raw materials of success. The committee's first thought was to use local stone quarried from close to Toro Point; but they soon found this was too small and too soft to withstand the pounding of the "northers", and that the nearest quarry with rocks sufficiently large and durable was twenty miles down-coast at Porto Bello. Sibert and his committee looked into the possibility of transporting Porto Bello rock by rail; but they decided in the end that it would be quicker and cheaper to ship it by sea. Rocks of from twelve to eighteen tons were therefore blasted from the Porto Bello quarry, loaded into barges and towed direct to the site. Here, off the western horn of Limon Bay, they were dumped overboard to form the loose or seaward wall of a breakwater which was pushed slowly out toward the centre of the bay. As soon as these rocks began to form a ridge high enough to counteract swell, a series of creosoted piles eighty-five-feet high were driven in along their sheltered or inland side. These piles were lashed together and interlaced so as to form a trestle sufficiently wide at the top to carry two lines of railroad track. Then came the spectacular part. As soon as the outer wall and trestle had been pushed well into the bay, local stones from the quarries round Toro Point were loaded into flat-cars, the flat-cars were shunted along the trestle and the stones swept off by Lidgerwood plough. It was, to quote Sibert, "an impressive sight to see these great boulders, hundreds at a time, cascading into the sea". In this way the landward side of the breakwater was constructed of local softstone, and the seaward side of durable rock.

The work proceeded with neither hitch nor respite through 1910, 1911 and 1912, with the breakwater being extended slowly but surely across the mouth of the bay. It was never spectacular work, but it was pleasantly satisfying. For to quote the engineer in charge: "There were no slides, no heaving of the bottom and next to no subsidence ... and the breakwater was completed without accident, ahead of schedule and at less than the estimated cost." And it has stood the test of time. For the barrier passed by ships today as they enter the canal is the same sixteen-foot loose stone wall—albeit heavily patched and reinforced—that was built close on sixty years ago by the engineers of the U.S. Army.

The east breakwater remained in abeyance until the west was virtually complete. Its basic design was similar—a soft inner core encased in an outer armour of durable rock—but its method of construction was different. For when Sibert analysed costs, he came to the conclusion that moving stone by sea had been uneconomic. For the eastern breakwater, therefore, stones were quarried from Sosa Hill on the Pacific coast brought some forty miles across the isthmus by trains of the Panama Railroad, and tipped into place direct from Lidgerwood dump-cars. To make this possible the following sequence was adhered to. First, the dredges operating in Limon Bay deposited a "blanket" of excavated debris along the line of the proposed breakwater (this was to discourage settlement in those places where the bottom was soft); into this blanket, pile-drivers then built a trestle wide enough to carry two lines of track; cars loaded with rock from Sosa Hill were shunted along either track and the rocks were ploughed off, away from the centre, to form the outer armour. Finally, the space between was filled by suction dredge with a mixture of coral-cum-sand excavated from the approach-channel. This method of construction was cheap, but it was none too strong; and in the early spring of 1915 a series of "northers" carried away nearly 4,000 feet of trestle and part of the half-constructed wall. After this setback, twenty-five-ton concrete blocks (made on the spot out of cement, Limon Bay sand and Chagres River gravel) were used in place of the Sosa rock. This created a more solid structure, and the breakwater was finally completed in 1916 at a cost of under four million dollars.

Both the east breakwater and the west terminate exactly 1,000 feet short of the centre line of the dredged channel, and as a vessel passes between them she enters Limon Bay and the confines of the actual canal.

The work to be done in Limon Bay and its hinterland was simple and relatively easy. It was basically dredging: the excavating of a channel forty-one feet deep and 500 feet wide from the entrance between the breakwaters to the site, three and a half miles inland, of Gatun Dam. In this section, therefore, operations soon took on a nautical flavour. The equipment consisted of dredges, clapets, tugs and scows; the working parties were frequently referred to as ships' companies, and activities were controlled by watches, shore-leaves and sea and harbour routine.

Limon Bay consists of a shallow, pear-shaped bite out of the

(*Above left*) Comte Ferdinand de Lesseps

(*Above*) Adolphe Godinde Lépinay

Philipe Bunau-Varilla

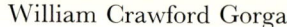

Caribbean, roughly two and a half miles wide and four miles long; in 1907 over fifty per cent of it was less than six feet deep. The French had already done a great deal of excavation here. They had dredged a deep-water channel close to the wharves of Cristobal and constructed a mole (on the foundations of an old coral reef) to protect the mouth of their canal. This French canal, however, was sited nearly a mile to the east of the proposed American channel; it ran not through the centre of the bay but inshore of Telfers Island, and because of this it has often been claimed that the French excavation was of little value to Goethals. This is not so. The French canal was an important asset, since it served for five years as the waterway down which material was assembled for building Gatun Dam. Work on the American approach channel was therefore able to continue uninterrupted, while supplies for the dam moved freely to and fro along the French and roughly-parallel waterway.

It was a complex armada of vessels which carried out the excavation of bay and hinterland: ladder-dredges, pipeline dredges, and suction-dredges; barges, clam-shells, clapets and scows; tugs, tenders, lighters and launches; crane-boats, drill-boats, gasoline-tenders and self-propelling dumps: manned in all by over 1,500 men. Their work fell naturally into three divisions:

From Mile 0 to Mile $3\frac{1}{2}$ (i.e. from the entrance between the breakwater to the shore) where the ground consisted of mud-cum-silt, and was excavated almost single-handed by the suction dredge, *Ancon*. From Mile $3\frac{1}{2}$ to Mile $4\frac{1}{2}$ (i.e. from the shore to the end of the coastal mangrove swamps) where the ground consisted of silt, coral, soft blue rock and clay, and was excavated by pipeline and dipper-dredges such as the *Sandpiper* and *Chagres*. And from Mile $4\frac{1}{2}$ to Mile $6\frac{1}{2}$ (i.e. the cutting through the Mindi Hills and the approaches to Gatun) where the going was harder—blue rock, heavy clay, gravel and boulders—and the ground had to be first blasted by drills, then excavated by ladder-dredge, suction-dredge or steam-shovel.

In the first section the work was unspectacular: the *Ancon* sucking mud-cum-silt from the bed of the channel, carrying it away to the open sea, and discharging it through her storage bins into deep water. Unspectacular but effective. For the *Ancon*, between 1907 and 1912 excavated the amazing total of thirteen million cubic yards of silt. Indeed as regards sheer yardage, this sturdy 3,000-ton dredge built by the Maryland Steel Company (see Figure 19 on page 178) was undoubtedly the piece of equipment which made the biggest contribution to excavation. The *Canal Record* is eloquent in her praise:

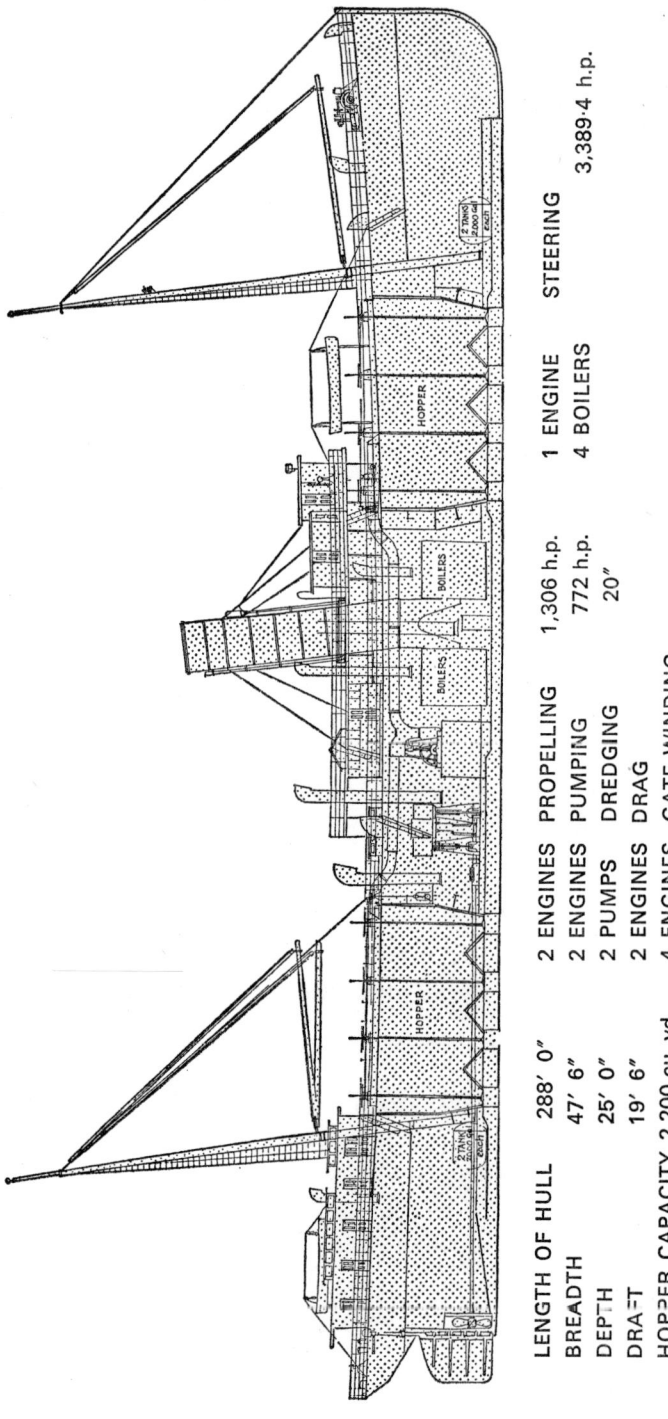

LENGTH OF HULL	288' 0"	2 ENGINES	PROPELLING	1,306 h.p.
BREADTH	47' 6"	2 ENGINES	PUMPING	772 h.p.
DEPTH	25' 0"	2 PUMPS	DREDGING	20"
DRAFT	19' 6"	2 ENGINES	DRAG	
HOPPER CAPACITY	2,200 cu. yd.	4 ENGINES	GATE WINDING	
		1 ENGINE	STEERING	
		4 BOILERS		3,389.4 h.p.

Figure 19. The sea-going suction-dredge *Ancon*—"undoubtedly the piece of equipment which contributed most to excavation"

The dredges *Ancon* and *Culebra* work twenty-four hours a day, six days a week, and the seventh day they spend not in rest, but in making ready for the week ahead. In constructing the canal each of them is doing the work of eight good steam-shovels and more than a hundred dump cars, for their average day's excavation is a clear 15,000 yards. Each has its own quarters, mess-halls, machine-shop, power-house, and equipment for excavating; and the spirit of the men in each is like that of every Zone settlement—to make next week's work count for more than the week that has passed ... They are big ships, 288 foot long, 47 foot beam, 25 foot draught and 3,015 tons in weight. The *Ancon* is working in Limon Bay, from the entrance between the breakwaters in toward the shore. Already [by the summer of 1909] 4,175,340 cubic yards of earth have been pumped into her bins and deposited in deep water in the Caribbean. A similar amount of work on land would make a very big cut in a very big hill, and people would see it and comment on it. But the *Ancon* leaves no trail behind her, no visible sign of her work; for the channel in Limon Bay does not show even at low water. Only the men on the ship, the engineer who takes measurements and the occasional leadsmen who cast for curiosity, know that the channel is there, from one to twenty feet below the adjacent bed of the sea ... On Sunday morning the *Culebra* ties up at La Boca to make light repairs, to coal and to give her crew a few hours ashore. The *Ancon* ties up at Cristobal for like purposes. First thing on Monday they are at work again, and until the following Sunday morning their engines never rest.

By the summer of 1912, eighty per cent of the work in Limon Bay had been completed, and a cutting 500 feet wide and nowhere less than thirty-two feet deep had been dredged from breakwater to shore at a cost of under eighteen cents per cubic yard—by far the cheapest excavation along the forty-odd miles of the canal. All credit for this to the *Ancon*'s designers, builders, skipper and crew: especially her crew, whom their captain described as, "a grand bunch; not a single loafer among them".

In the second section—the mangrove swamps which lay between coast and hills—the work was more complex and was carried out by a greater variety of vessels. In fact nearly all the fleet listed on the following page were engaged either in this section or in redredging the adjacent French canal.

This fleet didn't come into being overnight. It was built up slowly between 1906 and 1910, with the French dredges being systematically rebuilt and returned to service, while the American dredges arrived one by one from yards in the United States. To start with only a single Belgian ladder-dredge was at work, keeping open the channel to Cristobal's wharves. But in the spring of 1907 the equipment ordered by Stevens began to come through, and work was gradually extended along the whole of the old French canal, "which had become so silted up that in places only a row-boat could pass along it". At first, excavated soil was carried by clapet to the open sea and dumped, but from 1909 onward it was used either as part of the fill (or soft inner core) of Gatun Dam, or as a "blanket" for the base of the eastern breakwater.

THE DREDGING FLEET OF THE ATLANTIC DIVISION

Type	Number in Service	How Acquired	Complement	Cost
Sea-going suction-dredges (*Ancon*)	1	Purchased from Maryland Steel Co.	66	$362,425
Ladder-dredges	3	From French: rebuilt	45	35,000 each
Pipeline dredges	6	2 from French 4 purchased	69	98,550 each
Dipper-dredges	2	Purchased	31	98,500 each
Clam-shell dredges	1	From French	24	25,000
Self-propelling barges	5	From French: rebuilt	24	20,000 each
Tugs	4	Purchased	30	60,000 each (approx.)
Supply tenders	2	From French: rebuilt	12	10,000 each
Dump scows	9	Purchased from Newport News Shipbuilding	15	26,000 each
Crane-boats	1	From French	12	23,500
Drill-boats	1	From French	6	3,000

Plus sundry launches, pile-drivers, lighters, etc.

Early in 1910 the channel dredged by the *Ancon* was extended inland through the low-lying ground behind Limon Bay. This was the world of mangrove swamp and mosquito where so many of the railroad workers and French engineers had died. Now, however, thanks to Gorgas and his sanitary squads, the crews of the American dredges had a mortality rate of less than one per cent, and work was pushed steadily forward, with occasional disruptions due to wear-and-tear or flood, but no major setback. Typical of the ex-French dredges used in this section was the *Mole* (Figure 7 on page 71). These dredges worked in conjunction with mud scows or clapets—barges with a capacity of 250 cubic yards—soil being brought up in the *Mole*'s buckets then tipped via a shute into the clapets which were moored alongside. Many of these former French dredges were twenty-five years old, but they surprised the Americans by their capacity for work. To quote Bishop: "In point of efficiency the French dredging equipment approached more nearly to the modern standard than their dry excavation plant . . . their dredges were extremely well built and did excellent service for many years." It is pleasant to record an instance where French technology had its just reward; and it would be no exaggeration to say that this section of the canal was built very largely with French equipment.

By the summer of 1912, more than eighty-five per cent of the approach-channel through the swamps had been excavated.

It was the final section which proved the most recalcitrant, for the soil was difficult and flooding a problem. The Mindi Hills were sandstone, with the occasional conglomerate of gravel and boulders: terrain which the ladder- and dipper-dredges were not strong enough to excavate unaided. A system of advance-blasting was therefore experimented with and finally perfected by William Gerig (the divisional engineer). First, a section was bored by well-drills, the holes being roughly thirty feet apart and forty-five feet deep; about a hundred and fifty of these holes were drilled at a time, filled with sixty per cent dynamite, and exploded by detonator, the current being provided by the nearest dredge. The resulting debris was then removed by dipper- and ladder-dredge or by steam-shovel. In this way a cutting was pushed steadily through the hills—which at this point were no more than 100 feet high—until it debouched onto the flood plain of the Chagres roughly a mile and a half from Gatun.

The problem in these last few thousand yards of the Atlantic channel was flooding. The soil in the Chagres valley was soft—mud, clay and alluvial silt—and it could be excavated easily enough by pipeline or suction dredge. But there was water everywhere. Water in the already excavated channel, which was now some forty feet below sea-level: water in the old French canal, which at this point intersected the American cutting: and water, above all, in the diversionary channels which funnelled away the Chagres while work was in progress on the dam. And the Chagres was unpredictable as ever: one day trickling peacefully along the bed of its channel, the next boiling in a ten knot mill-race over its banks. The Americans had a taste now of the floods which had bedevilled the French. To quote the *Canal Record*:

> During the night of November 16th [1909] the Chagres started to rise. On the 17th torrential rainfall was reported at all stations between Culebra and Cristobal, and a further rise was predicted to seventy feet above sea-level. [This proved, in the event, to be an under-estimate.] At Vigia the water piled up to such an extent that the house of the observer was flooded, and the observer himself had to take to high ground for safety. Communications broke down; and at Gatun the water reached the highest point ever recorded. All the cleared area in the anchorage basin south of the dam was flooded. Water was up to the roof of the pumping station, steam-shovels and locomotives were inundated, and bents in the spillway trestle carried away. In the west diversion channel the whole of the trestle along the toe of the Dam was also carried away, and the excavation pits at Mindi were flooded with water up to sea-level: i.e. the water in them was forty-two feet deep. The Panama Railroad was under eight feet of water and several men were drowned. Miraculously the damage is relatively slight and consists more in loss of time and a temporary disorganisation of forces than in actual devastation.

Nevertheless the floods covered an area of nearly a hundred square miles; it was several weeks before the cutting could be pumped dry and for almost a month tug-boats were unable to beat up the French channel against the current—"They had," Sibert tells us, "to run ahead for some 1,000 feet, make fast to a tree and with their winches pull the barges up, then repeat the operations over and over again. It was a long, hard haul; but thanks to the sterling work of the barge crews, Gatun was never allowed to run short of raw materials."

In spite of several such hold-ups, work on this final section continued largely according to schedule. By the summer of 1912 excavation was eighty-seven per cent complete, and only a narrow uncut belt of the valley, 1,000 feet across, held back the waters of the Atlantic from the half-constructed walls of the dam.

At the same time as the cutting itself was methodically pushed inland and deepened, work was carried out on the terminal facilities—for these, although not strictly a part of the canal, were none the less essential to its functioning.

As early as 1905 Stevens had begun to replace the half-rotten wharves of Colon with concrete piers, and this work was continued by Goethals, with the additional construction of a coaling plant, a fuel-oil plant, a mole and four deep-water docks; the channels in and around the unloading berths were deepened, and the already multitudinous railway sidings were extended the length of the waterfront. This work, which involved more than a million cubic yards of excavation and cost more than ten million dollars, was scheduled for completion soon after the opening of the canal.

By the summer of 1912 the Atlantic approach channel had been virtually completed, the figures being:

> By dry excavation 6,113,621 cubic yards at 67 cents per yard (steam-shovel)
> By wet excavation 30,103,104 ,,   ,, at 24 ,,   ,,   ,, (dredge)

From this table two facts are apparent. The work was relatively easy—compare the twenty-four cents per yard of the Atlantic dredges with twenty-two *dollars* per yard of Bunau-Varilla's steam-shovels in the Cut—and it was not typical; for in the Atlantic division alone was the bulk of the excavation carried out by dredge. The dredges involved were often old, and in the final analysis credit for what was achieved belongs very largely to their crews. "Men make the city," Thucydides wrote 2,500 years ago, "and not walls or ships without men in them;" and this was certainly true of the dredges in the Panama Canal. But perhaps a single story sums up the spirit of the dredgermen more eloquently than a panegyric.

The skipper of the *Gopher*, an ancient sea-going ladder-dredge, had been working on the canal for more than twenty years. In 1912 he slipped on a greasy hawser, fell overboard, and was crushed between two of the clapets moored alongside; he was taken to Ancon Hospital seriously injured. A week later, as soon as he was off the danger list, he was visited by the divisional engineer; and the first question he asked (according to Duval) was: "How many yards last week?" And the second question: "And the *Gopher*? Does she still hold the record for excavation?" It may be hard nowadays not to raise eyebrows at such loyalty to a mere construction project; but there is no reason to believe the story apocryphal, nor to suppose that the attitude of the *Gopher*'s skipper was not shared by a large percentage of those who manned the dredges in the Atlantic section of the canal.

(2) *Building Gatun Dam.*

No part of the canal aroused such controversy and violent opposition as Gatun Dam. It was attacked by Congress, the press, and a large number of armchair engineers, whose doubts can be epitomised in a single sentence: "how could a 'soft' dam composed almost entirely of earth be expected to contain a lake of 170 square miles fed by the flood waters of so mighty a river as the Chagres?" It *sounded* a fair question. And whenever a slide or a settlement temporarily disrupted work the sceptics were vociferous in condemnation. "Collapse of Gatun Dam", "Failure at Panama", "Gatun Dam a Fatal Blunder" were typical headlines; while the following extract from the New York *Times* is typical of a host of editorials:

> A gigantic and costly engineering blunder has been made in the construction of the Panama Canal. It is Gatun Dam . . . Only a few days ago an engineer of high standing and recognised ability went so far as to make the flat assertion that if the present plans are persisted in, the canal will be an utter and disastrous failure. It is discouraging to note that all the experts consulted by the *Times* agree that the dam is a great mistake. For even though a barrier might be constructed so as to hold water, the surrounding hills are so pervious that it will be impossible to impound the flow of the Chagres.

This vituperation was due to the dam's composition and site.

The idea of damming back the Chagres was not new; it was first put forward by the far-sighted Godin de Lépinay in 1879—though it must be admitted that de Lépinay's dam was an inspired principle rather than a detailed proposal based on surveys made on the spot. His scheme was initially rejected; but when in 1887 the French began to run into financial difficulties, it was revived; and the *Compagnie Nouvelle* carried out extensive surveys, and decided that the best site for a dam would be at Bohio, where the valley of the Chagres was comparatively narrow and a barrier could be built on a foundation of stable rock. The company, however, went into liquidation before construction got under way. When the Americans took over they too decided to dam the Chagres, and most people visualised their dam as a conventional masonry structure at Bohio. The Board of Engineers, however, came up with a very different proposal: for a "soft" dam, consisting of mud, sand and clay, with its foundations not on rock but in the marshes around Gatun.

It would be hard to imagine a scheme which conjured up, for the layman, more horrific possibilities. The dam, they lamented, would be squeezed flat by its own weight; it would become saturated; seepage would be cumulative; it would subside into the marshes, it would cause the formation of an underground lake. These doleful predictions were given widespread publicity and credence; and it needed a speech by Taft in Congress, an article by Stevens in the

Engineering News, and an official explanation in the *Canal Record* before the critics were temporarily silenced.

The *Canal Record*, on this point, is worth quoting in full; for it gives a clear picture both of the dam itself and the principles involved in its construction.

> In order that misapprehension as to the dams and locks at Gatun may be dispelled, the following official statement of conditions there is published. The purpose of the dam at Gatun is to impound the waters of the Chagres River and its tributaries in a lake which will be formed in the Chagres valley. The dam will extend from the ridge of the hills in the west, across the valley, to the ridge of hills in the east, and will be about one and a half miles long. It will be in two parts, being "anchored" at the centre by a small hill which rises from the middle of the valley—through this hill the spillway for discharging the Chagres will eventually be built . . . The plan for constructing the dam is to pump sand and clay onto the site selected until a hill 135 feet high and 1,700 feet wide extends across the valley. This sand and clay has been found in large quantities in the Chagres valley, and has been proved by thorough test to be good material for the construction of an earthen dam. The dam will be built by suction-dredges which will pump the material mixed with water upon the site, and the water, running off, will leave behind a closely packed deposit of homogeneous material. For the purpose of adding weight to the dam and of preventing the material from sliding north and south (as a great mass of earth is likely to do) two walls or "toes" of rock are being built across the valley. The north or downstream toe is composed of rocks from the cut through the Mindi Hills. The south or upstream toe is composed of even harder rocks from the cut at Bas Obispo, and this south toe will be forty-five feet wide and sixty feet high. Between these toes many million cubic yards of sand and clay from the Chagres valley will be pumped: the toes, it should be stressed, not being part of the dam proper but being built to hold the material of the hydraulic fill in place.

The idea that there is a lake under the site of the dam may have originated from the fact that test borings revealed water in roughly ten per cent of the holes sunk. This water, however, was found to be under pressure: it rose in the bore-holes, proving that it had no outlet but was encased in random pockets. In addition to these borings two test pits were sunk 100 feet below sea-level, and these confirmed what the borings had already shown: that the dam is being built in a firm foundation of impervious clay. What is true of the foundations of the dam is also true of the foundation of the locks, which are being constructed at the extreme east end of the dam where it abuts the hills. These locks will be built entirely of concrete in the form of three watertight boxes each divided into two parts; and beneath the level of their floors, curtain walls will be sunk to a sufficient depth to keep out water. The stone and sand necessary to construction can be delivered at the handling plant as required, and no trouble is anticipated in keeping to the schedule laid down.

The first step was clearing the site.

The area to be cleared consisted of roughly 600 acres of jungle-cum-swamp astride the valley of the Chagres. It was hard manual work to start with: three hundred native labourers armed with machetes hacking down the trees to knee-level, while a further three hundred followed in their wake burning the foliage and grubbing up the stumps. Monkeys chattered in protest, and a tiger cat was killed by one of the working parties within half a mile of Gatun. Then came the levelling, picturesquely described by Storrs Lee:

> It was an ugly denuded waste of land, across which the Chagres snaked. Stubble was everywhere, and standing out like pockmarks were hundreds of black ash heaps where the greenery had been burned. Across this soggy wasteland stretched miles of pilot line and spur track; steam-shovels bit into hills and piled up levees; a dredge in the Chagres sucked mud from one place and vomited it into another; and dynamite crews sent up enormous geysers of rock and water. Men in gangs of forty to a hundred swarmed about the valley, all in the blue shirts and khaki trousers of the Zone Commissary, while the air was filled with the babel of more than twenty languages.

The scene may have looked confused; but, there was no confusion about the overall plan, and by midsummer 1907 clearing had been completed and work progressed from valley to river.

This was the second step: the diversion of the Chagres.

In 1907 there were four routes through which the Chagres escaped to the Caribbean (see Figure 18 on page 174): the east diversion channel, the French canal, the river itself, and the west diversion channel; all of these cut through the line of the proposed dam. Sibert's plan was to block the first three, so that the whole volume of the Chagres was funnelled off via the west diversion channel. Once this had been done, work could be pushed ahead, without fear of flooding, on the east section of the dam and in the central (spillway) hill. As soon as the latter was reasonably complete, the Chagres would be diverted again, this time through the spillway, and work would then be continued on the west section of the dam.

Throughout the winter of 1907/8 the western channel was progressively enlarged until it reached a depth of forty feet and a width of more than 140. The French canal, the east diversion and the original river were then filled in, section by section, the work being carried out chiefly by Bucyrus shovels, ladder-dredges, and the suction-dredge No. 82. To quote Sibert: "No serious difficulties were encountered in building these dams; for the Chagres still flowed through its lowest-lying outlet (the west channel), and the water level in this was never substantially raised."

When the east and central sections of the site had been cleared of water, work was started on the third step: the construction of the solid "toes" which were to hold the dam in place.

These toes stretched the width of the valley, which at this point was roughly a mile and a half across, and were sited 1,200 feet apart. First their foundations were made stable and dry. This involved cleaning out, by suction-dredge, the beds of the various rivers and diversion channels which crossed their path; while as an added precaution solid layers of sheet-piling thirty feet deep, were driven into the channels to preclude the possibility of seepage. Swamps and water planes were filled in, and the whole area drained, levelled and ploughed. Then came the dumping of rock. A railway trestle was built across the valley following the thirty-foot contour of either toe; Lidgerwood dump-cars, filled with rock from the excavations at Mindi and Bas Obispo, were then shunted along the trestle and the rock was ploughed off, away from the centre of the dam. As soon as the lower slopes had piled up to a height of thirty feet, the trestle was raised to the sixty-foot contour and the operation repeated. By the end of 1908 a solid wall of rock, sixty feet high, had been constructed along the extremities of the embryo dam.

There then began the fourth and most spectacular step: the construction of the dam itself.

In December, 1908, a single suction-dredge began pumping clay from the bed of the old French canal into the centre of the dam; and at the same time a single locomotive began shunting in carloads of earth. It was a slow beginning. By December 1910, however, there were four dredges and a dozen locomotives at work, and they were emptying in between them a monthly total of 600,000 cubic yards of liquid fill and 500,000 cubic yards of soil. To quote Bishop:

The core thus created was built up gradually to a height of ninety-five feet. It was composed principally of blue clay, so impervious that it was slow to dry out; and in its watery condition it flowed into every interstice in the ridges of rock and earth, until the whole mass at the centre of the dam became like a rubble wall, each rock cemented to another. The argillaceous sandstone (or blue rock), found all over the isthmus, which is hard until exposed to air, is formed of such clay; and it is thought that in time the core of the dam will solidify into such rock. On top of this hydraulic material was dumped a denser clay, found in nearby borrow-pits, and this brought the core to the 105-foot level.

Slides and subsidences were frequent. It was frightening (and sometimes dangerous) to watch trestles, steam-shovels and dump-cars being tipped over and carried along anything up to a dozen yards. But in spite of alarmist reports to the contrary, most slides were confined to movement within the fill. As a result of tests carried out in the summer of 1911, the height of the dam was allowed to remain at 105 feet, while the slopes were flattened out to 1-in-8 and 1-in-12; and this, together with the compacting referred to by Bishop, reduced sliding to a minimum. By 1912 the work was virtually complete; and a wall, literally "more solid than the encircling hills", blocked the valley and the path of the once-irresistible river.

As the dam grew higher, plant and material were assembled for the fifth step: the construction of spillway and locks.

The plant was complex: docks along the line of the French canal at which barges could unload, storage sheds where the raw material could be stockpiled, cranes and conveyor belts for shifting the material from shed to mixer, and a series of cableways and tip-lines for lowering the concrete, when mixed, into position. In addition there were pumping stations, turbine-rooms, masonry yards and sheds for storing the delicate equipment which would soon be operating the gates of spillway and locks. The materials used were principally cement, stone and sand. And in what quantities!

The cement was shipped from New York in vessels of the Panama Railroad Company; it arrived at the rate of 2,000 barrels every five days, and before the spillway and locks were complete more than 2,600 barrels had been tipped into the mixers. The stone came from Ancon (by train) or from Porto Bello (by barge): it was stored 200,000 cubic yards at a time on the banks of the French canal. While the sand came from Nombre de Dios, thirty-five miles to the east-north-east.

A journey of thirty-five miles for sand and twenty-five miles for stone naturally put up the costs. But Sibert has left us an amusing account of the Commission's lack of success in finding a nearer source of supply:

> In searching for suitable sand, some of our field parties penetrated the country of the [Cuna] Indians. These people live on small coral islands, cultivating land on the main shore, and they did not look with favour on visits from the white men, whom they suspected were searching not for sand but for gold. Our survey teams soon discovered sand of good quality which could be easily worked, and a party of senior officials visited the Indians with a view to opening negotiations. When they landed on the largest of the islands they were led through a labyrinth of dwellings and into the Chief's quarters. The Chief, about seventy years of age, was seated on a block of timber, and he motioned his visitors to a seat on the sand at his feet. An air of great solemnity surrounded the proceedings. The Chief was told of the intention of the United States Government to connect the Atlantic and Pacific oceans by a canal so that boats could cross in a short time; he was told how this would improve the trade of the Indians, and how it would increase the price of their coconuts and ivory. The Chief listened; but when the story was finished he said that God had given the Indians their country, the land and the water and the sand that was under the water, and that which God had given to the Indians they would neither sell or give to the white man. When another attempt was made to argue, he waved his hand and said simply: "There is no need to talk further." From this interview it was evident that sand could not be procured from the Cuna without bloodshed. Permission was asked to anchor for the night, and this was granted on condition that the party left early next morning and never returned.

Sibert goes on to comment favourable on the Indians' strength, physical fitness and apparent immunity from malaria. This he rightly attributed to the fact that they visited the mainland only by day (when the *Anopheles* were inactive) and spent their nights on the coral islands (which the *Anopheles* never flew to because there was no fresh water on them in which they could breed).

As soon as plant and materials had been assembled work was begun on the construction of a spillway and sluice-gates which would discharge the surplus waters of the Chagres according to the dictates of man.

A spillway might have been cut at any convenient point round the perimeter of the now rapidly forming lake. But as luck would have it a favourable site was found along the line of the dam, and it was very sensibly decided to combine dam, spillway and locks in a single structure. The site selected was Spillway Hill in the centre of the valley: a mound of argillaceous sandstone and stable rock—almost the ideal formation through which to cut a channel. The purpose of the channel was to provide an escape route for the Chagres floods (i.e. to cope with a maximum discharge of 182,000 cubic feet per second), and also to control accurately the rate of discharge, so that in dry weather too much water was not allowed out of the lake. Sibert's solution was basically simple. He designed a structure with a semicircular crest which consisted of fifteen solid concrete piers connected by steel gates which could be raised or lowered individually as conditions required (see Figure 20 opposite). Beyond the crest, water was siphoned off into a carefully graded runnel, 300 feet wide and paved with concrete twelve feet thick. This runnel led to the bed of the Chagres River and thence to the sea.

Work was started in the spring of 1909, and the *Canal Record* gives us a glimpse of what was involved.

> Concrete work in the spillway will involve the laying of over 250,000 cubic yards of concrete, and will extend over three years. The forms are already in place and provide for the laying of monoliths forty feet by twenty feet, weighing 4,800 pounds... The concrete handling and mixing plant is distinct from the plant used at the locks. A dock has been built on the old French canal, and cement, sand and rock will be delivered alongside it in barges towed from Cristobal. A locomotive crane, operating along the front of the dock, will handle the material from barge to storage shed by means of clam-shell buckets. Cars on a belt-line railway running beneath the docks will be filled by gravity with sand, cement and rock in succession, and when loaded they will be pulled by cable to the mixers. These mixers, driven by an old French 75 h.p. engine, will mix the material and dump it into two-yard buckets, carried on specially designed flat-cars. And finally the flat-cars will run via 4,000 feet of track to the spillway, where the buckets will be lifted off by crane and the material placed. There will be two tracks, one for the loaded cars and one for the empties. It is expected that 500 cubic yards of concrete will be laid each day.

This expectation was realised. Throughout 1909 and the early months of 1910 work was pushed steadily forward, with the stumps of the fifteen piers rising toothlike out of the spillway crest, while the bed and walls of the runnel was concreted foot by foot. By April 1910 the runnel was complete, the piers were twenty feet above lake-level, and the stage was set for what was probably the most spectacular and certainly the most difficult operation carried out in the Atlantic Division: the diverting of the Chagres into its new spillway.

This diversion had to take place before the spillway was complete, because the west half of the dam could not be built until the west diversion channel had been closed and the waters of the Chagres excluded from the construction site.

Sibert has left a graphic account of the problems of this penultimate stage of the work.

> In forcing the Chagres from the west diversion channel into the spillway many difficulties were encountered. For the bottom of the spillway channel was ten feet *above* sea-level, and the bottom of the diversion channel ten feet *below*. This meant that during construction of the necessary dams, the river had no outlet until it had risen some twenty feet. The sides and bottom of the west diversion channel were difficult ground to work in—for they were mud to a depth of 200 feet—and it was therefore decided to close the channel by making barriers in two places simultaneously, one along the thirty-foot north contour of the finished dam and one

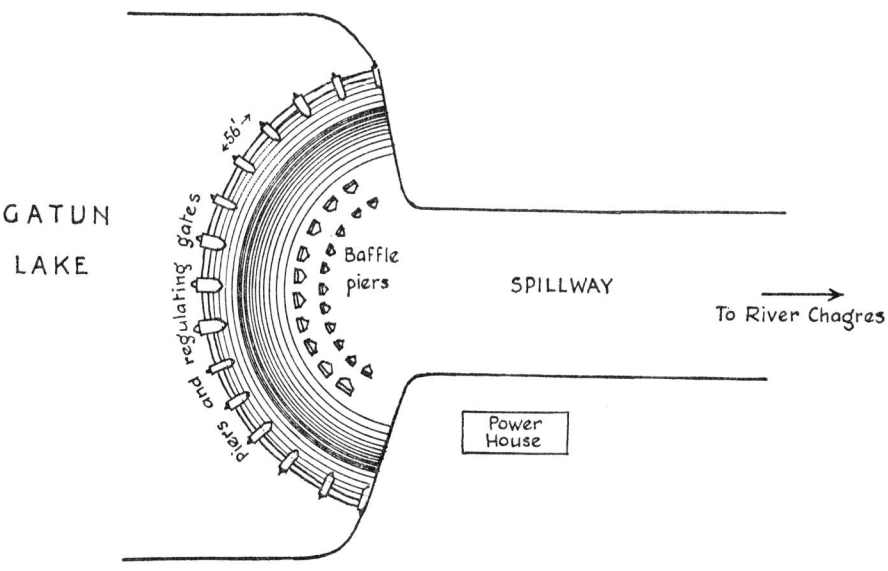

Figure 20. Gatun spillway

along the thirty-foot south contour. The reason for attempting to build two barriers at once was the hope that during construction the head of water which would result from the rising river would be divided between the two dams—that is, should the river rise six feet there would be a fall of three feet at the upper dam and three feet at the lower. These barriers were, of course, to be encompassed by the main dam when built; and an unlimited amount of rock and soil was available for their construction from the Culebra Cut.

The first step was to drive trestles across the stream at the selected locations, and to try to build the barriers by dumping rock direct from trestle to stream. [This was started on April 22nd], with the fill being gradually worked out toward the middle of the river. When the flow had been constricted sufficiently to create a strong current, medium-sized stone was dumped from the full length of the trestle, in the expectation that the current would distribute such stone downstream to form an apron. The rate of dumping was gradually increased; but when the stream had been compressed into a gap about eighty feet wide and six feet deep, the force of the water was such that all stones were carried far downstream, since none of the pieces was big enough to withstand the current. It was therefore decided to dump carloads of crooked rails into the river above the trestles, in the hope that these would form an entanglement which would stop the stones on the upstream side of the trestle. This operation was successful, and resulted in raising the barriers above water. On April 24th one of the trestles cracked and moved a few inches downstream, but not enough to prevent its use after minor repairs. After the flow of the river had stopped, the two barriers were raised to the top of the trestles and widened, and the Chagres commenced to flow through the spillway.

The river, however, was not to be tamed so easily. And on April 26th, Sibert tells us, a settlement occurred, the space between the barriers became flooded, and the whole of the north dam was washed downstream.

> Thus one of the barriers passed away, and the sudden release of water caused the bank against which the other barrier abutted to slide into the river. This slide was so great as almost to break the dam, a lip of earth about three feet wide being the only barrier which prevented the Chagres from resuming her old course. Trains were rushed onto the trestles, and an attempt was made to repair the damage, about 30,000 cubic yards of rock being

The Cucaracha Slide

(*Above left*) Theodore Roosevelt

(*Above*) George Washington Goethals

William Nelson Cromwell

dumped within twenty-four hours. But no sooner was the work completed than the entire body of rock slid into the river, the small lip of earth cracked, and it seemed as if the Chagres were victor . . . However, two suction-dredges were rushed to the scene; and they, pumping in material from some distance away, gradually filled the river bed with clay and sand until an island, three-quarters of an acre in extent, was formed immediately above the threatened place. [This created a safety factor; and in the shadow of its protection] repairs to the south barrier were completed and the north barrier was rebuilt to its full height. And the Chagres was at last permanently diverted into the spillway channel where man's control of her was complete.

This was another key moment in the building of the canal: when the mighty river was finally transformed from a demon of destruction to a beast of burden, its waters no longer threatening the canal but harnessed to serve it.

The spillway was finally completed during the dry season of 1911 and 1912, water from the lake being temporarily excluded from the site by bulkheads of timber and a coffer-dam. When finished it consisted of a convex wall 800 feet long and nearly 100 feet high. This wall was made up of masonry piers, forty-five feet apart, the openings between being filled by steel gates weighing well over forty tons. The gates were mounted on roller-bearings, and were operated by electricity; and each could be raised or lowered individually—like a window sliding up and down in its frame—so that the volume of water to escape could be regulated at will. Running longitudinally through the wall was a watertight tunnel which housed the operating machinery; this tunnel had an inner and outer shell, so that any leakage through the latter fell into an air space and was carried away by inset drains. The runnel below the wall was most skilfully designed by Caleb M. Saville, with water from different gates converging so as to neutralise thrust, and a series of cast-iron baffles robbing the mill-race of its force, so that by the time the water reached the bed of the Chagres, some quarter of a mile below the dam, it was flowing at no more than two to three knots. The spillway was completed in 1913.

And so to the last great work of the Atlantic Division; the construction of the three flights of locks which would raise vessels from the sea-level approach-channel to the eighty-five-foot level of the lake.

The initial task was to excavate the site: to dig a pit roughly a mile and a quarter long, 200 yards wide and fifty feet deep at the point where the eastern end of the dam abutted the hills. This involved shifting more than five and a half million cubic yards of soil, three-quarters of it by steam-shovel and one quarter by dredge. To quote Sibert:

> There was nothing difficult or unusual about this excavation until we came to the lower end of the bottom lock. Here the underground rock [which was the base on which foundations were laid] dipped steeply away until it was sixty-six feet below sea-level, and even at this depth its surface was irregular and consisted of miniature hills and valleys, the latter being filled with mud of the softest possible consistency. Slides were frequent, the debris flowing over or round the retaining walls and into the chamber itself; men were buried; shovels were overturned; and no one expected on returning to work in the morning to find things as they had left them the evening before. The excavation of this bottom chamber and its adjacent flare and guide walls was the most difficult problem technically in the Atlantic Division, if not in the entire canal.

It was solved eventually by building an elaborate series of barriers and soakaways, and by flooding the chamber so that suction dredges, working more than fifty feet below sea-level, could excavate down to solid rock. But—to quote Sibert again—"a pit some sixty feet below sea-level dug out of soft mud is difficult to maintain"; the banks slid in if graded at less than 1-in-12, and a succession of slides held up operations for almost a year and caused a sharp increase in costs. Goethals was not amused; and the story goes that on one of his tours of inspection he rebuked the engineer-in-charge. "Your schedule, sir, calls for these forms to be finished by the end of next month. You are not making much progress."

"I know, Colonel," the engineer said mildly, "but we are doing our best."

"I don't expect you to do your best," was the curt reply. "I expect you to complete your work on time."

And greatly to Sibert's credit the locks *were* completed on time, the slowness of excavation being counterbalanced by the speed of laying concrete.

The laying of concrete at Gatun was on a scale hitherto undreamed of in the history of engineering—indeed even today there are few structures in the world consisting of more than two million cubic yards of concrete. The technical problems involved were not unduly difficult; the difficulty arose in maintaining a constant and amazingly high rate of mixing and placing—3,000 cubic yards per day, week after week, month after month, year after year. A single fact puts this achievement in perspective. Up to 1909 the record amount of concrete ever laid in a single day was 1,700 yards. In other words Sibert and his engineers maintained for two years a daily rate of mixing and placing which was nearly double the rate which had been achieved previously in any single day.

The work fell into two phases: first, the assembling and mixing of raw materials; and second, the placing of the concrete itself.

The raw materials were crushed rock, sand and cement. Rocks were quarried and pulverised at Porto Bello, loaded into 150-foot barges and towed the twenty miles to Cristobal and thence via the French canal to the docks at Gatun. Because of the frequent storms which swept in from the Caribbean it was decided to create a vast storage area at the docks, so that in bad weather when sailings were cancelled, work on the dam would not be held up by lack of raw material. This storage area held 200,000 cubic yards of rock and 100,000 cubic yards of sand; and not once in more than three years of continuous construction were supplies allowed to run short. Sand was dredged at Nombre de Dios, loaded into barges and towed to the docks by the same route. The cement—2,250,000 barrels of it—came by lighter from New York. All in all more than three million tons of these raw materials was brought to Gatun.

The method by which they were mixed and delivered to the site was a triumph of far-sighted organisation. The key was an automatic electric-railway loop-line, brainchild of the imaginative Stevens. This line ran underneath the storage dumps of sand cement and stone, up an incline until it was directly over the mixers, and then back again to the dumps. Its rolling-stock consisted of roughly a hundred automatic cars of eighty cubic feet capacity; these moved round the loop-line unmanned, being driven by a three-phase current taken from overhead trolleys, so they could be stopped and started individually by men operating a simple knife-switch. Their cycle was first under the cement shed where each car was stopped and loaded by gravity with the correct percentage of cement; then under the sand store where it was loaded with sand, and then under the stone store where it was loaded with stone. The car then proceeded up a 1-in-15 ramp to the mixers where it was stopped by a man in the mixer shed; its contents were tipped straight into the mouth of one of the eight gargantuan machines, and the car was then restarted and run back to the storage sheds where it began its cycle again. As Sibert testifies: "After the correction of initial mechanical defects, these cars did excellent work, shifting more than a million tons of material in a single year."

The mixed concrete was dumped into two-yard buckets which

were placed on a flat-car. These flat-cars were then hauled by another railroad to the site of the locks. Here the buckets were hoisted onto an overhead cableway, run out to the point where concrete was needed, and lowered and dumped. The empty buckets (on another series of flat-cars) were then returned by a parallel railroad to the mixers.

If the key to mixing was the electric railroad, the key to laying was the overhead cableway (see Figure 21 opposite).

Sibert describes this apparatus as follows.

> The advisability of using cableways for building the locks was at first questioned by many for their disadvantages in placing concrete in a constricted space were well known. It was decided, however, that building walls sixty feet wide and more than a hundred feet apart could not be termed working in a constricted space, and the advantages of covering the working area with overhead lines of delivery were many. The men referred to one advantage as giving them a "sky hook" over all the work. For an overhead system keeps the working area relatively free of plant, and facilitates the delivery of material such as lumber, steel forms and ready-mixed concrete . . . Great towers were therefore erected on either side of the excavated pits; these were eighty-five feet high and mounted on tracks (like steam-shovels) so they could be moved backward or forward as the need arose. They were connected by two-and-a-half-inch lock-steel cables, guaranteed to carry six tons . . . It was decided to build the walls in monoliths thirty-six feet long: i.e. to complete a wall for thirty-six feet from top to bottom, then design forms which would box in this length of wall. Duplex cableways were used, which meant that all concrete could be delivered to within nine feet of its final destination; and it was found that by using wet concrete, the material flowed into place and no rehandling was necessary. By this method a monolith in each wall could be built with the towers in one position . . . No such massive walls had ever been built as those at Gatun, and the plant and method of construction met this exciting challenge in a very satisfactory way.
>
> [Sibert ends his account on a personal note] . . . The interest that the entire force took in this plant, and their enthusiasm when it came up to our expectations, was remarkable. And it extended not only to the workers but also to their families. In walking to my office in the morning I was frequently accosted by children in the streets of Gatun, who would proudly tell me how many cubic yards had been placed the day before.

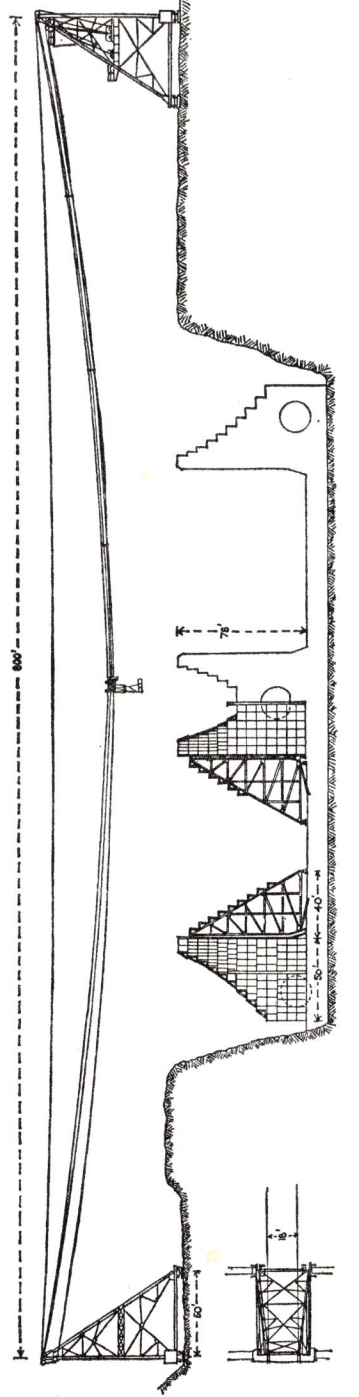

Figure 21. Overhead cable for laying concrete at Gatun

So the walls of the locks rose slowly, foot by foot, until by the autumn of 1912 the work was ninety-three per cent complete: all that remained to be done was to place the facings and install the gates.

It was now that the sceptics and trouble-makers launched their last, and most ludicrous assault on the work at Gatun. The lock-gates, they said, were "impossibly heavy . . . no machinery on earth could hoist them into position . . . they [would] be too cumbersome to operate . . . they [would] crash through the floor of the locks, destroying in seconds the work of years." The gates were indeed gargantuan, and by far the heaviest in the world (see Figure 22). The largest was sixty-five feet wide, eighty-two feet high, seven feet thick and weighed 730 tons; there were ninety-two of them in all, and placed end to end they would have made a tower a mile-and-a-quarter high weighing more than sixty thousand tons. Yet they were designed with such skill and ingenuity that each could be closed by the flick of a switch so that literally not a single drop of water seeped through its interlocking plates. For they floated like a ship. Each gate consisted of two leaves, hinged to the walls at opposite sides of the locks; each leaf was sixty-five feet wide, i.e. was wider than half the width of the lock, so that when the leaves were closed they formed a slight angle pointing against the water pressure. Each was built in the form of a webbed box, with its girders encased in a steel sheath. Each, in other words, consisted of a series of watertight compartments, and was so buoyant that it practically floated on the water. The gates were safely installed by the spring of 1913; and in close on sixty years continuous service have shown no sign of justifying the forebodings of the sceptics.

Early in 1912 there occurred two incidents which showed that completion of the Atlantic section was now only a matter of time.

On January 27th, the spillway channel was closed; not a drop of moisture escaped through spillway, locks or dam; and the waters of the Chagres started to rise. They rose slowly, inch by reluctant inch, as though unwilling to admit they were at last subservient to the will of man. They trickled first into the empty huts of the old Indian village of Gatun, then over the ties of the now re-routed railroad, then over the low-lying mangrove bushes, and finally up the trunks of the disbelieving palms. By March 2nd, a lake sixteen feet deep and three miles long extended up the valley of the Chagres, and the water was rising steadily at the rate of eleven inches a day.

After more than thirty years the dream of Godin de Lépinay had been realised.

A few weeks later, on March 15th, another milestone in the

Figure 22. The guard gate, Gatun

building of the canal was safely passed. Ever since the turn of the year the strip of land which divided the Atlantic approach-channel from the bottom lock had been progressively reduced by blasting. By the morning of March 15th only a narrow neck of soil, less than eight feet wide, remained. This was dynamited at noon. And the waters of the Caribbean came swirling up to the wall of the lock.

By the spring of 1912 a broad expanse of water, nowhere less than 500 feet wide and forty-one feet deep, stretched from the entrance of Limon Bay to the wall of the dam; while the dam itself rose 100 feet high and solid as the encircling hills. The work of the Atlantic Division was complete.

12

THE CENTRAL DIVISION

The Central Division was the largest of the three semi-autonomous kingdoms brought into being by Goethals: 31.7 miles of valley and low-lying hill between Gatun Dam overlooking the Atlantic, and Pedro Miguel Lock overlooking the Pacific. It consisted of two clearly defined areas: twenty-two miles of the Chagres valley (which had to be flooded) and ten miles of the continental divide (which had to be breached). The man in charge was Major David Du Bose Gaillard, a forty-eight year old graduate from West Point.

(1) *Flooding the Chagres Valley*
Flooding the middle reaches of the Chagres was the simplest and yet in some ways the most vital part of the American plan. If successful, it would provide a deep, broad and easily navigable waterway for half the length of the canal and would solve once and for all the problem of the Chagres floods; if unsuccessful, it would jeopardise the whole conception of a high-level waterway with locks. There were four prerequisites of success. Firstly, the building at the bottom of the valley (Gatun) of an impervious dam, and a spillway able to funnel away the heaviest conceivable flood. Secondly, the building at the head of the valley (Gamboa) of another and smaller dam, which would prevent the waters of the newly created lake from backing into the Culebra Cut during excavation. Thirdly, the sealing of any gaps in the lake's perimeter. And last, levelling the bottom of the lake, so that no underwater protuberances would endanger navigation.

A dam at Gatun was built by engineers of the Atlantic Division (see Chapter Eleven).

A dam at Gamboa, together with ancillary diversion channels, had been constructed by the French; but these, in time of flood, had proved inadequate. One of Gaillard's first tasks, therefore, was to deepen the diversion channels and to strengthen the seventy-foot dyke which had been designed to keep the Chagres out of the Cut. Figure 24 (page 203) shows a cross-section of the finished dam and its position relative to river and cutting. There was nothing remarkable about this work, and from 1907 to 1912 the dam caused no anxiety. In the summer of 1912, however, it was realised that the rising waters

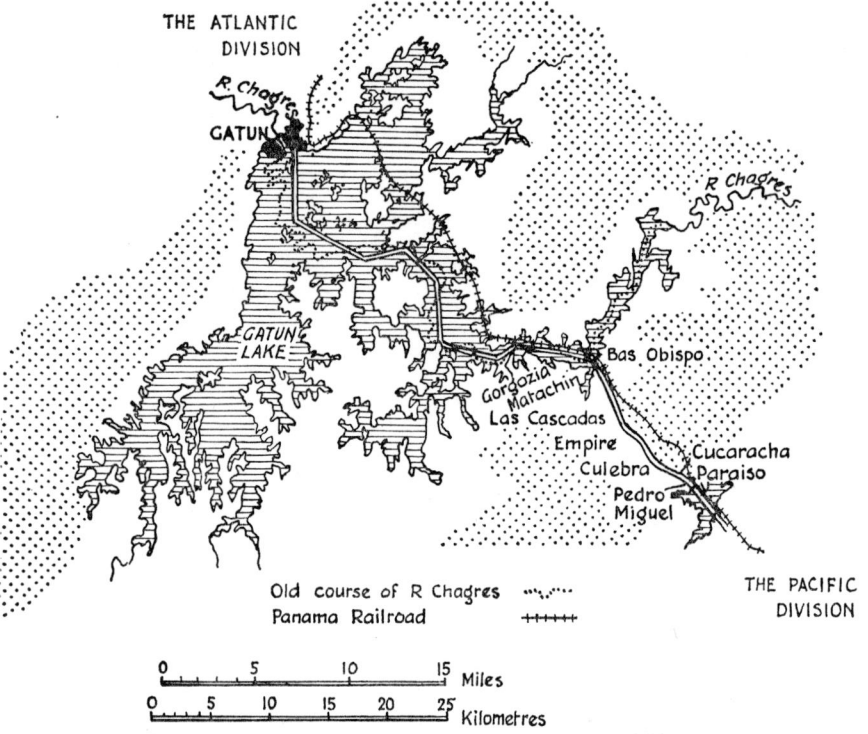

Figure 23. The Central Division

of the lake would impose an additional strain: *vide* the *Canal Record*.

Once the spillway gates were closed and the lake rose, the waters of the Chagres backed up to Palo Grande and came swirling high up the dyke at Gamboa. In consequence this dyke is being raised about five feet and widened fifty feet by the dumping of clay on the side facing the Cut. Its new elevation of 78.2 feet will afford a leeway of more than twenty-two feet against a rise in time of flood.

This enlarged dam successfully protected the Cut until October 1913, when it was blasted open by President Wilson, and the combined waters of river and lake were allowed to cascade into the finished Cut.

The perimeter of the lake had been carefully surveyed. Indications were that the encircling hills were virtually impervious and sufficiently high—although this was something which could only be proved by letting the waters rise to their full eighty-five-foot level.

THE CENTRAL DIVISION   203

In the event, the surveyors were proved correct—but by no more than a few inches—and a certain amount of strengthening (by sinking sheet piling) and heightening (by constructing dykes) had to be carried out around the perimeter before Gaillard was satisfied. Sibert and Stevens give an interesting account of this work.

> The rising lake was watched with no little apprehension, for on the watertightness of the basin depended the success of the entire project. Great satisfaction was therefore felt as the lake rose week after week, according to programme, with no trace of material leakage ... It was found, however, that in places the perimeter was only a foot or two above the final level of the lake, and it was necessary at these points to increase the height of the rim. [One trouble spot was the valley in the Trinidad] ... This valley was

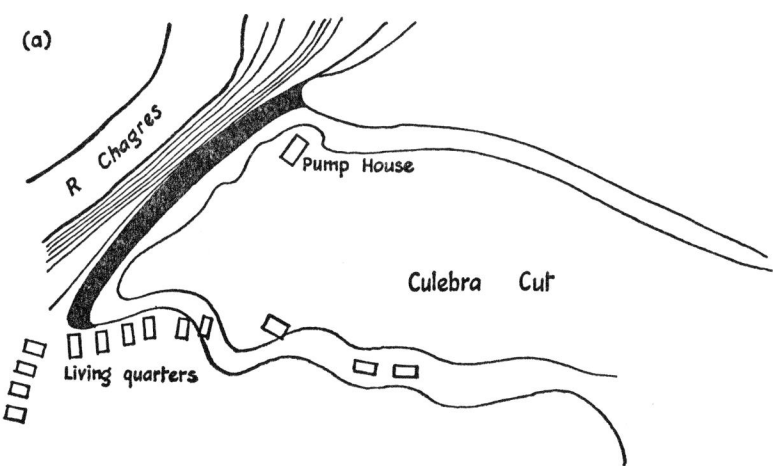

(a) Gamboa Dam and its relation to R Chagres and the Culebra Cut
(b) Cross-section of Gamboa Dam and its 1912 addition

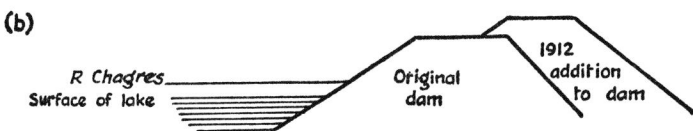

Figure 24. Gamboa Dam: its relation to River Chagres and the Culebra Cut

virtually inaccessible by land, and we therefore decided to wait until the lake was near its full height and then transport the necessary plant etc. by boat. It was no easy task, however, to locate the submerged valley by water, and our engineers had eventually to be guided there by Indians who built great fires, the smoke of which was visible from far out across the lake ... It was a queer sensation [Sibert adds] to travel by boat through the tops of trees, passing *en route* hills which (as the water rose) became converted to islands, congested with game.

By the autumn of 1913 the lake was at its full height and the perimeter at all points had proved impervious to seepage. And impervious in spite of the forebodings of the sceptics, it has remained.

The bed of the lake was levelled before the water was allowed in, some seven million cubic yards of soil being redistributed away from the line of the canal. This was a simple operation, the rising knolls being "topped" by steam-shovel and their soil dumped in near-by hollows and swamps; and by the autumn of 1910 the outline of a channel, some 750 feet wide had been excavated between Gatun and Bas Obispo. Then the spillway gates were closed, and the waters of the Chagres were allowed to back up-valley. This, however, gave rise to an unexpected problem. The area flooded was mostly swampland, made up of submerged logs, decayed vegetation and high grass, and as the water rose so a large proportion of the swamp bottom rose with it. This led to the formation of what were apparently islands—large bodies of land consisting of grass and even small trees—which were driven aimlessly about by the winds. It wasn't long before this floating material, some of it matted to a depth of fourteen feet, completely blocked the channel. The only practicable way to get rid of it was to tow it to the spillway dam and allow it to be swept over and out to sea. "It was an odd sight," Sibert tells us, "to watch a little tug chugging along, pushing in front of it acres of apparent land." By the autumn of 1913, however, the lake was at its full height, and cleared for transit.

The creation of this vast sheet of water laid for ever the ghost which had haunted de Lesseps: the ghost of the Chagres floods. For it transformed the canal from a narrow and tortuous channel constantly menaced by the Chagres, to a broad high-level bridge of water, with the Chagres a subservient beast of burden quietly carrying shipping to and fro. Looking at the lake today it seems (like the dam) to fit so naturally into its surroundings that it is difficult to realise it is created by man—witness Bishop's story of the celebrity who, as he was being shown over the newly opened canal, remarked naïvely: "You were extremely fortunate, you know, to find so large a body of water exactly here"! Yet made by man the lake undoubtedly is: a classic example of the forces of nature being metamorphosed from master to servant.

American engineers deserve, and have always been accorded, a great deal of credit for the creation of this vital lake. Equal credit, however, is due to the unsung inspector from the Parisian Department of Public Works out of whose inspirational dream Goethals and Gaillard, thirty-five years later, fashioned so successful a reality.

(2) *Excavation of the Culebra Cut*
It was here, in the heart of the continental divide, that the battle between man and nature reached its climax. For Culebra Cut was the nub of the canal, the kernel which had to be cracked.

By 1907 fever, forest and flood had been brought under virtual control. But the mountains themselves still remained to be moved—and because of their peculiar structure they proved unbelievably recalcitrant.

The French had planned to dig a ditch through the hills at Culebra with slopes of roughly 1-in-2, and had budgeted on twenty-three million cubic yards of excavation. The Americans, with a wider cutting and slopes of 1-in-3, had budgeted originally for fifty-three million cubic yards of excavation; this, however, was raised to seventy-eight million in 1908, ninety-four million in 1911 and 111 million in 1913. These too, however, turned out to be gross under-estimates for by the time the last of the twenty-six slides had been dredged away and the last of the slopes had settled, excavation in the Culebra Cut and its environs had reached the staggering total of 150 million cubic yards—enough to fill a train-load of flatcars which would stretch the width of the Atlantic.

To understand why excavation increased so dramatically, we need to understand the geology of the continental divide.

Figure 25 (on page 206) shows a simplified cross-section of the rocks between Gamboa and Pedro Miguel—note the two volcanic cores, the four faults and the eight fundamentally different types of rock all within the space of ten miles. This complexity set Gaillard two problems. In the first place, dealing with so many pockets of rock of a different hardness, he found it impossible to plan and keep to a uniform schedule. In the second place, he was bedevilled by slides; for at one spot the banks of the Cut would remain stable at a slope of 1-in-2, while in another spot they would come sliding into the prism at slopes of 1-in-6 or even 1-in-8. The first problem he overcame by a programme of extreme flexibility. The second frustrated

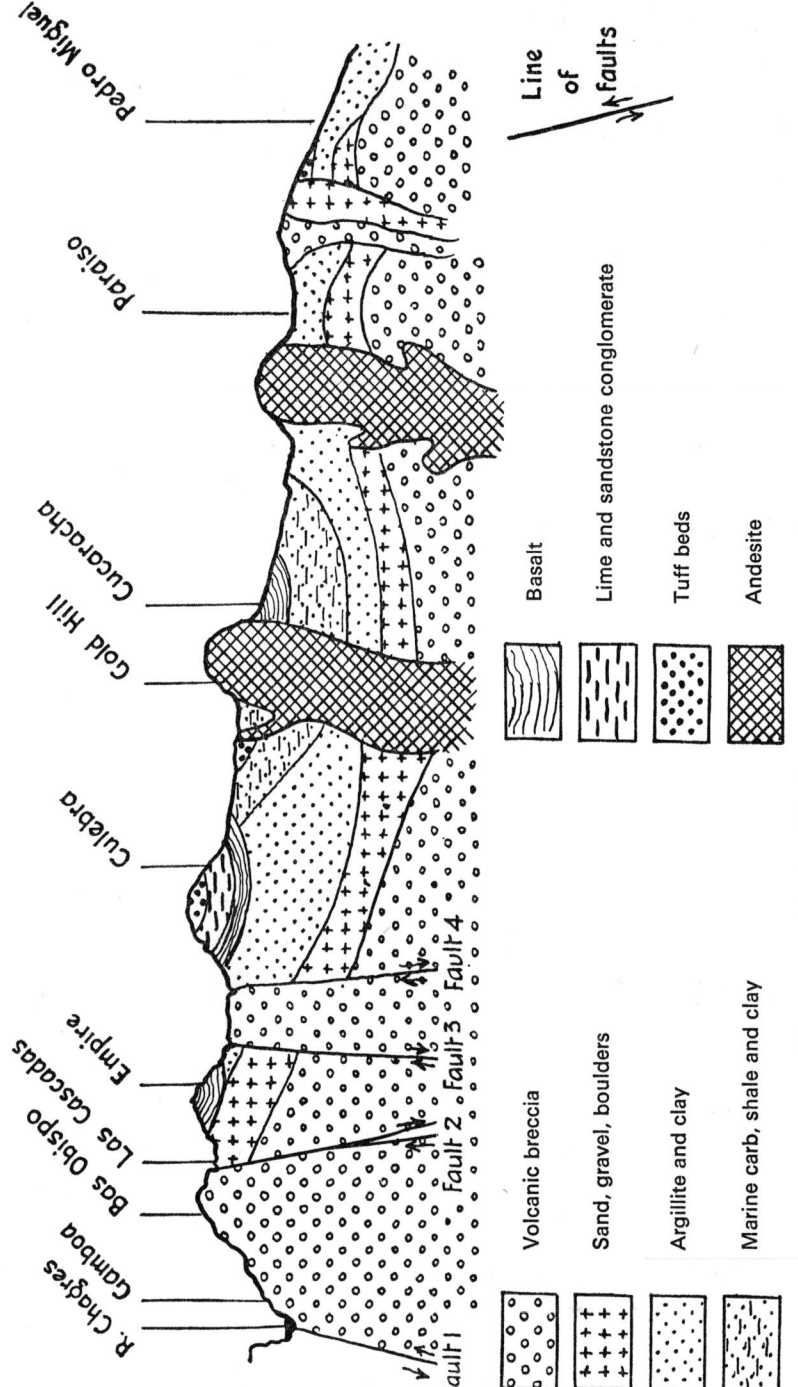

Figure 25. A simplified cross-section of rocks in the Culebra Cut

him year after year and hounded him in the end to a tragic and premature death.

It was these slides which were the isthmus's last and most obdurate line of defence. Bishop describes them with the eye of a layman.

> The Canal Zone was a land of the fantastic and the unexpected. No one could say when the sun went down what the condition of the Cut would be when it rose. For the work of months or even years might be blotted out by an avalanche of earth or the toppling over of a mountain of rock. It was a task to try men's souls; but it was also one to kindle in them a joy of combat which no repulse could chill, and a faith in ultimate victory which no disaster could shake.

A more technical description of the slides is given by Donald MacDonald, geologist to the Isthmian Commission and the U.S. Bureau of Mines. In the Culebra Cut, he tells us, there were four distinct types of slide: structural breaks and deformations, gravity slides, fault-zone slides, surface-erosion slides.

The first indication of a structural break or deformation was a fissure parallel to and set back some thirty yards from the edge of the Cut. Next, a series of solid blocks would tilt away from the bank; these would then become squashed out of the base, and finally a whole section would disintegrate and slough down into the excavation. These slides had a primal cause—the unstable geological condition of the materials involved—and a subsidiary cause—the oversteepness of the slopes. Instability was brought about by a number of factors—the formations involved consisted of very soft and weak rocks (indurated volcanic clays, friable bedded tuffs, and slippery lignitic shale); these rocks were frequently weakened by faults; ground-water would seep into the disturbed material and add to its instability; the lignitic shale beds, where they inclined toward the canal, were planes of weakness along which the overlying materials tended to slide; also chlorite particles in the clay served as a lubricant. For this type of slide there was only one remedy: to make the slopes less steep by removing material from the upper portions, so that pressure on the foot of the slopes became less. MacDonald adds that the Culebra slide was the most troublesome of this variety, and says with some justification that, "in the first plans and estimates, geological conditions were not sufficiently considered."

Gravity slides were caused by the fact that along the line of the Cut, porous material frequently lay on top of beds of relatively impervious clay or igneous rock. Rain and ground-water would

Figure 26. The Cut at Bas Obispo

saturate the porous mass, but would then be impeded in their downward course by the rock. This caused a muddy slippery zone to form along the plane of contact; and where this plane sloped toward the cutting a slide of the normal or gravity type would result. This type of slide had certain distinguishing features. The rocks were not weakened below the plane of actual sliding; for the material moved off a solid base and was not squeezed out by frictional pull; hence these slides were nothing like as destructive as deformation slides, for they affected only the material which actually moved. It was found better and cheaper not to remove their upper portions, but to let them run their course and to excavate the resulting debris from the bottom of the Cut. The only effective remedy was better drainage. The most troublesome slide of this sort, MacDonald tells us, was the Cucaracha which was active over a period of thirty years.

Fault-zone slides occurred where sheared faults cut diagonally across the line of the canal. They appeared in rocks which were normally strong enough to stand at a steep slope, but were in places weakened by diagonal canalward-sloping faults which left overhanging masses of rock resting insecurely against slippery fault-planes. Slides of this type were La Pita and Las Cascadas, and the only practicable remedy was to lessen the slope in the vicinity of the fault and to prevent excessive seepage.

Surface-erosion slides were of nuisance-value only, and were a minor and purely temporary problem. They were caused by heavy rain washing down the slopes which initially were unprotected by vegetation. It was estimated that over 50,000 cubic yards of sediment were swept in this way into the prism. But as soon as the slopes were carpeted with grass and shrubs no further trouble was experienced.

MacDonald ends his account with a warning and a reassurance.

> In all the work of canal construction nothing attracted a wider public attention than the slides. It may be as well, therefore, to state in conclusion that slides which require considerable dredging are likely to continue for the first few years of canal operation. These, however, will not be sufficiently large to endanger traffic passing through the canal, nor to menace its ultimate utility.

Both warning and reassurance turned out to be justified.

The next most serious obstacle which Gaillard had to surmount was the excessive rainfall.

Precipitation in the Zone was heavy, especially in the upper reaches of the Chagres. The number of days on which it rained a measurable amount was between 250 and 270 a year, and much of this fell in the form of torrential afternoon thunderstorms. In the

Central Division, the following table shows the average rainfall during the period of construction:

1906	......	105 inches
1907	......	83 ,,
1908	......	95 ,,
1909	......	130 ,,
1910	......	129 ,,
1911	......	80 ,,
1912	......	90 ,,
1913	......	85 ,,

These figures may not make spectacular reading when compared, say, to the 470 inches which fall each year in Assam. But because the hills of the isthmus are so steep-sided and their rocks lie so close to the surface, precipitation led to flooding out of all proportion to its intensity. Add to this the fact that the labour squads had to work in a cutting some three hundred feet deep, and it will be realised that rainfall was an embarrassment from which Gaillard was never free.

The final problem was that of having to work in a constricted space. There is nothing an engineer likes less. And in the case of the Cut it was not only the working area that was restricted it was also the surrounding terrain, where a solitary railway-line through precipitous hills was the only channel both for bringing up equipment and taking away soil. Sibert puts the case very clearly.

> The problem in the Cut was how to plan operations—such as drilling, blasting, shovelling, track-laying and hauling away—so that no element of the work interfered with another element. This, in a confined space, required very careful study. Every drill, dump-car and shovel, etc. was located daily on a map, and an accurate estimate made of its work and movement. Track was the key. About 275 miles was shifted each year with the consequent relaying of more than 1,600 frogs; and this had to be carried out without interruption to the movement of some 160 trains a day.

It says much for Gaillard's efficiency that in spite of these difficulties, he was able steadily to reduce the cost per cubic yard of excavation—from $1.03 in 1908, to 75 cents in 1910 and finally to 55 cents in 1912.

These then were the problems of the Central Division: heavy rainfall, a vast amount of difficult excavation, and a constricted field of operations. The solution was meticulous planning and hard, back-breaking work.

There was no short cut to success.

The hills never yielded. They had to be conquered foot by hard-won foot.

When Gaillard took over the Central Division, the first problem he dealt with was rainfall; and the way he dealt with it was by creating an effective system of drainage.

The *Canal Record* tells us that the drainage of the Culebra Cut presented two distinct tasks: how to prevent water from the surrounding country entering the Cut; and how to rid the Cut of rainfall and water collecting in it from seepage. The first task was solved by a system of diversion channels, the second by gravity-drains and centrifugal pumps.

Among the hills of the continental divide the Rivers Obispo, Masambi, Sardanilla, Mandinga and Comacho continually cross and recross the line of the canal. It was no easy task therefore to clear the Cut of water. The French had built two diversion channels, the Obispo parallel to the east bank, and the Comacho parallel to the west. Neither of these, however, was conceived as a permanent feature, and it was envisaged that even when de Lesseps' canal was complete a number of streams would empty into it. The Americans, however, felt that water entering the canal would tend to block it with silt and would create potentially dangerous currents. Permanent diversion channels were therefore designed, the Obispo Diversion draining water into the Chagres at Gamboa, and the Comacho entering the same river at Matachin. The former was the more important. It drained a bigger area (ten square miles), and was built on a bigger scale. Its construction entailed a million cubic yards of excavation, the creation of a mile-and-a-half of carefully revetted dyke, and the sinking of more than 900 feet of sheet piling. Indeed Sibert says: "This work would ordinarily have been considered a major undertaking, but such was the magnitude of operations in the Cut that the Obispo Diversion was looked upon as a mere side-issue." The Comacho Diversion drained a smaller area, only five-and-a-half square miles. It did, however, include one engineering masterpiece: a tunnel through the Haut Obispo Hills which had been completed by the French and was subsequently utilised by Gaillard. These diversions did their work tolerably well; although with the knowledge which comes with hindsight it is easy to see that they should have been set farther away from the canal. For as the slopes were progressively flattened out on account of slides, so the cutting itself crept gradually nearer to the channels, until to quote Goethals, "These diversions eventually gave a good deal of trouble because of their proximity to the Cut, water seeping out of them being undoubtedly responsible for some of the slides."

As regards rain and seepage into the Cut itself, water was carried away by gravity from the central summit, being channelled into the

Chagres to the north and the Rio Grande to the south. When the Cut reached a depth of some hundred feet pumps were installed: eight to the north with a discharge-capacity of 55,000 gallons per minute, and ten to the south with a capacity of 39,000 gallons.

Having dealt with drainage, Gaillard's next problem was how to assemble his equipment and put it to methodical use.

He was lucky here in that his predecessor, John F. Stevens, had planned and laid a railroad system of unsurpassed efficiency, and had ordered a vast quantity of first-class equipment. Gaillard's job, therefore, was to harness this plant to an overall plan; and perhaps the best way to understand this plan would be to follow the work of excavation stage by stage.

First the drilling.

This involved the boring of some six hundred holes a day: holes which were subsequently filled with dynamite and fired so as to prepare the ground for excavation. For this task Gaillard had at his disposal 200 tripod-drills (which bored three-inch holes to a depth of thirty feet) and 200 well-drills (which bored five-inch holes to a depth of 400 feet); in addition, he had several dozen one-man portable air-drills for trimming. The larger drills were equipped with boilers, but it was soon found that they operated best by compressed air. The installation of air compressors and the provision of a constant and easily tapped supply of air was therefore essential. This Gaillard made the responsibility of a special division of more than 200 men. They tackled the job by ringing the perimeter of the Cut with a continuous circuit of six-, eight- and ten-inch pipes which were connected to compressors at Rio Grande, Empire and Las Cascadas. Gate-valves were placed in these pipes at intervals of 1,500 feet so that air could be shut off from any part of the circuit without interrupting supplies to the rest. At intervals of 500 feet lateral pipes were run down the banks and into the Cut, and these too were equipped with gate-valves and with connections to the various types of drill. At any one time there were more than 225,000 feet of piping in and around the Cut; and each year, to keep pace with excavation and slides, Gaillard's "Air Division" relaid the incredible total of 4,800,000 feet. The drills themselves generally operated in batteries of five or six, so that they covered simultaneously a width of roughly thirty feet. The holes they bored were, on average, six feet apart and twenty feet deep—although both depth and distance apart depended on the character of the rock. It has been estimated that between 1908 and 1913 the drills in the Cut bored more than 6,000 miles of hole.

The sharpening and maintenance of the drills was carried out initially at Rio Grande and Paraiso; but as the line of the prism widened and deepened, it was found more practical to bring mobile machine-shops (mounted on flat-cars) into the Cut itself. These, equipped with forges, dies, hammers, lathes and anvils, moved from point to point as they were needed by day and carried out routine maintenance by night. The *Canal Record* describes their work:

> To keep the equipment in good repair, the Superintendent of Mechanical Drills and Pipe Lines has at his disposal a force of 218 men. Day and night they patrol the edge of the Cut looking for leaks etc. . . . One night recently a portion of the bank opposite Culebra slid into the canal, carrying with it the air lines to a battery of drills. Within half an hour of the slide being reported a repair gang was at work; the gate-valves were shut, and emergency lines were run over ditches and under railway track to the drills. Although it was after midnight when the slides occurred, by seven a.m. water and air were available, and the drills were able to start as usual on time.

A not very remarkable incident, but one which epitomises the efficiency of Gaillard's organisation.

After the holes had been drilled, they were filled with explosive and fired.

There are two points of interest in this second stage: the difficult nature and unprecedented scale of the blasting, and the efficiency of the safety precautions. Difficulties stemmed from the fact that the terrain was never uniform, so that the powder-men found themselves handling the hardest rock one hour and the softest clay the next; they had therefore to learn by trial and error the right amount of explosive for the different formations of rock. As to the scale of the work, it was astronomic. In a representative month (March, 1912) 200,000 holes were drilled and packed with 415,000 pounds of dynamite, and when exploded this dynamite pulverised more than 870,000 cubic yards of soil. It had been estimated that in the three peak years of excavation nineteen million pounds of dynamite were exploded in the Cut, breaking up more than forty million cubic yards of rock and soil.

With continuous blasting being carried out in a crowded area, one would have expected accidents to be commonplace. In fact they were remarkably rare; and in the three busiest years of construction only eight men were killed and forty-seven injured. Goethals has left us an account of safety measures.

> Dynamite was brought to the isthmus on chartered steamers and unloaded at Cristobal. It was then taken by special train to one

of the four magazines (at Mindi, Gamboa, Gold Hill and Cocoli Hill). These magazines were constructed of concrete blocks, were bullet proof, and were looked after day and night by special guards; also the ground about them was kept clear of rubbish and vegetation in case of fire. The temperatures of the magazines were carefully watched, the boxes were periodically turned, and the fuses were kept in separate buildings—in short the strictest possible regulations were enforced with a view to reducing the chances of accident.

Experiments were carried out with different grades of powder, different types of fuse and different methods of firing. And it was eventually found that Trojan powder, made up in half-pound cartridges, was best suited to conditions on the isthmus; that the fuses were safer when connected in series or multiple arc; and that the best way of exploding them was by electric current from the dynamos. It says much for Gaillard's efficiency and good sense that even during the heaviest floods blasting operations were never held up, and that during the touching off of thirty-three million pounds of gun-powder there were only two serious accidents.

When the dust of the explosions had settled, steam-shovels moved into the blasted area. This was the third stage: grubbing up the earth and pulverised rock.

Gaillard's steam-shovels worked to an overall plan. And here we have the big difference between the French and the Americans. In the 1880s the former performed prodigies of valour as individuals, whereas in the 1900s the latter performed prodigies of valour as members of a highly organised team. Not a yard of soil was excavated until there was a dump-car into which it could be loaded and a well-laid track ready to carry it away. The basic plan was as follows. The method adopted by the French of working up-grade from either end of the Cut towards a central summit was continued; for this not only helped drainage, but had the advantage of providing a down-grade for the loaded trains as they pulled out of the Cut. Work proceeded on two levels. On the upper level, a pilot cut thirty-four feet wide was excavated to a depth of twelve feet, and track was laid along it close to its outer edge; dump-cars were then shunted along the track. On the lower level, steam-shovels pushed steadily forward excavating soil and swinging it into the dump-cars, until the latter were full and ready to be towed to the tip. This excavation proceeded until a cut thirty-four feet wide and twelve feet deep had been shovelled away for the length of the cutting from Gamboa to Pedro Miguel. As soon as this cut was complete it

THE CENTRAL DIVISION 215

became the new level for track, cars were shunted along it, while the steam-shovels started work on another and lower cut. In this way the bed of the canal was gradually lowered and widened in parallel strips. The shovels worked virtually non-stop, biting out from two to five cubic yards at a time; and so proficient did their operators eventually become that the machines were able to claw up and dump a shovel-load of soil every eighteen to twenty seconds.

These shovels were the sinews of the American assault, the driving force on which all other facets of the work depended. In the years of peak activity (1909-12) there were sixty-nine of them at work in the Cut, mostly seventy-ton or ninety-five-ton Bucyruses. These splendid machines (see Figure 15) held both the daily and monthly record for excavation, and the *Canal Record* sings their praise—"Bucyrus shovels hold all records of output, and worked satisfactorily year after year even when the most difficult digging conditions were encountered." Samuel G. Blythe of the *Saturday Evening Post* has left a picturesque description of them in action.

> It is King Yardage who is doing business now, with his sixty-nine steam-shovels and 7,000 men ripping a cutting through the hills of the continental divide. I watched a steam-shovel at work in the Cut. It was one of the smaller machines, but it took up at a scoop two and a half cubic yards of dirt. Every eighteen seconds its big claw grabbed two waggon-loads of soil and dropped it on a flat-car. It worked with the precision of a clock: out against the bank, ripping up through it, swinging over the car, dumping its load and going back for another. The man who manoeuvred it was an Irishman. The man on the crane, who attended to the dumping, was an American. The two stokers at the engine were Jamaican negroes. And the six members of the move-up crew [the men who levelled the ground where the shovel stood and placed the track so that it could move forward and keep its nose to the bank] were Sikhs from the north of India, men who wore white turbans, worked like automatons, and observed all the requirements of their religion, even throwing away their food if the shadow of an unbeliever fell on it. Nobody has kept count of the different races at work on the isthmus, but there are more than fifty. You can hear all their languages as you walk along the line. You can see men from India, the Argentine, British Columbia and Siberia hard at work together, all paying tribute to King Yardage, and all motivated by the demand that this month's excavation shall be greater than that of the month before.

Coaling and maintenance of the shovels were carried out at night.

Most of the coaling was done by negroes, who dumped forty to fifty tons direct from the coal-cars into the bins of every shovel. Maintenance was entrusted to mobile working gangs equipped with forge, drill, shaper and lathe; these moved into the Cut at sunset and worked until dawn, carrying out even such major repairs as replacing boilers, so that the shovels could remain at work month after month.

The mind boggles at the sheer volume of work carried out by this comparative handful of machines. For of the yardage listed below over sixty per cent of the French excavation and over ninety per cent of the American was by steam-shovel.

EXCAVATION OF THE CULEBRA CUT

By the Old French Company	
1881–1888	38,642,107 cubic yards
By the New French Company	
1889–1903	10,498,008 ,, ,,
By the Americans	
1904	243,472 ,, ,,
1905	1,084,428 ,, ,,
1906	2,702,991 ,, ,,
1907	9,177,130 ,, ,,
1908	13,912,453 ,, ,,
1909	14,557,034 ,, ,,
1910	15,398,599 ,, ,,
1911	16,596,891 ,, ,,
1912	15,028,413 ,, ,,
1913	9,348,190 ,, ,,
Total:	147,189,716 cubic yards

While Figure 27 shows a cross section of the work (a) originally planned, (b) carried out by the French, and (c) carried out by the Americans. It will be seen from this that, even allowing for replacements, the steam-shovels at work in the Cut averaged more than a million cubic yards of excavation apiece—an eloquent tribute to the men who designed, built and operated them.

Every bucketful of this vast quantity of earth had to be disposed of. And this was the final phase of Gaillard's plan: the carting away of the ton after million ton of soil and rock.

Spoil trains ran out of the Cut either north at Gamboa or south at Pedro Miguel. On the north gradient twenty-one steam-shovels were continually at work, loading into cars on fourteen parallel tracks; and the sequence of events was as follows. A train of empty cars was hauled into the Cut on an up-grade, it reached the summit and started back on a track running down-grade. At the point where work was in progress, it would stop beside a series of shovels; it was at the start now of what was known as its "run around". The cars were shunted slowly past the shovels until they were filled with earth and rock—this might take anything up to an hour, or even, if the rock was recalcitrant, two hours. Still on a down-grade, the train would then proceed out of the Cut, onto the railroad and thence to one of the dumping grounds. Here the cars were turned over to the dump engineer; unloaders and ploughs were adjusted, cables were winched taut, and the soil was swept off the side of the cars and onto the dump. Meanwhile the locomotive which brought the train in would couple onto a line of empties and push them to the nearest repair yard; here the "bad orders" (cars damaged during the loading or unloading) were taken out and good cars substituted. The train was then pushed up-grade along the empties' track until it arrived once again at the summit. The process was then repeated.

On the south gradient the procedure was much the same. And the *Canal Record* tells us that between 150 and 160 trains, each consisting of eighteen to twenty cars, were hauled to the dumps each day; also that transportation stock consisted of 135 locomotives and 1,930 cars, each train being crewed by a white engineer, conductor and flagman, and a negro foreman and brakeman.

The successful handling of what, in the 1900s, was an unprecedented volume of traffic bears witness to the excellence of Stevens's layout and the efficiency of the staff of the Panama Railroad. There was no waiting now for cars, and none of the frustrating derailments which had bedevilled Dingler, Bunau-Varilla and

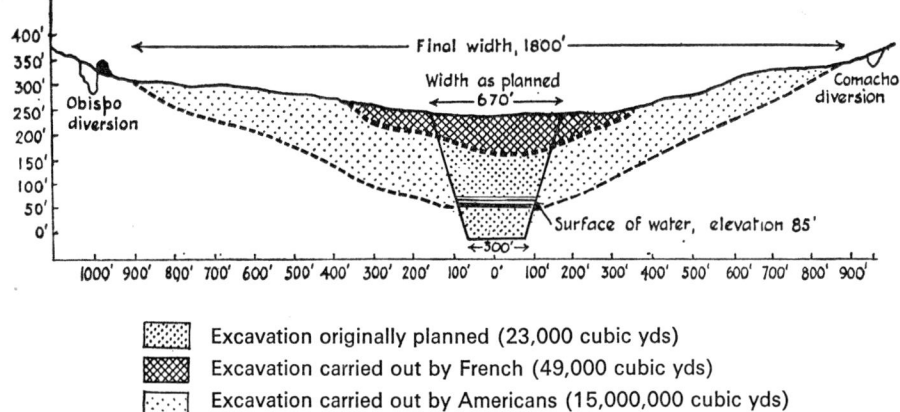

Figure 27. Excavation in the Culebra Cut

Wallace; only the non-stop operation of a smooth well-oiled machine.

From 1908 to 1913 work proceeded steadily without a break, six and a half thousand men streaming each day into the Cut, working their ten-hour shift in temperatures of anything up to 120 degrees Fahrenheit, and then in the cool of the evening moving back to their quarters in the surrounding hills. Bishop quotes a visitor's impression of the scene by day.

> The spectacle exceeded all my anticipations, for nowhere else on earth is there to be found a display of human activity on so large a scale and in so marvellous a setting. It was this combination [of activity and setting] which added a touch of the extraordinary to the picture. For to stand at the southern end of the Cut, between the majestic hills of the continental divide, was an experience which no one could ever forget. On either side were the green, near-perpendicular walls of rock and in the steadily widening and deepening chasm between, a swarming mass of men, rushing railway trains and monster-like machines, all working with ceaseless activity and all seemingly animated by human intelligence. Everybody knew what he had to do and was doing it. It was organisation reduced to a science—an endless chain system of activity in perfect operation . . . He who did not see the Culebra Cut during the work of excavation missed one of the great spectacles of the ages: a sight the like of which man may never again be given to see.

The same feeling of wonder is expressed more succinctly by Sir James Bryce, British ambassador to Washington. "Never before have so much labour, so much scientific knowledge and so much administrative skill been concentrated on a work designed to serve the interests of mankind." It is hard to find anyone who visited the Cut by day who was not impressed.

What is not generally realised is that the Cut was equally impressive by night. And here the usually prosaic *Canal Record* waxes eloquent.

> Five o'clock in the afternoon is "quitting time" in the Culebra Cut. The shovels cease to dig, spoil trains lay up for the night, and the men who have been working since seven a.m. start up the steep banks for their homes in the villages along the edge of the canal, or gather in little groups to wait for the labour trains. Yet the work does not altogether cease; for "quitting time" for the 6,000 day workers marks the beginning of labour for the four to five hundred who work in the Cut by night. As the labour trains creep along the tracks in the bottom of the Cut, so coal

Figure 28. The Cut at Paraiso

trains start running down the canal, the repair trains set out from the shops at Empire, new gangs climb into the batteries of drills and the track-repair squads stand by for their work.

For the night is spent in preparing for the day; and it is because of this unceasing work right round the clock that the great excavation-machine moves smoothly week after week, month after month, year after year.

It is the duty of the coal-train crew to see that every steam-shovel has sufficient coal in its bin to last through the following day. A dozen cars of coal are hauled each night from the storage piles to the Cut. A train runs alongside a shovel, uncouples a car and leaves it there with two negroes whose work is to fill the shovel bin. As soon as this car is uncoupled the train moves on. It stops alongside shovel after shovel until all the cars have been distributed—"spotted" the men of the coal-train say. By the time the last car is "spotted" the first shovel has been filled, and the locomotive begins to collect the cars and distribute them again to other shovels. If the shovels are favourably situated for coaling, if the tracks are clear of trains and free from rocks, if no derailment occurs and if all the men work fast, the coaling is finished by midnight. If, however, all does not go well, day may be breaking before the last shovel is supplied. But no matter how long it takes, the coaling must be done, and it therefore sometimes happens that the train of empty coal-cars is crawling back to the storage pile at sunrise, at the same time as the labour trains are bringing day-workers to the Cut.

Anyone who has watched the steam-shovels in action will realise that there must be much work for the repair men. For although the shovel crew are warned that a "record yardage" is not so desirable as a fair average with a small repair bill, emulation among the men is intense, and repair bills are intangible whereas records stand and are talked about. And in the end, the usage given a steam-shovel is determined by the man who operates it. Sometimes the steel teeth of the dipper are run into a bank of rock apparently well shattered by dynamite, only to find firm resistance. Whether he will wait till the rock is further broken, will attack another part of the bank, or will draw back the dipper and with the force of a long blow attempt to drive the teeth into the rock and lift it out—these are items in the steam-shovel man's knowledge. A hundred times a day he must make such decisions. It is not unusual, therefore, to see a ninety-ton shovel stagger under the work it is set to do, or to see its dipper-stick stand rigid because there is not power enough in the engine to force the teeth into the rock. Even without these unusual burdens, the shovel's work is racking, and scarcely a day passes without the need of strengthening or replacing some part of it. All night the repair men are at work with crane, forge, drill, wrench and hammer, because tomorrow may always be a record day in the Cut and each shovel must be ready to do its best.

Anyone who spends the night in a village along the Cut, and who has not become used to the sensation, is startled about midnight and again about daybreak by a series of explosions. Buildings shake as though in an earthquake, and the pattering of small bits of mud and rock on the iron roofs heighten the illusion that the town is under bombardment. Residents of the villages know that the explosions are only blasts of dynamite down in the canal, where the men at work on the tracks use surface charges to dispose of the larger stones, or where the mines placed by the powder gangs are being set off.

The watchmen getting steam up for the morning, the tenders of the drainage sumps, the men who repair tracks and shovels and the men who drill holes and break up the rock with dynamite, all have their work and each makes some noise in doing it. Yet on the whole the Cut is quiet by night; and it is more by the lanterns moving here and there, and the glare of the locomotive headlights, that a person standing on the bank divines the amount of labour which darkness hides. A few evenings ago, the repair gangs had a long job under the shadow of Gold Hill, and the searchlights of the locomotives played steadily down the Cut for more than an hour. It threw into eerie relief the crumpled mass of rock and earth which is moving slowly into the canal at Culebra, lighted up the labour quarters along the edge of the Cut, blotched the west bank with alternate light and shadow, and in the bottom of the trench showed scores of moving shadows where the night men were at work. This was a clear night; but there are many nights when blinding rain arrests the rays of the searchlights, and the rush of water drowns the sound of labour. And there are nights too when a heavy mist settles in the Cut, when the opposite bank is visible but in the trench below one can see only a white river of fog, so dense that it looks like water. Then trains move slowly along the hidden tracks, lanterns are held close to the faces of the repair gang, and the powder-men move cautiously from hole to hole. When the morning sun disperses this fog, the night gangs have disappeared, but they have left the Culebra-Cut-Machine ready, as always, for whatever demands may be made on it during another day.

And so the Machine ground on, steadily, one might almost say inexorably, year after year. There were few heroic achievements—for Goethals frowned on efforts at record-breaking because they wore out equipment and put up costs—and few spectacular highlights; simply the churning away of drills and the non-stop scooping up and carrying away of millions of tons of rubble and earth. It is difficult to wax eloquent over the shifting of some 150 million cubic yards of dirt.

It was not until 1913, when excavation was nearing completion, that the work was highlighted by drama.

First, the tragedy of Gaillard. On January 17th 400,000 cubic yards of soil sloughed down the Cucaracha slide and into the Cut; the bed of the prism bulged under the strain, steam-shovels were buried, and drills, flat-cars and track disappeared in a holocaust of destruction. Three days later a rock bluff 290 feet high toppled off the face of Gold Hill, cascading a further million tons of debris across the line of the canal. It looked as though the work of years had been negated in a few catastrophic hours. And Gaillard, already a sick man, broke under the strain. For months he had been fighting not only the Cut, but dizziness and headaches of increasing severity; it was now found that he was suffering from a brain tumour. The discovery, however, was made too late; operation was impossible and by the end of the year Gaillard was dead. Goethals wrote his obituary.

> Lieut. Col. D. D. Gaillard died on the morning of December 5th at Baltimore, Md. His period of canal service coincided with the years of most active construction work. To this work he brought trained ability of the first order, untiring zeal, and unswerving devotion to duty . . . His associates mourn him as a valiant soldier, a true man, and a well-loved companion.

The king of the Central Division was dead. But his work lived on. And on May 20th there took place a landmark in the history of the canal. In spite of the slides, steam-shovels boring toward one another through the central summit met for the first time at the bottom level of the cutting. The *Canal Record* describes this event in prose which does less than justice to an historic occasion.

> Steam-shovel No. 222 (manned by J. S. Kirk, engineer, and U. L. Hill, craneman) and steam-shovel No. 230 (manned by D. J. MacDonald, engineer, and J. V. Rosenberry, craneman) met at canal grade in the Culebra Cut at 4.30 p.m. on Tuesday, May 20th almost opposite the residence of Col. H. F. Hodges.

These are the first through steam-shovels to meet at the lowest grade in the Culebra section.

A statement which gives little indication of the blood, sweat and tears which made the meeting possible.

Five months later, at the end of September 1913, steam-shovels and equipment were removed from the Cut so that water could be admitted via pipes under the Gamboa dyke. After more than thirty years of endeavour the waters of Atlantic and Pacific were about to meet.

The *Canal Record* describes the preliminaries to blasting the dyke—an event which was, at the time, considered almost tantamount to opening the canal.

> All steam-shovel operations in Culebra Cut proper will be discontinued on Friday, September 15th, and between this date and October 5th all equipment and material must be recovered including over thirty-six miles of track. At the present time about thirty shovels are at work in the Cut, all on bottom excavation with the exception of two on each side of the canal which are engaged in "lightening the load" on the higher levels as a preventive measure against slides. The shovels formerly at work on the Cucaracha have been withdrawn, and the remaining debris will be removed (after flooding) by dredge. The remaining bottom material is being drilled and blasted, and this too will subsequently be removed by dredging . . . Water will be admitted to the Cut on Tuesday, October 5th, five days in advance of the date set for the destruction of Gamboa dyke. The means employed will consist of four twenty-six inch pipes which extend under the dyke and have up to now been used to pump drainage water out of the Cut. The water thus let in is intended to act as a cushion against the inrush when Gamboa dyke is dynamited on October 10th.

The dynamiting of this last barrier was the climax of thirty years' work among the hills of the central divide.

October 10th was a holiday. All through the morning special trains and an armada of tugs, barges, dredges and scows converged on Gamboa; thousands of engineers and V.I.P.s congregated on the hills overlooking the dyke, and at two p.m. Washington time Woodrow Wilson pressed a button installed in his desk in the White House. A signal sped 4,000 miles to the isthmus, and the eight tons of dynamite let into the dyke was detonated. The New York *Times* waxed eloquent: "With an explosion which shook the surrounding hills and threw huge rocks into the air, the dynamite was set off by

President Wilson, the last obstruction in the Panama Canal was swept away, and the dream of centuries became a reality. By this simple act the President caused the greatest spectacle in the history of the world's greatest work of engineering." As the dust settled, it was seen that a gap 125 feet wide had been blasted out of the dyke, and through this the combined waters of river and lake were swirling in an irresistible flood. Or, to be more precise, in a flood which was *almost* irresistible. For close to the centre of the Cut the water was checked by the soggy mass of the Cucaracha, which even eleven tons of dynamite had failed to breach. Tugs and barges came to a reluctant halt, the pleasure boats returned to Gamboa, the dredges set to work; and the dream of uniting the oceans was still, for the moment, unfulfilled.

For a week engineers struggled with the Cucaracha, exploding charges of such violence that houses from Empire to Pedro Miguel rocked on their foundations. But to no avail. "The use of dynamite is futile," wrote Gaillard's successor. "For such is the sodden nature of the material that it merely seeps back into the holes thrown out by the explosion." It seemed as though the opening of the canal might be seriously delayed.

Then the Chagres came to the rescue.

Between October 19th and 23rd a force of two hundred men and four dredges struggled night and day to excavate a channel through the unyielding clay, and eventually on the night of the 23rd they managed to coax through a reluctant trickle. But the channel silted up as fast as it was dug. Next day, however, it rained continuously for eight hours, the Chagres rose, and, backing into the Cut provided the head of water which was needed to maintain a constant flow. The trickle was metamorphosed first to a steady effluence, then to a flood which carried before it thousands of tons of rock and silt. The centre of the slide began to disintegrate; on the night of October 24th it finally broke and by dawn a continuous sheet of water at the eighty-five-foot-level stretched from Gatun overlooking the Atlantic to Pedro Miguel overlooking the Pacific.

After one of the most prolonged and arduous struggles between man and nature which the world has ever known, the work of the Central Division was complete.

13

THE PACIFIC DIVISION

This division extended from Pedro Miguel at the end of the Culebra Cut, to the forty-five-foot mean tide contour in the Bay of Panama, a distance of eleven miles. In many ways it was a pleasant area to work in: the climate was relatively dry, Panama was the social centre of the isthmus, and as regards construction the work was technically easy. There was, however, a less satisfactory side to the coin; for progress in the valley of the Rio Grande was retarded by a long and acrimonious dispute about the siting of the Pacific locks, and in the end they were built in the wrong place.

The original plan, drawn up by the International Consulting Board in 1906, had recommended that a dam and three tiers of locks (similar to those at Gatun) should be built between Sosa Hill and Corozal, thus creating a lake of seven square miles on the Pacific side of the continental divide. If this recommendation had been carried out, the canal would have had a pleasing simplicity in design, and large man-made reaches of water on either side of the Culebra Cut would have facilitated navigation. Secretary Taft, however, chose this moment to make one of his unfortunate sallies into the affairs of the canal.

> The great objection to locks at Sosa Hill [he wrote to the President] is the possibility of their destruction by the fire from an enemy's ships. If, as has been suggested to me by officers of this Department entitled to speak with authority on military subjects, these locks may be located against and *behind* Sosa Hill in such a way as to use the hill as a protection against enemy fire, then [the lake could be retained] . . . If, however, Sosa Hill will not afford a site with such protection, then it seems to me wiser to place the locks at Miraflores.

This apparently innocuous letter sparked off a year and a half of investigation, experiment, claim, counter-claim and special pleading.

Without doubt, a dam and a three-tier lock close to the sea would have been the happiest solution. This, however, was found to have technical as well as military disadvantages; for the soil to seaward of Sosa Hill turned out to be not stiff clay (as was thought from the

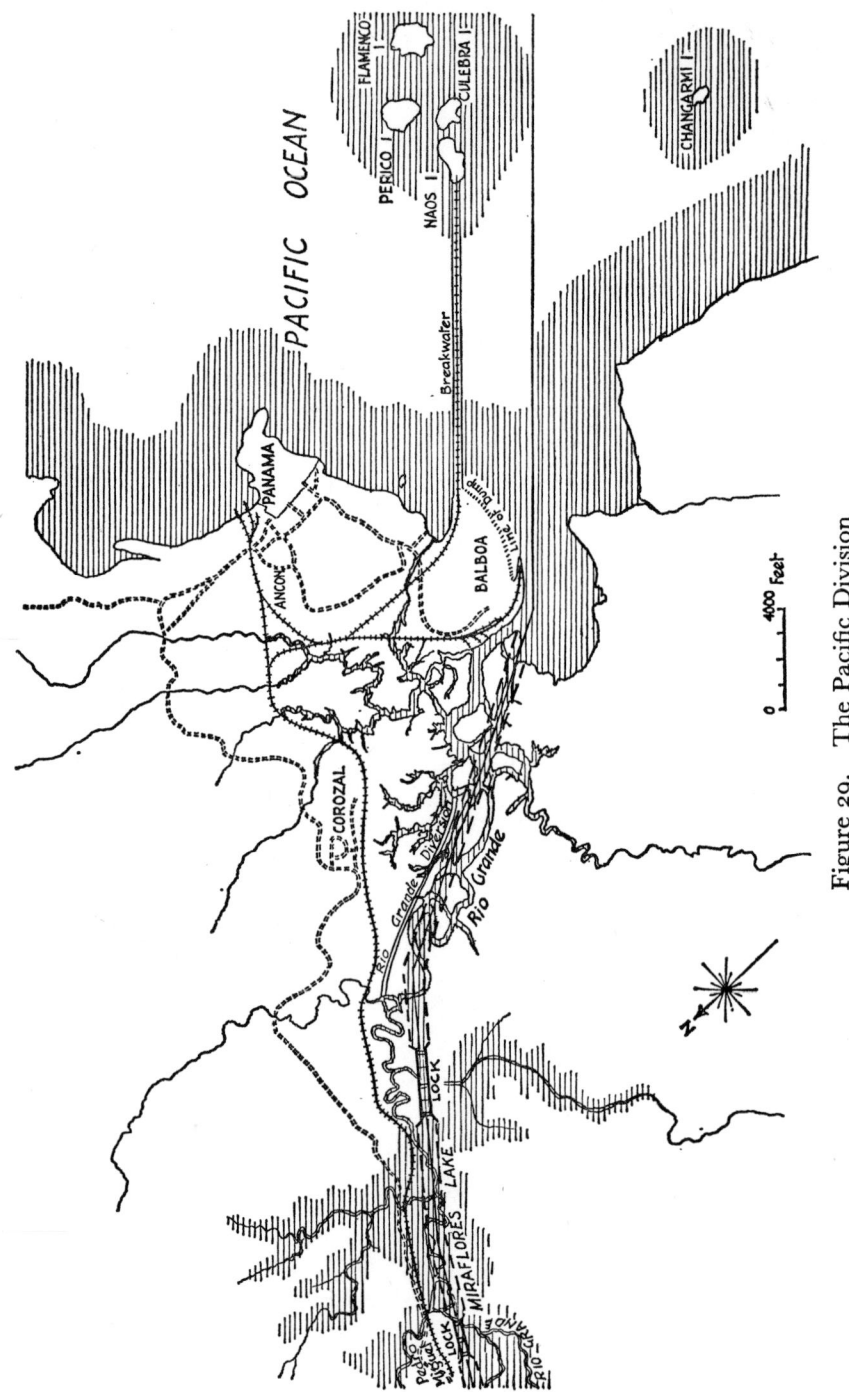

Figure 29. The Pacific Division

original borings) but unctuous blue clay with little supporting power; locks here, in other words, would have been not only vulnerable to bombardment but costly to construct, and the surveyors were ordered to search for an alternative site. Foundations were found to exist for one lock at Pedro Miguel and for two at Miraflores, both sites being screened from gunfire. Many prominent engineers pointed out that the creation of locks at these places would virtually do away with the Pacific lake, would add to the accident hazards, and would lead to serious congestion at the end of the Culebra Cut. Taft, however, was adamant; and on December 20th, 1907 the President authorised the proposed changes. The whole affair was summarised in a single sentence by John F. Stevens: "The advantages of a commodious lake at the Pacific terminus were many from a navigation and commercial standpoint, but the military features were considered paramount." It is ironic that the least satisfactory aspect of the finished canal should have nothing to do with the much publicised slides at Culebra or the much criticised dam at Gatun, but should have been brought about by the preoccupation of Secretary Taft with defence.

Because of these fundamental changes of plan, work in the Pacific division didn't get under way until early in 1908. The head of the division, Sydney B. Williamson, was, therefore, always struggling to make up for lost time; and it was only because of his technical ingenuity that this section of the canal was completed on schedule.

The work consisted of two quite separate undertakings—the excavation of an approach-channel, and the construction of locks, dams and guide walls at Miraflores and Pedro Miguel.

(1) *Excavation of the Pacific Approach-Channel.*
Panama Bay is as different from Limon Bay as chalk from cheese. It is virtually an open anchorage in the centre of a shallow indentation in the coast, with a cluster of tiny islands lying roughly three miles offshore. The standard work on the coastline states categorically that "no storms likely to injure shipping ever visit the Pacific terminal", and this seemingly improbable claim the years have proved. The need to construct the usual type of sheltered anchorage has never therefore arisen. Tides and currents, however, are another matter.

There is a maximum tidal range at Panama of twenty-one feet, and a steady littoral current running from east-north-east to west-south-west; and the latter, it was estimated, might deposit annually more than half a million cubic yards of silt across the mouth of the canal. It was therefore recommended by the Consulting Board that a breakwater three miles long be run from Balboa Point to Naos Island, thus screening the channel-entrance from both currents and silt.

This breakwater was designed by Gaillard, and was constructed by engineers of the Central and not the Pacific Division. The reason for this apparent anomaly is that material used in its construction came from the Culebra Cut; the breakwater was therefore both a dumping ground for Gaillard and a building project for Williamson; and when Army and civilians were in confrontation, it was the latter who stepped aside.

Work started in the autumn of 1907. At first all went well, with a trestle of creosoted piles being extended slowly seaward from Balboa Point, track being laid on the trestles, and cars full of spoil being shunted along the track to tip their contents over the side. It was soon found, however, that the mud of the sea bed had an unusually low coefficient of friction, and was quite unable to bear the weight of the debris dumped. The *Canal Record* describes what happened next.

> Progress was reasonably rapid until the trestle reached the old channel made by the French as an entrance to Balboa docks. Then slide after slide occurred to retard the filling. Time and again a whole section of trestle and track would disappear overnight into the mud, and a new trestle would have to be built before dumping could continue. In some places the vertical settlement was as much as 125 feet and the lateral displacement was as much as 300 feet, so that soon not a single foot of trestle remained at the place for which it was intended . . . In the last year [1909] 82,000 cubic yards of earth and rock have been dumped, yet the breakwater is not yet a quarter completed.

In 1910 more than half a million yards of spoil were poured into the breakwater, but at the end of the year it was still a mile short of Naos Island. It was not finally completed until September 1914, by which time more than two and a quarter million cubic yards of rock and soil had been tipped into the unstable mud of the bay—more than ten times the amount originally estimated.

Naos breakwater, in fact, proved a microcosm of the canal as a whole. For the finished wall, forty feet wide at the top and rising eighteen feet above high water and having revetted slopes of 1-in-1, has an appearance of simplicity which gives little hint of the hazards and difficulties experienced in its construction.

At the landward extremity of the breakwater, work was started in 1909 on the fuel plant, coaling plant, dry dock, repair shops, wharves and piers which were to turn Balboa into one of the leading ports in the world. The main task of Williamson's division, however, was excavation: the digging out first of a deep-water harbour, then of a channel through the low-lying valley of the Rio Grande.

This excavation was carried out in three ways. Two and a half million yards were extracted by steam-shovel at an average cost of eighty cents per yard; two-and-a-half million yards were extracted by hydraulic jet at seventy-two cents per yard; and thirty-five million yards were extracted by dredge at twenty-five cents per yard.

Excavation by steam-shovel followed the same pattern as in the Culebra Cut, the seventy- and ninety-five-ton Bucyruses biting out the earth and loading it direct into dump-cars which were emptied into swamp land round the mouth of the river. There were no major problems here, and the cost per yard was less than one-twentieth of that in the Cut.

Excavation by hydraulic jet was an innovation perfected by the ingenious Williamson. It was first used in the channel south of Miraflores locks, where, to quote Williamson himself, "it proved impracticable to move earth and rock by dredging or subaqueous methods, since the requisite number of dredges, barges, drills and rock-breakers could not have been assembled in such a confined space so as to complete the work within the allotted time." The earth, therefore, was first dislodged by means of powerful jets of water, then carried (water-borne) to a series of suction pumps which raised it out of the channel and disgorged it onto the adjacent embryo dams. The *Canal Record* gives details.

> This plan involves (a) the disintegrating and sluicing of the soil into sumps—which is done by a series of monitors or hydraulic giants; and (b) the lifting and conveying of the resultant semi-liquid material to its place of deposit—which is done by centrifugal dredging pumps mounted on concrete barges . . .
>
> The hydraulic giants are of the latest type used in mining operations in California. They weigh 1,500 pounds apiece, and consist of a base for attachment to a sixteen-inch gate valve at the terminus of a pipeline, a horizontal and vertical joint, and a long conical reducing piece. Frictional resistance is decreased by a ball-bearing, and a weighted lever is attached to control the direction of the jet. A deflecting nozzle is fitted to the discharge end of the giant, and this permits deflections through a small angle without changing the position of the main body. The tapering piece of the giant is also fitted with two sets of guide vanes

which prevent a scattering or rotary motion of the water after it has left the nozzle. The nozzles used will vary from four inches to six inches in diameter, and at full head the water coming through them will exert a pressure of 130 pounds to the square inch—the equivalent of a ton and a half of pressure on the bank a hundred feet away. The giants will operate from eight feet above to forty-five feet below mean tide level, and will wash the material down into sluices which will carry the water-cum-earth to a sump where barge pumps are constantly at work.

[There will be three of these pumps, each mounted in a concrete barge sixty-four feet long, twenty-four feet wide and five feet eight inches deep.] While the construction of barges out of concrete is not entirely new, having been pioneered in Italy, it has never hitherto been attempted in American engineering. Wooden forms will be used, and wall construction will consist of half-inch mesh wire-cloth, with transverse and longitudinal rods fastened to a reinforced framework. Plaster will be laid on the outside first, then the inside. When the barges are complete they will be launched sideways, and the dredging pump, motor and equipment (weighing in all 60,000 pounds) will be installed near the centre of the barge. Each unit consists of a suction-dredge pump directly connected to a Westinghouse motor. The manganese steel impeller on each pump has five blades, and is designed to handle 10,000 gallons of water and fifty cubic yards of solid matter per minute, i.e. 110 cubic feet of water to one cubic foot of sedimentary material. The motors are of the three-phase type, 2,080-volt with automatic starting equipment; while power will be supplied by Miraflores central station via armoured submarine cables.

This costly and complicated apparatus proved its worth in no uncertain manner, excavating from the Miraflores channel alone more than two million cubic yards of soil in two years. It was subsequently transferred to the Central Division, where it worked on the Cucaracha slide.

Steam-shovels and hydraulic jets, however, reliable and ingenious though they were, carried out between them barely a tenth of the Pacific excavation. The bulk of the work was done by dredge.

A glance at the table opposite tells us that there were four main types of dredge in the Pacific fleet: sea-going dredges, rebuilt (i.e. French) ladder-dredges, self-propelling clapets and scows, and finally the highly specialised rock-breakers and drills.

THE DREDGING FLEET OF THE PACIFIC DIVISION

Type	No. in Service	How acquired	Complement	Cost $
Sea-going				
(i) *Culebra*	2	Purchased from Maryland Steel Co.	68	330,000
(ii) *Corozal*		Purchased from Wm. Simons, Renfrew.	72	399,500
Ladder-dredges	4	Purchased from French and re-built in Balboa.	45	65,000
Clapets	9	Purchased from French and re-built in Balboa.	24	22,500
Tugs	6	American-built.	30	approx. 50,000
Dump scows	3	Purchased from Newport News Shipbuilding.	12	28,000
Dipper-dredge	1	Purchased from Atlantic Gulf and Pacific Co.	31	94,500
Dump-barges	7	Purchased in U.S., knocked down and reassembled.	—	24,300
Rock-breakers	1	Purchased from Lobnitz and Co., Renfrew.	12	50,000
Drill-barges	1	Purchased in U.S.	46	35,700

The two sea-going dredges, *Culebra* and *Corozal*, had little in common and were used for very different purposes.

The *Culebra*, sister ship to the *Ancon* which did such sterling work in Limon Bay, was a suction dredge, having two twenty-inch pumps discharging into self-contained hoppers or bins. She worked the seaward extremity of the canal, excavating loose material and silt which, before the completion of Naos breakwater, was continuously swept into the approach-channel by currents and tide. This she did to such good effect that by the spring of 1911 the first four miles of the channel had been excavated to their final width and depth.

The *Corozal* (see Figure 30 on page 232) was a ladder-dredge, specially ordered from William Simons of Renfrew, Scotland to excavate not only mud but also the more difficult gravel, rock and heavy clay found in the upper reaches of the Rio Grande. She left the

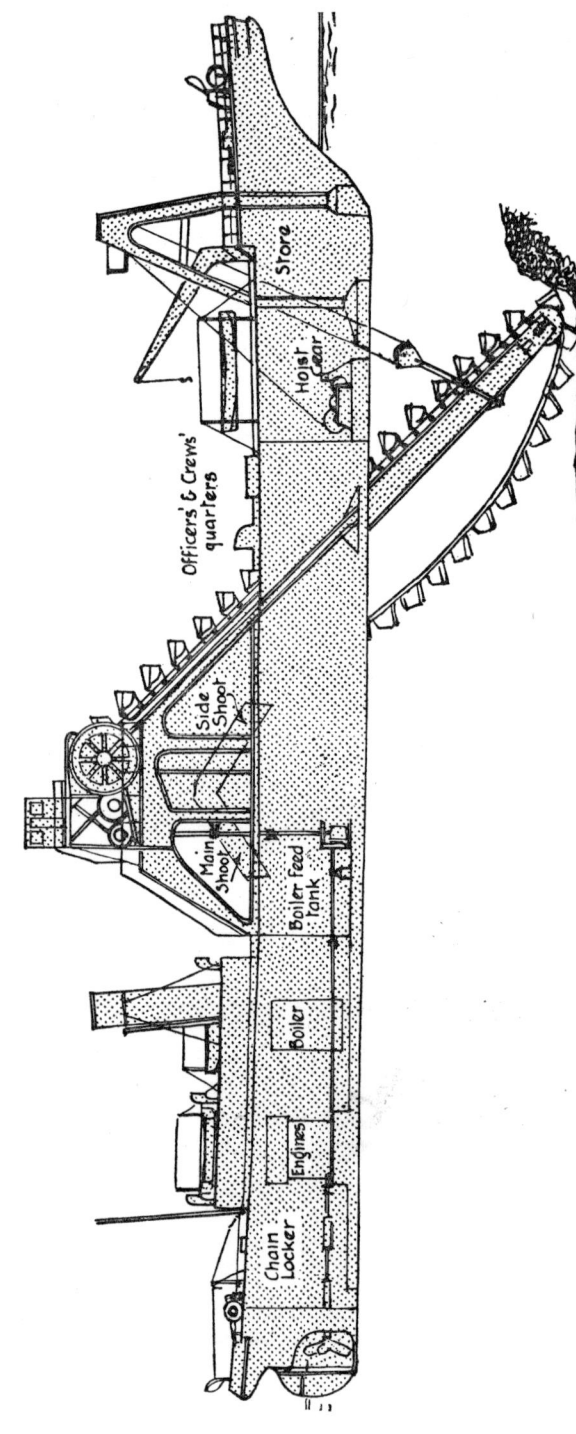

Figure 30. The sea-going ladder-dredge *Corozal*

Clyde in December 1911 and arrived in Balboa at the end of March after a trip of 12,000 miles—a voyage which, according to her master, was the longest ever made by a dredge with her superstructure in place and ready for operation. The *Canal Record* details the *Corozal*'s statistics.

> She is a twin-screw hopper dredge built of steel, 268 feet overall length, forty-five feet moulded breadth and nineteen feet depth; her mean draft when loaded with 1,200 tons of spoil is fifteen feet nine and a half inches. Her boiler plant consists of two Scotch marine boilers, and she has two triple expansion engines which either propel the ship or run the dredging gear. Her ladder, upon which the continuous chain of buckets revolves, is 115 feet long and weighs 100 tons. The bull wheels, by means of which the turning power is applied to the chain, weigh twenty-five tons each, the top tumbler weighs fifteen tons and the bottom thirteen tons. Two sizes of bucket are provided: of fifty-four cubic feet for excavation in soft soil, and of thirty-four cubic feet for working in rock or clay; the buckets are constructed with cast steel backs and tempered lips of manganese; there are thirty-nine in a chain, and the vessel brought with her ten spares of either kind. The work for which the dredge is to be used is the digging of four million cubic yards of hard material—rock, clay and boulders—from the approach-channel between Balboa and Miraflores locks, excavation which cannot be done by the ladder- or dipper-dredges now in service because of the character of the material and the depth at which it is found. The *Corozal*, however, has a centre well ladder so that she can make her own flotation . . . and in the tests all requirements were met, the dredge handling even the most difficult combinations of rock and boulder clay with apparent ease.

Although she was a late arrival at the workings, the *Corozal*—together with the *Ancon* and *Gopher*—was probably among the trio of machines responsible for the greatest volume of excavation. For in three years she more than fulfilled her target by removing 4,193,000 cubic yards of difficult spoil from the bed of the Pacific channel.

The ladder-dredges of the Pacific fleet were the *Marmot, Badger, Gopher* and *Mole*: vessels which twenty years earlier had done such valuable excavation for the French. Having been stripped down and partially rebuilt in Balboa, they embarked in 1907 on another decade of service, and surprised everyone by their capacity for hard and continuous work. The *Marmot, Badger* and *Mole* did most of their excavating in and around La Boca, where the soil was relatively easy. The *Gopher*, however, was despatched for more specialised work to Chamé.

Chamé beach lies twenty-five miles to the west of Panama: a sheltered arc of clean, white silica sand. Early in 1909 a sample of this sand was sent to the U.S. Geological Survey at Pittsburgh for analysis; Pittsburgh pronounced it "eminently satisfactory", and a couple of months later excavation was under way. It was hoped at first to handle the sand by pipeline dredge, but this proved impossible because of the heavy and continuous swell. It was Williamson who suggested that one of the "tough old French dredgers" might prove more seaworthy, and towards the end of summer, the *Gopher* hove-to off Chamé beach. To quote the *Record:* "[She] proved extremely well-suited to the work here, and was continually in service throughout the entire period of construction"—i.e. for another five years.

Chamé sand was used in enormous quantities for concrete-making throughout the Zone. It was dredged by the *Gopher*, loaded into an armada of barges and towed for storage to the sand-handling plant at Balboa. In five years of more or less continuous operation the *Gopher* excavated 2,007,590 cubic yards of sand at the remarkably low cost of thirty cents per yard. This, of course, was in addition to the very considerable work she had already done for the French; and few dredges before or since can have performed such continuous and valuable service.

Of the fleet of barges, clapets and scows, six were used on the Chamé sand run, the remainder worked principally in and around La Boca, performing valuable but unspectacular service in ferrying supplies, repairing the breakwater or transporting the spoil dug by ladder-dredges out to sea.

There were also two rock-breakers working in the channel: the *Teredo* and the *Vulcan*.

The *Teredo* was a drill-barge: length 127 feet, breadth thirty-two feet and depth twelve feet; she had three drill towers rising to fifty feet above her deck, each supporting an Ingersoll Rand rock-drill which could be lowered to a depth of sixty feet. Whenever the orthodox dredges were brought up short by a stratum of rock which their buckets couldn't bite into, the *Teredo* was moved into position; she then proceeded to drill the rock in five-foot sections, and the resulting holes were filled with eight-inch by two-inch dynamite cartridges, and exploded. It says much for the *Teredo*'s safety regulations that in five years' service she never had an accident.

The *Vulcan* was a less sophisticated vessel. Her equipment consisted of a $22\frac{1}{2}$-ton ram, fifty-six feet long, which was raised by a powerful winch and then allowed to fall, again and again, until the rock was pulverised. She was used chiefly on thin strata, since she could only break the rock to a depth of some two feet.

Ram-drills, rock-drills, barges, clapets, scows and five different classes of dredge: the diversity of the Pacific fleet is an indication of the diversity of Williamson's work. It wasn't difficult work; there was no intransigent technical problem like the Gatun Dam or the Culebra slides; instead there were a large number of highly specialised projects all of which had to be co-ordinated and completed according to schedule. The *Canal Record* of December, 1912 gives a good picture of the work in progress.

> Fortifications and breakwater work, dredging, and the construction of terminal docks and wharves are all in simultaneous progress at the Pacific entrance. The mainland has at last been connected with Naos Island, the gap of 17,000 feet having been closed after many setbacks occasioned by the rock and earth subsiding into the mud. Dumping of spoil continues, however, because the breakwater, although stable, is not yet completed to its full width. Cranes for the new steel pier are in process of erection; and the new concrete wharf, covered throughout, is being used for general cargo. Little remains of the old village of Balboa; for steam-shovels have levelled the site for the railroad and highway which are being run through it parallel to the dry dock . . .
>
> The dredging fleet is stretched out along a distance of $2\frac{1}{2}$ miles, from the steel pier to the dyke which separates the entrance work from that at Miraflores locks. The old ladder-dredge *Mole*, under the command of the master who has been dredging in the Pacific entrance for twenty-five years, is scraping hard rock from the bottom of the canal, forty-five feet below mean tide. The rock must first be broken by blasting, and nearby the drill-barge *Teredo* is hard at work, making holes in the rock bottom for the charges of dynamite. The *Vulcan* also works here, raising its steel ram to a height of some ten feet and letting it drop on the rock. This hammering is repeated upon one spot until the ram reaches the desired depth of forty-five feet below mean tide; then the *Vulcan* moves on—a plan on board showing the area to be covered from hour to hour.
>
> The dipper-dredge *Cardenas* is at work on the channel opposite the new concrete wharf. It is too light for effective work at a great depth, but its output is still sufficient to justify its retention in service.

At the end of the channel, with its nose touching the dyke [that guards] Miraflores lock, the new ladder-dredge *Corozal* is digging earth and rock which have not been blasted. It has been at work since last April, and its buckets—though none has required renewal—show the effects of hard service. It digs out both earth and rock without ceasing, although some of the ledges struck at the greatest depth make the engines turn slowly, while the whole ship quivers with the effort. Digging is carried out at all stages of the tide twenty-four hours a day, six days a week; and the output in heavy clay and sandstone interspersed with strata of rock is as much as 150,000 cubic yards a month.

The seagoing suction-dredge *Culebra* is also at work in the channel, clearing mud and silt from the rocky bottom of the canal. While a pipeline suction-dredge has been specially brought from Gatun Dam and re-erected at Balboa, and is pumping mud and silt from the site of the new terminal docks and depositing it onto the nearby flats.

Dredging continued until August 1913, by which time the approach-channel had been cleared to its full width and depth from the forty-five foot tide contour right up to the dyke which held the water back from Miraflores lock.

On August 31st work on the seaward face of the lock was also completed, and the dyke was blasted open by 37,000 pounds of dynamite—the size of the charge being yet another indication of the vast scale on which construction was planned and carried out. The sea poured in; within an hour the rush of water had scoured out an opening 300 feet wide; and by dawn on September 2nd a broad channel of navigable water lay motionless between sea and lock. After five years of patient excavation the Pacific approach-channel was complete.

(2) *Construction of Locks, Dams and Guide Walls at Miraflores and Pedro Miguel.*

The Pacific locks consist of two quite separate structures divided by a small, man-made lake.

The upper lock is at Pedro Miguel, close to the end of the Culebra Cut, at a spot where the hills of the continental divide begin their slope to the Pacific. Since the lock is situated at the end of a long and narrow cutting, it was thought that the emptying and filling of it might create surges which would endanger shipping; the canal was therefore widened from 300 feet to 600—the first of a host of niggling modifications brought about by the split-level design of the locks.

Pedro Miguel itself is connected to the near-by hills by a core wall to the east and a dam to the west. The former is unremarkable; but the latter is a massive structure, 1,400 feet in length, with slopes of 1 in 8; it was comparatively simple to build, except where a stratum of gravel, lying in the old bed of the Rio Grande, had to be dug out of its foundations and replaced by impervious clay.

Miraflores Lake has a surface elevation of fifty-five feet above sea-level and a surface area of only 1.6 square miles. The lake is so small in fact that in the dry season the loss of water due to lockages and evaporation is less than the inflow from the streams which empty into it, while in the wet season there is a surplus of rain water which has to be siphoned away. In the former case, water is let in from Gatun Lake; while in the latter it is discharged through a spillway in the dam connecting the Miraflores locks to the adjacent hillside. This spillway carries the water away via the Rio Grande diversion channel for one and three-quarter miles, then, enters the old bed of the river which it follows to the sea.

The locks at Miraflores consist of two tiers, one immediately above the other. The lower pair are not provided with the usual dividing gate on account of tidal variations in the level of the approach channel. The locks are connected to the hills in the west by a dam consisting of two rock ridges filled hydraulically with 1,750,000 cubic yards of waste, and to the hills in the east by a concrete wall, 500 feet long, with the spillway close to its centre.

The construction of these locks and their ancillaries posed no great technical problem. Williamson's only worry in fact was how to complete the necessary work as cheaply as possible within the allotted time. Excavation was never difficult—except perhaps in the case of the lower lock at Miraflores where the soil had to be sluiced away by hydraulic jet. The concrete work, however, called for a vast amount of placing in a short time and a restricted space; and it was here that Williamson proved both his administrative and technical skill. For the plant which he devised for producing and placing the two and a half million cubic yards of concrete which went into the locks was a model of efficiency—"by far the most advanced apparatus of its kind that has been used anywhere in the world". As regards production, it consisted of a stone-quarrying plant, a sand-dredging plant, and transportation and storage equipment; as regards handling there were berm-cranes for mixing and chamber-dredges for placing.

Stone was quarried at Ancon hill, a few miles inland from Panama. Ancon was chosen rather than Cocoli, Corozal or Sosa partly on account of its better quality stone, and partly because its quarries

Figure 31. The floor and gates at Pedro Miguel

were open and easy to work. A quarry-floor and crusher-shed were constructed on the south-west slopes of the hill at an elevation of 175 feet—test borings having indicated that two million cubic yards of stone could be quarried between this height and 400 feet. The stone was first pierced by air-driven well- and tripod-drills, and blasted with charges of forty-five per cent dynamite. It was then hauled by means of a Lidgerwood unloader onto the quarry floor. Here it was fed to the crushing plant: one No. 12 McCully gyratory crusher, and four No. 6 McCullys; the former reducing the blocks to five-inch diameter or less, and the latter passing it through a screen and reducing it still further. The product, pulverised to the semblance of powder, was finally carried off via a moving belt to the storage bins. These bins held 1,750 cubic yards of crushed stone, which was loaded by gravity into trains through twelve hand-operated chutes in the floor. It says much for the efficiency of this plant that not once in four years' continuous work was the concreting held up because of shortage of stone.

Sand from Chamé Point was stored in a special unloading dock in Balboa. This dock was of wood, with elevated storage bins designed to hold 2,600 cubic yards of sand. There were three bins, and three unloading cranes. The latter operated on runways, their hoisting, trolleying and bridging movements being actuated by direct-current motors, with an air compressor controlling the brakes; they were manoeuvred from a cabin high up in the tower, so that the operator had his clam-shell bucket in constant view. Between 1910 and 1914 the Balboa unloading dock handled over two million cubic yards of sand; and, as was the case with crushed stone, there was never so much as an hour's delay in supplying whatever quantity was needed.

Sand, stone and other building material was delivered to the lock sites by rail: not by the Panama Railroad, but by a special track laid by the Pacific Division Transportation Department. This track extended virtually the whole length of the division from Balboa to Pedro Miguel, with dump sites, sidings and storage yards at strategic points. It ran parallel to the Panama Railroad, about half a mile to the west, and the two lines were connected at Pedro Miguel, Miraflores, Corozal and Balboa, so that the blocking of any section need never interfere with the transport of material and supplies. The two lines, in fact, using the same gauge and rolling-stock, were virtually interchangeable; and here again there was hardly a single serious delay in five years of continuous operation.

Once it arrived at the lock-site, the material for concreting was mixed by berm-crane and placed by chamber-crane.

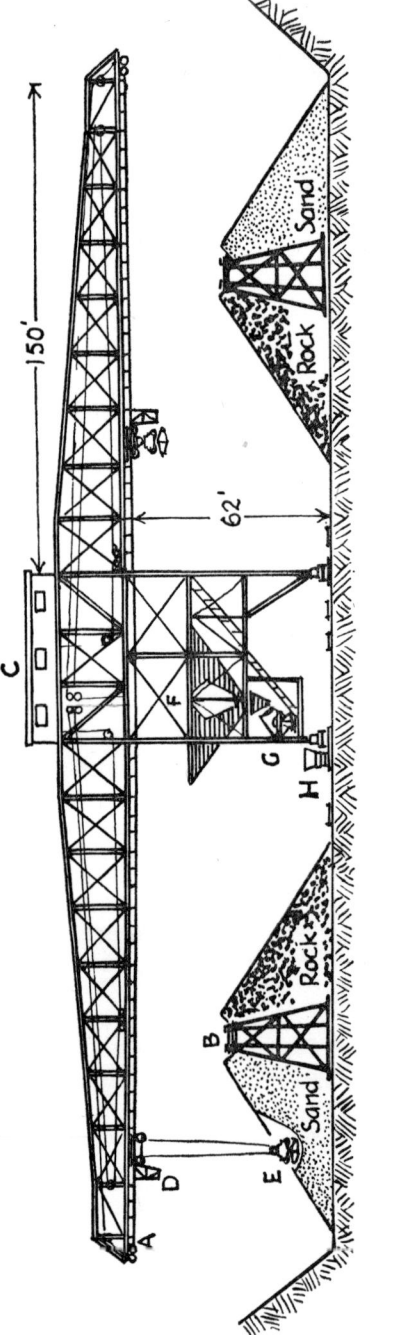

A Travelling trolley
B Storage trestle for rack and sand
C Machinery house containing electrical operating apparatus
D Operator's cab
E 2½ cu yd Hewlett excavating bucket
F Bins for sand and rock
G Two 2-cu yd concrete mixers
H Small flat-cars for transferring buckets of concrete from berm to chamber-cranes

Figure 32. Berm-crane at Pedro Miguel

The berm-cranes were massive structures of steel, each weighing 470 tons (see Figure 32 opposite). The *Canal Record* gives us details.

The construction plant consists of four berm-cranes and four chamber-cranes manufactured by the Wellman-Seaver-Morgan Company of Cleveland.

The berm-cranes are so-called because they are designed to travel on tracks located on berms which run outside of and parallel to the lock walls . . . They are of the balanced cantilever type, and the towers which support the arms are forty feet by fifty feet at base and sixty-two feet high. The truss in the upper part of the tower supports both the operating machinery and the underhung trolley-tracks for conveying sand and crushed rock. There are two trolleys to each crane, and each trolley carries a 2½-yard bucket which digs out sand and rock from the storage piles along either side of the forebay, beneath the outer ends of the cantilever arms. Each trolley has the capacity to deliver fifty yards of sand and 100 yards of rock to the bins per hour. There are four of these bins in each tower, two for sand and two for crushed rock. Beneath them is a housed-in platform where the bags of cement are emptied into the hoppers. Hoppers are located immediately below the cement room, and each contains three compartments—for sand, rock and cement respectively—each with its own chute. These chutes are provided with gates: the gates to the cement and sand chutes being operated by a wheel, and the gate to the rock chute by a lever. Operators on the platform can control the discharge from the hoppers, and also the gates, by compressed air; while water is fed to the mixers from automatic measuring tanks. [These mixers were equipped with an electric recording device which showed by means of a graph the proportions used and the time taken to mix and discharge them—which may sound simple today, but was a technically brilliant innovation in the early 1900s.] The motive power for all machinery is supplied by seven Westinghouse 500-volt d.c. motors . . . And the cranes can be moved by steel ropes so as to give 700 feet of lateral travel.

The concrete, when mixed and ready for placing, left the berm-cranes in specially-built flat-cars which were shunted one after another in endless succession onto track laid along the bottom of the excavated lock pits. Here it was taken over by the chamber-cranes (see Figure 33 on page 242), so-called because they were situated in the lock chambers.

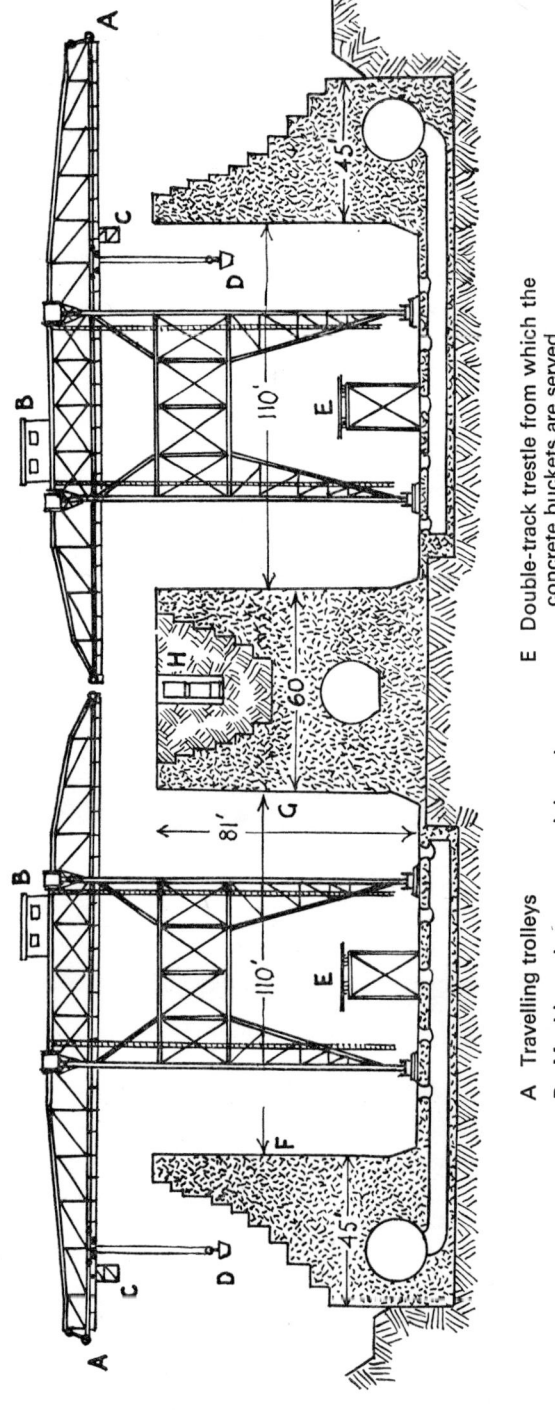

A Travelling trolleys
B Machinery houses containing electrical operating apparatus
C Operators' cabs
D 2-cubic yard bucket for placing concrete
E Double-track trestle from which the concrete buckets are served
F Side walls of locks, showing side wall and floor culverts
G Centre wall and centre wall culvert
H Operating tunnel

Figure 33.   Chamber-cranes at Miraflores

There were two of these cranes at Miraflores and two at Pedro Miguel; they were used not only for placing concrete but also for handling the steel and wooden forms and other items of equipment which had to be swung into position; and since their octopus-arms could reach to any corner of the site, they provided the same sort of "sky-hook" as the cableways at Gatun. Williamson describes them as follows:

> Each crane weighed about ninety-five tons, and was mounted on four heavy freight-car trucks for running on two parallel five-foot tracks extending the full length of the lock floors. The towers were fifty-six feet by forty feet (at base) with bracing designed to give ample clearance over the inclined trestles connecting the upper and lower lock chambers; each tower supported cantilever arms $53\frac{1}{2}$ and $81\frac{1}{2}$ feet long, which extended over the middle and side walls of the locks. The trolley (from which was suspended the buckets for placing concrete) thus operated over a continuous runway 191 feet long ($81\frac{1}{2}$ feet plus $53\frac{1}{2}$ feet plus 56 feet—the width of the tower) suspended from the cantilever trusses; and all movements, including the manipulation of the bottom-dump concrete-buckets, was controlled by an operator in the cage attached to the trolley. Motors of 47, 21 and 15 h.p. were located in a house on top of the tower, for hoisting, trolleying and traversing respectively. Traversing was controlled by a stationary switch on the tower frame, within reach of the operator when his cage was in a certain position only, the object being to prevent traversing simultaneously with other movements and so avoid torsional stresses.

These machines placed concrete with a speed and precision hitherto undreamed of in civil or military engineering: *vide* the *Canal Record:* "The four chamber-cranes are designed to pick up the buckets, deliver them to the lock walls, dump their contents and return them emptied to the cars at a combined average rate of 320 cubic yards of concrete an hour."

It is not surprising that, with such efficient plant, work at Pedro Miguel and Miraflores proceeded smoothly—once it got under way. The delay in siting the locks did, however, mean that little construction was carried out prior to 1909.

At Pedro Miguel excavation started in December, 1908 and was virtually completed within the year, more than a million cubic yards of spoil being removed from the site at a cost of eighty cents a yard. The excavated material was part soil, part rock, the former being dumped in the near-by west dam, and the latter being carried by rail to the Naos Island breakwater. The most difficult parts of the work were the final levelling, and the preparing of the culverts. This had to be carried out largely by hand through faulted trap rock, and special care needed to be taken with blasting, because concrete-laying on the adjacent guide walls was already under way; also the base of the lock-site was well beneath the drainage level, and pumps had to be constantly in use.

Since the sides of the lock-pits were high and unstable, the berm-cranes were moved into position only in the forebay or approaches to the locks. This forebay was lined on either side with huge wooden storage troughs, twenty-eight feet high and 800 feet long, which held respectively 45,000 cubic yards of sand and 55,000 cubic yards of rock. When the berm-cranes had taken material from these troughs and done their mixing, the aggregate was passed into a concrete bucket. These buckets were conveyed from berm-crane to chamber-crane via a double-track railroad, specially laid with seventy-pound steel rails to ensure quick and safe transportation. The rolling-stock consisted of twelve Porter locomotives and twenty-four flat-cars, and before long the following technique was perfected. A car, carrying two empty buckets, would be halted beneath a berm-crane; the buckets would be filled simultaneously from the crane's two discharge spouts, and the car would then proceed to the locks where it would stop under the first of the chamber-cranes; this crane would pick up one of the full buckets (soon to be poured into the appropriate form in the lock wall) and replace it with an empty one; the car would then move on to the second chamber-crane where the procedure would be repeated; finally the flat-car, with its two buckets empty, would return to the berm-crane.

So the concreting went on, with neither let nor hindrance. There was nothing spectacular about the work, no records to be broken, no hardships to be endured; simply the grinding away of an efficient machine. And the quantities placed were, according to the standard of the time, astronomic:

Year	Cubic Yards of Concrete laid at Pedro Miguel
1910	166,869
1911	498,187
1912	182,870
1913	58,162
1914	1,087
Total:	907,175 cubic yards

And while the walls of the lock rose foot by methodical foot, work was pushed forward on the adjoining dams.

These were commonplace structures. The dam to the west, in fact, was little more than a dump, and would never have been built if the site had not been earmarked by Williamson as the ideal site for disposing of spoil, which was tipped onto it in thin layers, wet down, compacted, and left in its natural state. This dam now contains nearly 700,000 cubic yards of spoil, yet it fits so perfectly into the surroundings that few people today realise it is not a natural spur of the hill. The dam to the east was also something of a luxury, for the ground here is well above water-level. There was, however, a minimal risk of seepage, and to obviate this Williamson designed and built a core wall, founded on rock, containing 1,500 cubic yards of concrete. Both these structures were completed by the end of 1913.

At Miraflores, work was complicated by the fact that the site was low-lying, and crossed by the valleys of the Cocoli and Rio Grande. The first task therefore was to divert these rivers and protect the site with embankments. As soon as this had been done (early in 1908) work was started on excavating pits for the locks. Conditions were more difficult than at Pedro Miguel, partly because of the complex nature of the soil and partly because the work was below sea-level. Williamson experimented with new techniques—such as excavation by hydraulic jet—and these, by and large, were successful. Nevertheless it was spring 1911 before the pits were dug and the berm- and chamber-cranes could be moved into position. Then it was the same story as at Pedro Miguel: year after year of placing yard after yard of concrete. Statistics tell virtually the whole story:

Year	Cubic Yards of Concrete Laid at Miraflores
1910	1,630
1911	272,933
1912	751,540
1913	450,792
1914	2,844
Total:	1,479,739 cubic yards

It will be seen from these figures that the concreting at Miraflores was on an even larger scale than at Pedro Miguel. It is hardly surprising, therefore, that the locks here were among the last items to be completed in the canal, their gates and operating machinery not being installed until the summer of 1913.

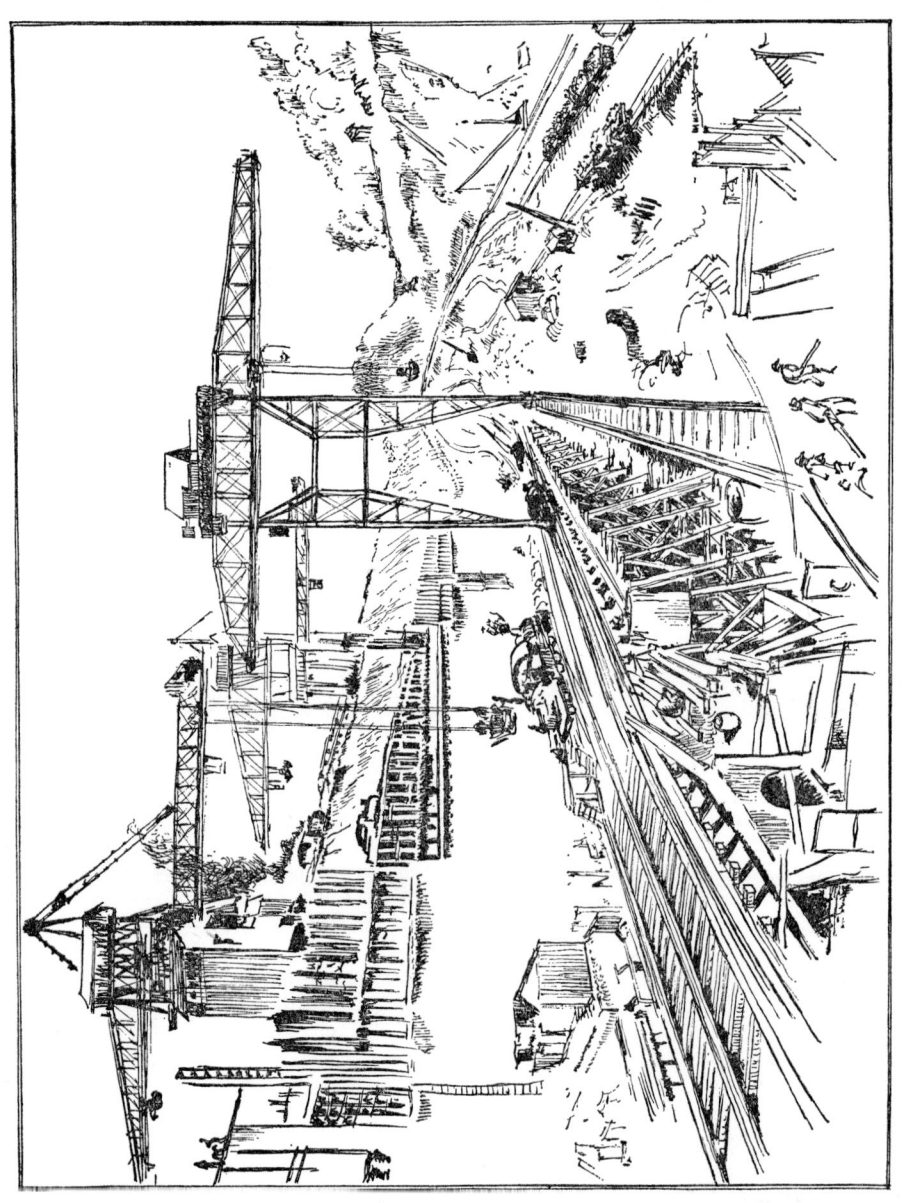

Figure 34. The walls at Miraflores

The installation of these gates was Williamson's final task.

The twelve lock chambers in the Panama canal are virtually identical: eighty-one feet high, 110 feet wide and 600 feet long. They were, at the time of their construction, by far the largest of their kind in the world, and their size gave rise to two problems: how to devise gates which were not inordinately heavy, and how to regulate the flow of water so that lockages didn't take too long.

The gates were masterpieces of skilled design and careful construction: *vide* the *Canal Record*.

> The gate leaves are shells of structural steel covered with a sheath of steel riveted to the girder framework. They are sixty-five feet long, seven feet thick and from forty-seven to eighty-two feet high. Each leaf is divided horizontally into two separate compartments. The lower compartment is watertight, and this makes the leaf so buoyant that it will practically float on the water, thus relieving stress on the bearings by which it is hinged to the wall. This watertight compartment is subdivided vertically into three sections, each independently sealed off, so that should the shell be broken or begin to leak, only one section would be affected. An air shaft and case twenty-six inches in diameter runs from the bottom compartment up to the top of the gate, and this also is watertight where it passes through the upper half of the leaf. After placing the steel plates on the frame, the rivets are driven in with care, the edges of the plates are caulked, and inspectors examine each portion of the work. Six million rivets are required in the lock gates, and every one of them is sedulously inspected before the contractor is paid . . . Within the great steel shell, made intensely hot by exposure to the sun, inspectors make their way examining and testing each rivet, and marking those that are defective. Sometimes the head has been driven too far into the steel, sometimes it is off-centre, sometimes it may be loose or broken. All imperfect rivets are rejected, cut out and replaced. Watertightness is determined by filling the gate leaves with water: a severe test in as much as the leaves were built to withstand pressure from without rather than from within. Yet so well has the work been done that hardly a rivet weeps. This is most surprising to the chief inspector who has had many years' experience in ship building where rivets in the hulls usually exhibit a far greater propensity to weep.

By the end of 1913 all thirty leaves at Miraflores and all forty at Pedro Miguel had been safely erected, and work was under way on installing equipment to control the inflow and outflow of water.

The emptying and filling of the locks is achieved through circular openings in the chamber floor roughly four feet in diameter. There are 105 of these openings in each lock, arranged in five rows of twenty-one. Each row of five communicates to a cross-tunnel under the floor, and half of these cross-tunnels lead to a culvert running the length of the inner wall (see Figure 35 opposite). The ends of these culverts open into either lake or approach-channel, so that water can be discharged or inducted at any time. It is thus possible to equalise the water-level in any two adjoining locks by leaving the cross-tunnels open to the central culvert; and this effects a considerable saving in water.

All locking machinery is controlled by electricity. There are 114 rising-stem valves to be opened and shut, 120 cylindrical valves and ninety-two leaves; there are also twenty-four water-level indicators. All this machinery is equipped with remote control and position indicators, which show on a control switchboard the exact position of every gate and valve. There are also a number of local and hand controls for use in emergency. This equipment was, before it was installed, put through the most exhaustive tests; the highest standards were insisted on; and indeed in sixty years of operation there has been hardly a single electrical failure—which helps to explain the canal's unique safety record.

This safety record, however, is also due in part to the extremely sensible arrangements for towing: arrangements which have altered little since they were first laid down in 1913.

The percentage of accidents when passing a vessel through locks is usually small, and about ninety per cent of those which do occur are due to failure in signals between the ship's bridge and engine-room. This possibility was eliminated at Panama where vessels never move into a lock under their own power, but come to a halt at the approach wall; from then on their movement is controlled by lock operators. Should a vessel fail to halt, collision with the lock gate is prevented by a three-inch chain which stretches from one side of the approach wall to the other; this chain is connected to hydraulic cylinders built into the wall, and its resistance is sufficient to stop a 10,000-ton vessel moving at four knots in seventy feet. There is also a guard or safety gate, and, as a final precaution, an emergency bulk which can be lowered from a turntable at the side of the lock.

Once a vessel is halted, it has two lines attached to its bow and two to its stern; it is then towed through the canal by four electric locomotives, very much as from time immemorial mules and oxen have towed barges through the waterways of the world.

These locomotives are an essential part of the canal operating

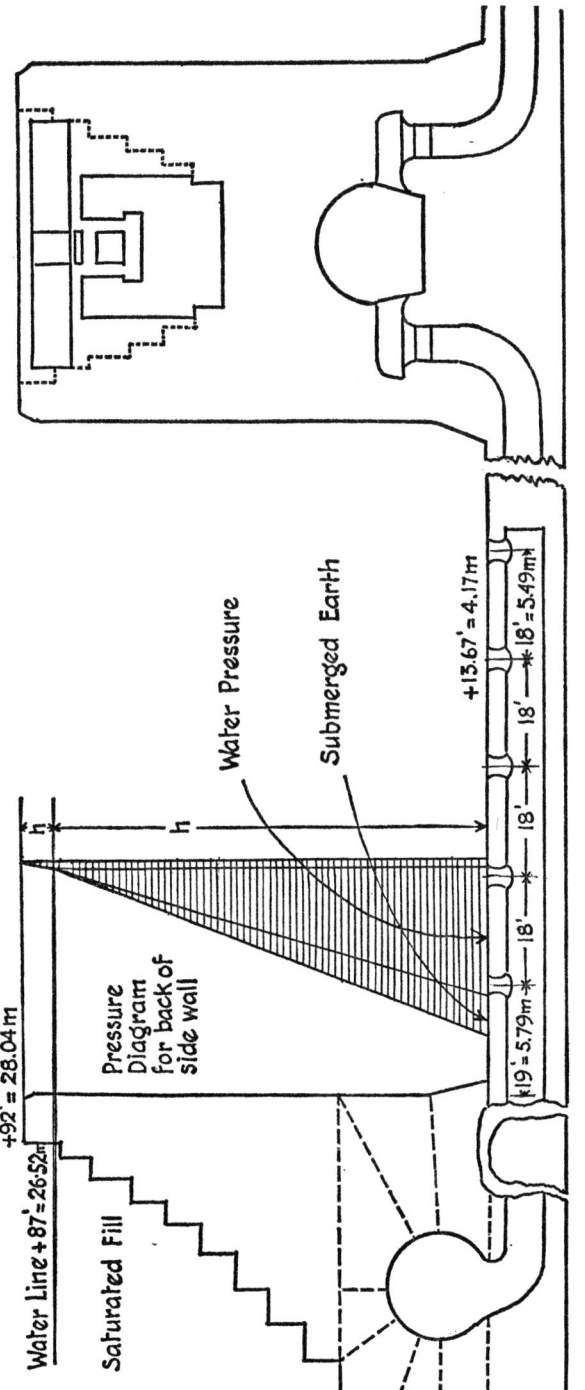

Figure 35. Cross-section of the culvert system for filling and emptying the locks

machinery. Few books give them a mention, but the *Canal Record* has preserved their statistics:

> Specifications and plans for the locomotives which will tow ships through the locks have been sent to Washington, so that bids may be made for the forty locomotives which will be required for the locks at Gatun, Pedro Miguel and Miraflores. The system of towing outlined in these specifications is the invention of Edward Schildhauer of the Canal engineering staff, and patent has been applied for . . . This system provides for the passing through the locks of a ship at the rate of two miles an hour, the vessel being held steady between four lines of taut hawsers. A ship will come to a full stop in the forebay of the lock, where four hawsers will be attached to it, two forward and two aft. At their other ends, these hawsers will be attached to the windlasses of four towing locomotives operating on the lock walls, two forward towing and the two aft holding the vessel steady. These locomotives will run on the level, excepting where they pass from one lock to another . . . There will be two systems of tracks, one for towing, and the other for the return of the locomotives when not towing. The tracks will be of the five-foot Panama railroad gauge, laid with ninety-pound Bessemer steel rail on Carnegie ties, each tie being anchored into the concrete by a bolt on the side farthest from the lock chamber. The towing track will have a centre rack, which the locomotive will always operate on . . .
>
> Each locomotive will consist of three parts [see Figure 36 opposite]: two tractors, and between them a windlass. The windlass will not be mounted on a truck, but will be supported by two arms resting on bearings immediately over the rear wheels of the tractors. The windlass is joined to the tractors by a drawbar and trunnion which is, in effect, a universal joint and permits free movement of the parts. The tractors will be alike in every particular, each consisting of a four-wheel truck upon which are mounted motor and control apparatus. When towing, motion is communicated from motor to rock pinions by means of a system of gear reduction in which there are no clutches. There is no means of disconnecting the train of gears, and, as a result, the rack pinions are in motion only when the motors are. A soleroid brake, which closes on the wheels whenever the current is cut off, provides against accident in case the current should fail while the locomotive is on one of the inclines.
>
> The electrical equipment consists of one motor for each tractor. Alternating current will be used, so that synchronous speed can

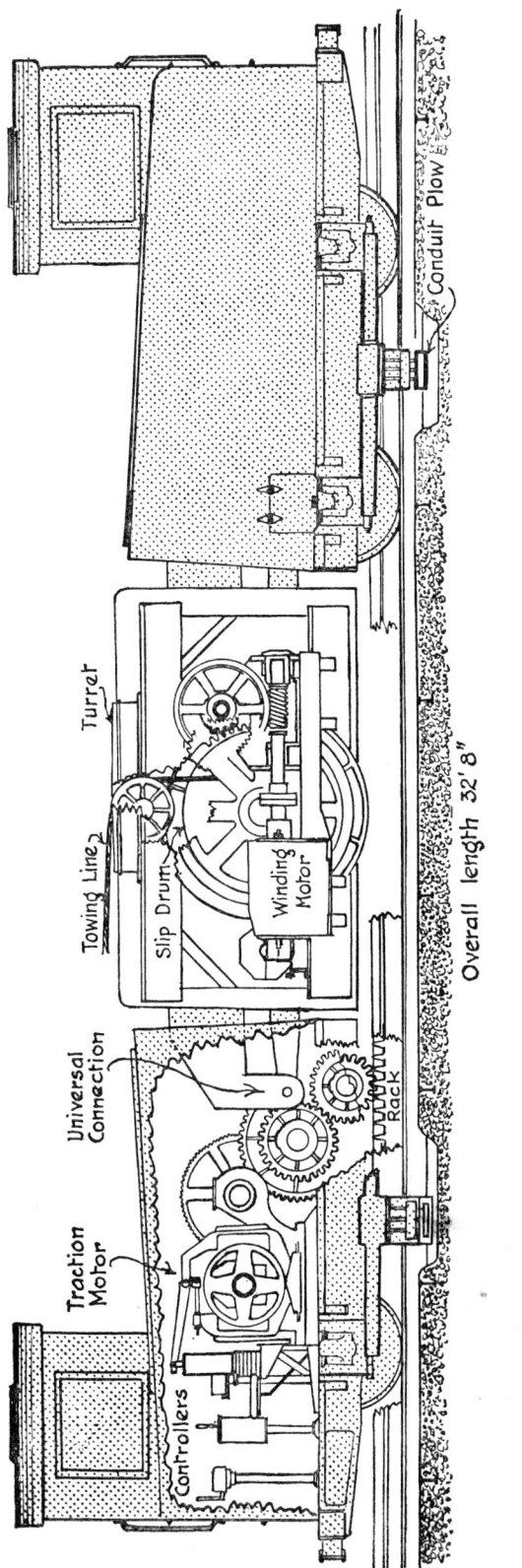

Figure 36. Electric towing locomotive

be maintained on all locomotives in a tow. The windlass motor will have a full-speed torque of 120 pounds at one foot radius, will be capable of fifty per cent greater torque for one minute, and will have a full load speed of 630 revolutions per minute. The towing line will be of plow-steel wire, composed of six strands of thirty-seven wires each, with a hemp centre; it will have a tensile strength of 225,000 pounds per square inch and a breaking strain of 70,000 pounds.

The installation of this equipment in 1913 marked the virtual end of construction.

A few weeks after the final tie was bolted in place, there occurred the last spectacular operation in Williamson's division—the forming of Miraflores Lake. This was started on October 1st, by the closing of the spillway through which, up to now, the Rio Grande and the Rio Cocoli had been escaping to the sea. The water rose quickly—far more quickly than at Gatun, for the lake was barely one-hundredth the size—and by mid-December a broad sheet of navigable water, fifty-five feet above sea-level, stretched between the walls of Miraflores and Pedro Miguel. The approach channel had been opened up a couple of months earlier; so by the end of 1913 the work of the Pacific Division had been completed—on schedule and according to plan.

14

THE LAND DIVIDED

The canal was formally opened in August, 1914, when the S.S. *Ancon* made the passage from Cristobal to Balboa in a little over nine hours. The *Ancon*, however, was by no means the first vessel to cross from sea to sea. This honour belonged to a canoe, paddled, appropriately enough, by Gorgas.

It was in the summer of 1912 that Gorgas, Le Prince and Colonel Mason, the three inseparables of the Sanitary Commission, set out from the Pacific end of the canal. Their journey could not be made entirely by water, since the locks at Miraflores and Pedro Miguel were still being built, and the canoe at these points had to be carried for several hundred yards over dry land. Once in the Culebra Cut, however, their course was virtually unobstructed.

The journey was not without incident. Le Prince wrote:

> [After lifting] our canoe up the steep sides of the Cut, we re-embarked at the Obispo Diversion Channel. We were dripping with perspiration by now, but enjoying [ourselves] immensely; and soon we reached some deep pools and got into the water to cool off. We then went down the Chagres River towards Bohio, now under Gatun Lake. Here a surprise awaited us. The river was in flood, and the current very rapid. It was all we could do to steer clear of the boulders. After a while we saw a number of men waving their arms as if suggesting we turn back, but we were in the grip of a strong current, and too busy dodging obstructions to pay much attention to them. Suddenly there was a terrific crash, and rocks were flying in every direction. We realised then that the men had been trying to warn us that fuses were lit and a blast about to go off. Rocks, stones and dirt rained about us as we were swept at full speed down the channel. We had intended to follow the river bed, but the flood through a diversion cut suddenly caught our boat and whisked us through. It was a thrilling and exciting moment, but Gorgas simply remarked, 'A rather warm reception!' . . . When we reached Colon, friends asked us where we came from, and thought we were joking when we replied that we had made the trip from Pacific to Atlantic in a canoe. About two years later I was invited to see the first (so-called) boat go

through the canal, and was amused that the large concourse of people who lined the banks were under the impression that they were watching the first vessel to pass from one ocean to the other.

Without wishing to denigrate Le Prince, the passage of a 10,000-ton vessel was a more meaningful event than the passage (with portages) of a canoe; and it was the former, inevitably, which caught the eye of the world.

There was a rehearsal on August 3rd, when Goethals himself directed the transit of the *Cristobal*, a small ocean-going vessel owned by the Panama Railroad Company. Two hundred V.I.P.s had been invited to attend the rehearsal; and among them was Bunau-Varilla, now well past middle-age but flamboyant and ebullient as ever. As the *Cristobal* backed clear of the docks, the little Frenchman was handed a telegram. He crushed the paper in his hand, stepped clear of the crowd, and theatrical and madly patriotic to the last, gestured at the disappearing vessel: "Gentlemen," he declaimed, "the two consuming ambitions of my life are fulfilled on the same day. The first, to see an ocean liner sail through the Panama canal: the second, to see France and Germany at war."

The passage of the *Cristobal* was far from plain sailing. At the end of the Atlantic approach-channel she was slewed off-course by currents caused by the mingling of salt and fresh water; as she was drawn through the upper lock at Gatun one of the towing locomotives burnt out its motor; while at Pedro Miguel a cable parted, and she all but rammed the wall of the lock. Goethals realised, only just in time, that the Army engineers in charge of the locks were landlubbers, altogether unqualified to supervise the passage of ocean-going ships. So he handed over, reluctantly, to the Navy.

It was the chance Captain Rodman had been waiting for. For more than a year this outspoken marine superintendent had advocated the forming of a special and exclusively naval corps to ensure the safe transit of vessels; and now that he was at last put in command he ordered that "qualified pilots should henceforth take charge of the towing and handling of every vessel which enters the canal". These pilots should, he decreed, board a vessel before she reached the first of the approach walls, and should under no circumstances leave her until she was in open water. He also prohibited mooring to the sides of the canal; "every vessel," he said, "should make the passage from ocean to ocean without touching a single wall."

Rodman's pilots were not, of course, fully trained by the time the *Ancon* made her inaugural voyage; but they had sufficient know-how to get the vessel through; and the unique safety record of the canal, from that day to this, is ample justification of Goethals' decision to give control of lockage to the Navy.

It was overcast and oppressive as early on Saturday, August 15th the *Ancon* steamed slowly into the Atlantic entrance of the canal. Aboard her were the Secretary of War, the President of the Republic of Panama and several hundred V.I.P.s. Their transit was uneventful—there being according to the prosaic *Canal Record*, "no unscheduled delays"—and nine hours forty minutes later the *Ancon* nosed out through the end of the dredged channel in Panama Bay, three miles beyond the Pacific seaboard. It was a historic moment: the culmination of four centuries of thought and thirty-five years of dedicated and backbreaking work. But there was little pomp and circumstance. For the outbreak of the First World War had stolen Goethals' thunder. A few people waved from the banks. A few flags and a few self-conscious cheers; and the Panama was open.

And open it has remained, to the ships of every nation, from that day to this: a tribute not only to the technical competence with which it was built, but also the idealistic spirit in which it was conceived.

Indeed in a changing world the Panama canal has, in sixty years, changed surprisingly little. Here and there it has been made a little wider or a little deeper; but the waterway which tens of thousands of travellers pass through today is basically the same as the waterway that de Lépinay dreamed of, Stevens planned and Goethals built: a bridge of water, dividing a continent, uniting the world—indeed the seal of the Canal Zone has as its motto the words, "The Land Divided, the World United."

Certainly the *Ancon*'s passengers, if any of them are still alive, would find few differences between their voyage of 1914 and a voyage through the canal today. Approaching from the Caribbean, they would see first the same green mountains, veiled in thunderheads, rising out of the same mist-encompassed shore. The breakwaters they pass through at the entrance to Limon Bay would be the same great barriers, albeit heavily revetted, which Sibert built of Porto Bello rock and Sosa stone. Now, as then, they would catch only a fleeting glimpse of the French canal—where half-way down the Atlantic approach-channel a deserted backwater meanders off, on one side to the suburbs of Cristobal, on the other to lose its way in jungle lush and green as any that faced Balboa. Men sweated, suffered and died to build the French canal; but no one uses it today, except perhaps for a handful of small boys fishing from home-made rafts, or the occasional party of American soldiers exploring in a canoe. David Howarth evokes its nostalgic charm:

The jungle leans out over both its banks. Trees have fallen into it, and nobody has any reason to dredge them out. Flocks of huge blue butterflies drift along it. It is as quiet and still and empty as any slow stretch of a Darien river a hundred miles from anywhere. But suddenly, now and again, a ship's siren bellows and frightens the birds, and one may catch sight of a monstrous disembodied funnel or a mast incongruously passing beyond the tops of the trees. The canal that succeeded, is close to the one that failed.

Both end abruptly at the spot where Stevens's huge man-made dam blocks the valley of the Chagres.

The dam is on a historic site: at the spot where the gold-rush prospectors of 1849 changed from train to canoe. But the passengers of the *Ancon* and the travellers of today can see no sign of railroad, river or indeed of dam; for so massive and gently sloped is the artificial barrier that it blends naturally into the surrounding hills. Only the unusually observant will notice, away to the west, the spillway, where surplus water from the high-level lake is funnelled away, via the old bed of the River Chagres, to the sea.

So to the broad waters of Gatun Lake: the 164 square miles which absorb and harness the mighty river whose floods de Lesseps was never able to contain. It is hard to realise the lake is man-made. It is dotted with islands, fringed with trees, and alive with reptiles, birds and fish. One could sail it for a week and see no trace of man—except perhaps for the occasional stretch of railroad skirting the shore, or, above Las Cruces, the paving stones of the old Spanish trail, leading up from water to jungle.

At its southern extremity the lake, hemmed in by hills, narrows to a tortuous channel. And here river and canal part company: the former slanting away into the Attos de Maria Enrique, the latter curving south to the Culebra Cut. This again is historic ground: the isthmus's redoubt, where Bunau-Varilla's "corps of specially dedicated men" laboured in vain, Wallace's dump-cars were derailed by the thousand, and Gaillard laboured and died. Its slopes are uneven today: in some places, where the rock is hard, steep and barren; in others, where the mud again and again came sloughing down like a slow-moving glacier to bury machinery and track, gentle and green with vegetation. It still looks a big excavation, even with the water in it eighty-five feet above sea-level; and one can visualise how gargantuan the cut would have had to be before de Lesseps' dream of a canal at sea-level could have been realised.

Beyond the cut, to quote David Howarth:

the canal descends by locks to what was [once] the valley of the Rio Grande. From the canal, it is hardly recognisable today as a Darien valley. The jungle and the old savannah lands have disappeared: [and in their place] are suburbs, housing estates, an airfield, barracks, mown lawns and ornamental gardens, all with the confident masculine neatness of a military installation.

But civilisation in the Zone is still no more than a veneer that exists on sufferance. Within a few hundred yards of Gatun Lake, indeed in places within a few hundred yards of the canal itself, jungle, lush and formidable as any that faced the conquistadors still holds sway.

Who were the men who did most to tame this jungle, divide the continent, and unite the two greatest oceans of the world?

If asked to name the dozen figures who contributed most to building the canal, I would nominate in order of importance, de Lesseps, Stevens, Gorgas, de Lépinay, Theodore Roosevelt, Goethals, Bunau-Varilla, Cromwell, Wyse, Dingler, Jackson Smith and Sibert.

De Lesseps, at Panama, failed. And it may seem strange to give pride of place to a failure: any fool, it could be argued, can start something he isn't able to finish. Yet de Lesseps was the source from whom all subsequent endeavours and achievements flowed; his was the vision, energy and courage which launched the greatest attempt man has ever made to alter the physical configuration of the world he lives in; and his, too, was the idealistic conception of a canal "for the benefit of all mankind" which has persisted from that day to this. It is true that as an engineer he had serious deficiencies; it is true, too that he was over-confident and obstinate. But there was nothing petty about him. Even his faults were on a heroic scale. And in the final analysis he was defeated not by the isthmus, but by the machinations of politicians and financiers. When one thinks of the appalling difficulties he was faced with, the wonder is not that he failed but that he came so close as he did to success.

"John F. Stevens," wrote the Speaker of the House of Representatives in 1907, "will never get credit for the work he has done [at Panama]; or if he does, he will never get enough." It is time the record was righted. Stevens inherited chaos; he bequeathed homogeneity. He inherited discontent, he bequeathed *esprit de corps*. When he came to Panama, success was a chimera; when he left, it was assured. His contribution was threefold. Because of the strength and magnetism of his personality, he provided the working force with a leader they could respect and trust. Because of his expertise as an engineer, he provided a transportation system par excellence which was the key to success. And because of his sound common sense he was able to push through a workable overall plan—for a high-level canal with locks. Without him, the canal would never have been built.

William Crawford Gorgas was, perhaps, the most attractive personality associated with the canal. Humble, gentle and unstinting in his praise of others, he didn't at the time receive the recognition he deserved; for he was first ridiculed by the old men of the Army and Navy Commission, then belittled by Goethals. Late in his life, however, when his achievements were seen in perspective, he was showered with honours and awards from almost every country in the world. His last days in a London hospital epitomise both the sweetness of his character and the regard in which he was held. He had just been awarded the Order of Saint Michael and Saint George, but was too ill to attend the investiture. His wife was afraid he might be disappointed, but he replied, "No. Think how lucky I am to be here . . . I might have died at sea, or on the way to Africa, separated from you." A few days later he had an unexpected visitor. "If General Gorgas is too ill to come to the palace to see me," King George V is reputed to have said, "then I shall go to the hospital to see him." And there took place at Gorgas's bedside a simple but deeply moving ceremony. "General Gorgas," the King said, "it gives me very great pleasure to present you with the insignia of this Order; and believe me, I very sincerely appreciate the great work which you have done for humanity." A month later Gorgas died—and was given the almost unique honour of a state funeral in St. Paul's Cathedral—one of the few great men in history who was wholly and unequivocally good.

Adolphe Godin de Lépinay is unknown today outside France, and several books on Panama fail even to mention his name. Yet he was the prophet who cried in the wilderness; and after the biblical forty years his prophecy, with uncanny accuracy, was fulfilled. For the canal which was finally completed in 1916 was in every essential detail the canal which he advocated in 1879. Here is Duval's description of the original proposal he put to *Le Société de Géographie*:

> De Lépinay's concept was of unbelievable simplicity. He proposed to create a large lake on either side of the continental divide by erecting one dam across the Chagres River and another across the Rio Grande, as close to the seas as configuration of the land permitted. The water in each lake would be allowed to rise to the approximate level of eighty feet, the two lakes would be joined

by a channel across the hills of the divide, and on each side of the isthmus locks would be constructed [to raise and lower vessels] between the lakes and the sea level.

It would be hard to find a more concise description of the canal which the Americans eventually built. De Lépinay, in short, lacked only one of the prerequisites of greatness: luck. If he had had his due, his scheme would have been adopted in 1879, and he would be honoured today as the masterbuilder of a successful—and French—canal.

Theodore Roosevelt once told a press conference that he regarded the two most important events in his country's history as the Louisiana Purchase, and the building of the Panama canal; he believed wholeheartedly, he said, in his predecessor's dictum that "the policy of this country must be for a canal under *American* control". There was nothing reprehensible *per se* in Roosevelt's goal of a canal which was American-built and American-controlled. What was reprehensible was the means he stooped to in order to achieve this. For there is no doubting that—albeit deviously and passively—he fostered the secession of Panama from its parent state; and no doubting either that he took advantage of Bunau-Varilla's machinations to establish a suzerainty over the Canal Zone which has neither legal nor moral justification. His heavy wielding of the big stick is at the bottom of much of the ill-feeling which exists today between North and South America. Having said this, it is only fair to record that Roosevelt's other interventions in the affairs of the canal were invariably on the side of the angels, and that twice in particular he prevented a blunder which could have been disastrous—supporting Gorgas and his anti-mosquito campaign (against the advice of the Commission and Secretary Taft), and supporting Stevens and his campaign for a canal with locks (against the advice of the majority board); also his choice of Goethals as "Tsar over all" turned out to be something of an inspiration.

George Washington Goethals was not, on the face of it, an attractive personality. He lacked the magnetism of Stevens or the dedicated kindliness of Gorgas. It is tempting therefore to play down his contribution to the canal, pointing out that he merely reaped where other and better men had sowed. This, however, would be less than fair. For Goethals had two outstanding qualities: he was a superb administrator, and a forceful leader of men. For sheer day-to-day efficiency his management of the highly complex programme of construction could hardly be faulted; while he handled his labour force with the authority of a strict but fair-minded autocrat.

He was the right man in the right job at the right time. And all credit to him for seizing his opportunity.

Bunau-Varilla would be affronted to find his name so lowly placed in the roll of those who helped to build the canal; for nothing short of the premier position would have satisfied his ego. And indeed as regards sheer volume of work his contribution is unsurpassed; since for close on twenty-five years he devoted himself body and soul to the fulfilment of what he describes as "the most perfect flower of French genius". And if this, today, sounds too high-flown an epithet for a somewhat mundane stretch of water, it must be remembered that the canal, to Bunau-Varilla, was a sort of Grail: a desideratum for which he was willing to sacrifice everything: health, friends, legality, morality, the lot. Witness his description of the signing of his iniquitous treaty.

> Two strokes of a pen were sealing forever the Destiny of the Great Thought which had daunted Humanity for centuries . . . In an instant I beheld, focussed before my eyes, all those heroes, my comrades in the deadly battle, who fell in the struggle against Nature, a smile on their lips, happy to sacrifice their lives to this work which was to render still more dazzling the glory of French genius . . . I thought of the shameful league of all the passions, of all the hatreds, of all the jealousies, of all the cowardices, of all the ignorances, to crucify this great Idea, and with it all those who had hoped, through its realisation, to give France one more glorious page in the history of Humanity . . . I had fulfilled my mission, . . . I had safeguarded the work of French genius; I had served France.

The tragedy was that Bunau-Varilla (like Roosevelt) stooped to such nefarious means to achieve so commendable an end.

William Nelson Cromwell is one of those shadowy powers behind the throne whose influence is difficult to assess; but at a time when most people had written Panama off he, almost singlehanded, kept the flame of de Lesseps' dream alive. It has sometimes been insinuated that because he made a great deal of money out of the canal his championship of it was in some way suspect or even discreditable. This is nonsense. An astute lubricator of political wheels is as worthy of his hire as the engineer who designs a technically brilliant spillway or dam. And without Cromwell's machinations to advance Panama and retard Nicaragua, it is highly probable that the canal would not be where it is today.

Lucien Napoléon-Bonaparte Wyse is another shadowy figure. It was his feat in securing a concession from Colombia which transformed the canal project from pipe-dream to practical proposition; and if he had been as good a surveyor as he was a diplomat, his name today might be as revered as de Lesseps'. In the event, however, his sketchy and suspect survey got the project off to a contentious start; and as the difficulties which he had glossed over but his critics had warned of came one by one to roost, his reputation suffered an eclipse. His role, therefore, was never as prominent as he himself wished or posterity might have expected.

Jules Dingler was the epitome of the thousands of Frenchmen who sacrificed everything—comfort, wealth, health and eventually their lives—in pursuit of de Lesseps' dream. He was a man of upright character, a skilled engineer, a sound administrator, and he devoted himself wholeheartedly to the task he had been assigned. He failed. But his failure should not blind us to the heroic extent of his achievements. For, like Stevens a generation later, he brought order out of chaos; and during the two and a half years of his administration the French assault on the isthmus built up to what ought to have proved a triumphant climax. It was not Dingler's fault that his labour force was decimated by a scourge no one as yet knew the cause of, nor that he was forced by de Lesseps' obstinacy to work to plans for an impossible (sea-level) canal. He did all—and more—that could have been expected of any man. And his failure was a great deal more meritorious than many a so-called success.

Jackson Smith is unremembered today. Yet it was due to his fair-mindedness and administrative skill that tens of thousands of labourers were, for the better part of a decade, well fed and adequately housed. If "an army marches on its stomach", the same could be said of a construction gang; while a decent roof over one's head is a prerequisite of a decent day's work. "Square-foot" Smith provided these essentials quickly, cheaply and efficiently; he was a key figure in a key position, and he ill deserves the obscurity into which he has fallen.

William L. Sibert was Stevens's right-hand man and a technically brilliant engineer. It may seem invidious to select a single star from so distinguished a galaxy of designers; but Sibert was acknowledged by his contemporaries to be outstandingly brilliant; also he had to cope with both the most difficult technical problem (excavating the lower chamber at the end of the Atlantic approach-channel), and the most controversial (designing Gatun Dam). His inclusion, however, should be regarded as a tribute not to him alone, but also to the great multitude of engineers of many nationalities, who helped to complete what even today still ranks as perhaps the greatest feat of engineering in the history of the world.

Any list invites criticism; and if asked to add to mine, I would include the unfortunate Charles de Lesseps, for the help and support he gave his father; Theodore Shonts, for the expertise he brought to the affairs of the Panama Railroad; David Gaillard, for his unremitting struggle with the Culebra slides; and finally Henry L. Abbot for his skilled and invaluable research on the regimen of the Chagres.

Behind these key figures were the great multitude of unremembered labourers through whose efforts success, in the final analysis, was achieved. The American "gold" employees were rewarded at the time with good pay, service medals and widespread recognition. The "silver" employees, however—unskilled workers from the West Indies and southern Europe—have seldom been given their due. The isthmus was not an easy place to work in—hot, humid and enervating—labour, in those days, was not safeguarded by the mass of union regulations which are now taken for granted; and it is surprising that under the circumstances there was so little absenteeism and discontent. The reason seems to be that both the French and Americans were able to imbue their labour force with a quite remarkable *esprit de corps*, so that they really *cared* about the canal: witness Bunau-Varilla's account of the death of his successor Léon Boyer. "On the following day Boyer was seized with yellow fever. He died like a hero. In the midst of his agony he wrote, 'Do not abandon Panama'. It was the last word from the great engineer." Few Americans found it necessary to die for the canal. But they were quite prepared to work for it: nine, ten, sometimes twelve hours a day, in temperatures often up to 110 degrees Fahrenheit. They worked partly, of course, for money, and partly for the fringe benefits of better accommodation and food. But without doubt a large number of them put an extra "something" into their work, because they realised that what they were doing was both important and worthwhile.

For de Lesseps' dream of an oceanic Bosphorus whose waters would unite the nations of the world still lingered on; modified in detail and tainted by political expediency, but with its inherent altruism unchanged through the years. And when at last the land was finally divided, it was this altruism which was acclaimed in a world-wide paean of praise, epitomised by Stafford's "Hymn of Panama":

>Thou who didst give our hand the might
>   To hew the hemisphere in twain
>   And level for these waters bright
>   The mountains with the main:

> In freedom let the great ships go
>   On freedom's errand, sea to sea—
> The oceans rise, the hills bend low,
>   Servants of liberty.

It had taken almost exactly four hundred years for the dream of Alvaro de Saavedra to be realised.

EPILOGUE

RETURN TO DARIEN

Today, after more than fifty years' invaluable use, the Panama canal is too small. Its locks are 110 feet wide and 1,000 feet long—large enough, when built, to take any ships which seemed likely ever to exist, but not large enough now to take some 700 of the world's heaviest merchantmen: not large enough, either, to take big oil-tankers or the strategically important aircraft carriers of the U.S. Navy. So either the canal will have to be enlarged, or a new canal will have to be built.

In 1964 the President appointed yet another commission to study the problem, and all the old routes were surveyed again: Tehuantepec in Mexico, Senator Morgan's brain-child through Lake Nicaragua, the routes via San Blas, Caledonia Bay and the Atrato River, even Bunau-Varilla's scheme for dredging the existing canal down to sea-level was resurrected. The routes were the same. But the problem was different. For the new canal will almost certainly be excavated by nuclear explosion.

Whose homes will melt in the holocaust? Whose water and food will be irradiated beyond redemption?

Research on harnessing nuclear power for excavation began in the United States in 1957 under the Plowshare programme, run by Livermore Laboratory. By the early 1960s it had been established that a one-megaton bomb, exploded a little beneath ground-level, would, in alluvial soil, produce a crater 1,000 yards in diameter and 690 feet in depth; and to these figures was added an even more impressive statistic—"the cost of such excavation would be under three cents per cubic yard." Now nuclear explosives, even in megatons, are small enough in bulk to be lowered through boreholes drilled by a conventional oil-rig. A new canal could, in other words, be built simply and cheaply by running a temporary access road across the isthmus, sinking boreholes at suitable intervals, burying nuclear devices in them, and firing them in series, perhaps a dozen at a time. By calculating the depth and explosive-power of each device according to the height and nature of the ground, a sea-level canal could be roughly excavated with none of the blood, sweat and tears which, a hundred years earlier, turned de Lesseps' dream to a nightmare.

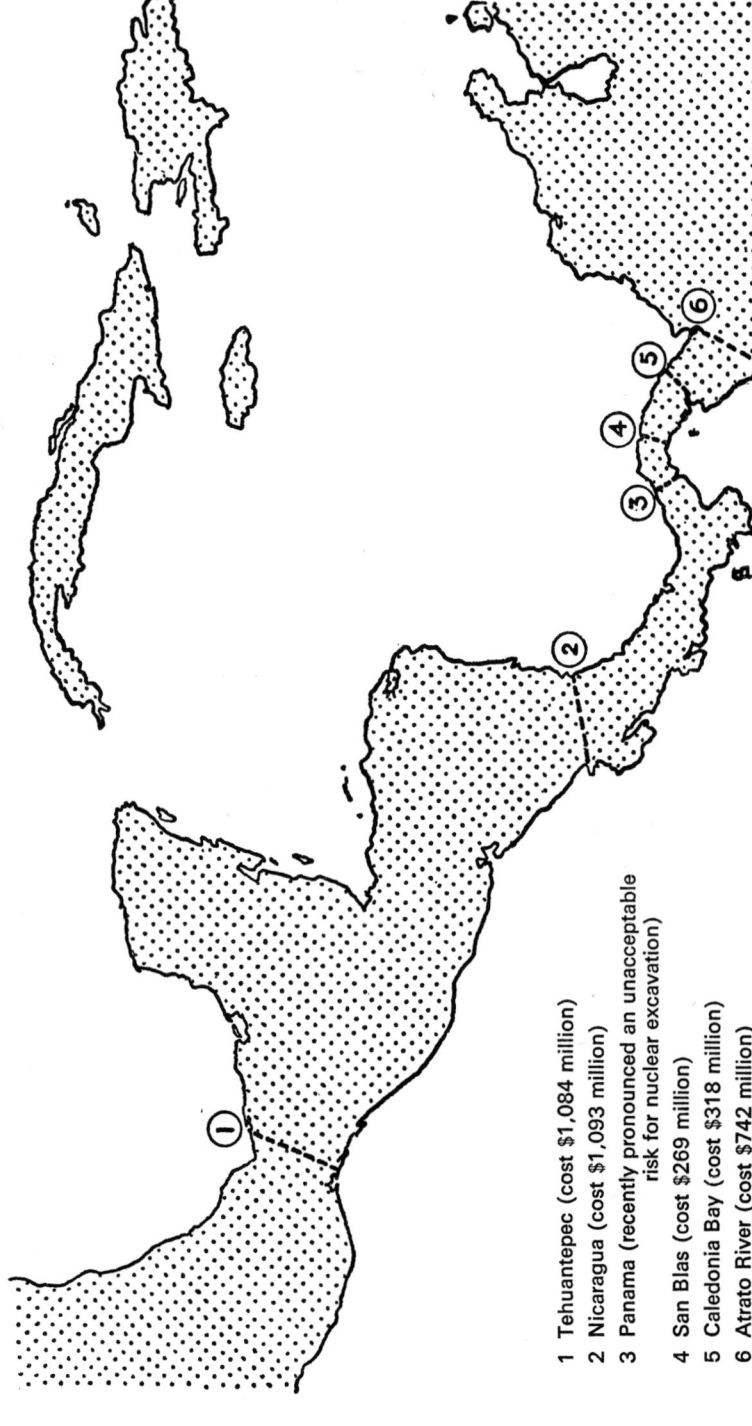

1 Tehuantepec (cost $1,084 million)
2 Nicaragua (cost $1,093 million)
3 Panama (recently pronounced an unacceptable risk for nuclear excavation)
4 San Blas (cost $269 million)
5 Caledonia Bay (cost $318 million)
6 Atrato River (cost $742 million)

Figure 37. Possible routes for nuclear excavation of a new canal

But there might, of course, be a nightmare of a different kind: that of an isthmus made barren by nuclear fall-out.

Scientists in charge of the Plowshare project claim that even with explosives in the megaton range, fall-out could be restricted to within a few square miles, and that atmospheric radiation would be negligible. But even if they are right, ground contamination would be another matter. What would happen, for example, to underground water made dangerous by radioactive waste, and the fish which lived in this water, and the birds who ate the fish, and the Indians who—perhaps a year later—ate the birds? To quote Hammond and Lewin:

> All radiation may cause generic damage to future generations, though the figures obtained are too controversial to summarise briefly; also there are many familiar and immediate side effects. Until the significance of these is better understood, extreme caution must be exercised, and before any Plowshare project is put into operation, those responsible must be quite sure that the money saved will be balanced against the human life that may be endangered.

Few people can be entirely happy at the prospect of the Darien hills being rent apart by nuclear explosion, and trees, rocks, streams and valleys, and all the primordial hierarchy of the jungle, being obliterated in a moment of time. But the fact remains: a nuclear-exploded canal could be completed at one-eighth the cost and in one-quarter the time of a canal dug by conventional methods; and if one man can, by pressing a button, achieve in a microsecond as much as a whole army of men with picks and shovels could achieve in a lifetime—well, that is progress. Progress is a god with vociferous followers today. So it seems likely that, after a period of careful survey and experiment, a nuclear-excavated canal will shortly be given the go-ahead.

The problem then becomes not how but where. Common sense demands a route that is short and sparsely populated; and provided the United States and Panama can reach a political agreement satisfactory to both, the obvious choice must be across the "neck" of the isthmus, at either San Blas or Caledonia Bay.

San Blas has one big disadvantage. The hills of the continental divide are, at this particular spot, over a thousand feet high; it would need a charge of forty-five to fifty megatons to blast them down to sea-level; and this hair-raising charge would have to be exploded only thirty-five miles from Panama and Colon. "The hazards to these cities," to quote a Plowshare report, "can not be fully determined until certain blast-safety work has been undertaken." It seems doubtful if they could ever be determined to the satisfaction of those who live there; and indeed the latest reports indicate that nuclear explosions within fifty miles of the present Zone have been declared "an unacceptable risk". Which brings us to Caledonia Bay—a low-lying route, a hundred miles from the nearest town, and populated only by a handful of half-breeds on the Gulf of San Miguel and a small number of Cuna Indians on the Caribbean shore.

This is historic ground: the site of Balboa's original crossing in 1513. And it will be a coincidence indeed if, after nearly five hundred years, a canal is finally blasted out along the very trail walked by the first white man to set eyes on the Pacific. Indeed there seems to be only one small let or hindrance to the route via Caledonia Bay: what will happen to the Cuna Indians?

Exactly opposite the mouth of the proposed canal is the little village of Mulatupo. Here is David Howarth's description of it:

> [Mulatupo] is not marked on the maps of the engineers, so insignificant does it seem to be. But there it is, a home, a centre of a little kingdom, placid and quiet now in the beautiful bay which [has seen] so many lifetimes of violence. On the shores of the mainland and on the other islands, are the banana groves and the coconut palms—each tree belongs to somebody—and on the reefs are fishing grounds, where the sea comes sparkling in incredibly blue and breaks incredibly white, and the young men balance their dugout canoes in the lee of the coral rocks. The life the Cuna lead there still seems as idyllic as it seemed to the buccaneers in the moments when they grew tired of gold and slaughter. Of course, a sophisticated person could never join [in] and enjoy it: but a glimpse of it can give him an uneasy feeling that this may be how mankind was meant to live.

If the canal is given the go-ahead, the Cuna will have to leave this terrestial paradise, which will vanish as though it had never been in a holocaust of fall-out and flame. One hopes they will leave willingly. But one can't help remembering the reply they gave Sibert's engineers who came, seventy years ago, in search of sand—"that God had given the Indians their country, the land and the water, and the sand that was under the water, and that which God had given to the Indians they would neither sell nor give to the white man." The engineers gave way gracefully in 1907. Will they, I wonder, give way as gracefully today? Will they be honest enough to admit the unpalatable truth: that dollars could never buy back what the Cuna would lose?

It doesn't seem likely. It seems highly probable in fact that the Cuna will be persuaded to leave, and that some time towards the middle of the 1970s a new generation of pioneers will land on the beaches of Caledonia Bay, perhaps on the very spot where Balboa landed in the summer of 1513.

They will push inland, these pioneers, through jungle lush and formidable as any that faced the conquistadors. And after a while they will come to the slopes of an inconspicuous hill: the hill where Balboa knelt and prayed and pointed out "the great maine sea, heretofore unknown to the inhabitants of Europe, Aphrika and Asia". And here, by an ironic twist of history, the strait that Saavedra dreamed of will eventually be blasted out, along the very trail which he hacked, 470 years ago, through the virgin forests of Darien.

BIBLIOGRAPHY

A complete bibliography on the Panama canal can be found in *The Land Divided* by Gerstle Mack; this contains details of almost exactly a thousand books, articles, documents, speeches and official and semi-official publications which cover every aspect of the canal and its history.

The following bibliography contains only material which I have read and used. It includes, I think, most of the original sources on which all histories of the canal are based, also a number of specialised works on construction.

CONTEMPORARY DOCUMENTS

Bulletin du Canal Interocéanique Nos. 1-127 (Sept. 1879 to Feb. 1889) a typical company magazine, eulogising its promoters and glossing over their shortcomings, dubbed by its denigrators *Le Moniteur des Chimères*, but none the less a valuable work of reference.

Canal Record Vols. I-IX (1908–1916) published weekly by the Isthmian Canal Commission: a detailed, painstaking but somewhat pedestrian account of construction and life in the Zone.

BOOKS

Abbot, Brig.-Gen. Henry L., *Problems of the Panama Canal*, Macmillan Co., London, 1905.

Arias, Harmodio, *The Panama Canal*, P. S. King and Sons, London, 1911.

Bakenhus, R. E., Knapp, H. S. and Johnson, E. R., *The Panama Canal*, John Wiley and Sons, New York, 1914.

Bishop, Joseph B., *The Panama Canal*, Charles Scribner's Sons, New York, 1920.

Bunau-Varilla, Philippe, *De Panama à Verdun: Mes Combats pour la France*, Plon, Paris, 1937.

—— *Panama, La création, la destruction, la resurrection*, Plon-Nourrit et Cie, Paris, 1913.

Cornish, Vaughan, *The Panama Canal and its Makers*, T. Fisher Unwin, London, 1909.

Dimock, M. E., *Government-operated enterprises in the Panama Canal Zone*, Cambridge University Press, 1934.

Drumont, Édouard, *La dernière bataille*, E. Dentu, Paris, 1890.
Duval, M. P., *And the Mountains Will Move*, Stanford University Press, 1947.
Goethals, Gen G. W., *The Panama Canal: an engineering treatise*, Vols. I and II, McGraw-Hill, New York, 1916 (contains 25 technical papers, each by an expert who took part in constructing the canal).
Gorgas, Masie D. and Hendrick B. J., *William Crawford Gorgas: his life and works*, Doubleday Page and Co., New York, 1924.
Gibson, J. M., *Physician to the World* (biography of Gorgas), Duke University Press, 1950.
Hammond, R. and Lewin, C. J., *The Panama Canal*, Frederick Muller, London, 1966.
Haskin, F. J., *The Panama Canal*, Doubleday Page and Co., New York, 1914.
Howarth, David, *The Golden Isthmus*, Collins, London, 1966 (the most readable and well-balanced general history of the isthmus, but contains relatively little on construction).
Lee, W. S., *The Strength to Move Mountains*, Putnam, New York, 1958.
Le Prince, J. A. and Orenstein, A. J., *Mosquito Control in Panama*, Putnam, New York, 1916.
Lesseps, Comte Ferdinand de: *Recollections of Forty Years*, D. Appleton and Co., New York, 1888.
Mack, Gerstle, *The Land Divided*, Alfred Knopf, New York, 1944 (the definitive history).
Nelson, W., *Five Years at Panama*, Sampson, Low, London, 1891.
Nicolay, H., *The Bridge of Water*, D. Appleton-Century Co., New York, 1940.
Otis, F. N., *History of the Panama Railroad*, Harper and Bros., New York, 1867.
Pepperman, W. L., *Who Built the Panama Canal?*, E. P. Dutton and Co., New York, 1915.
Robinson, T., *Fifty years at Panama 1861–1911*, Trow Press, New York, 1911.
Rodrigues, J. C., *The Panama Canal*, Charles Scribner's Sons, New York, 1885.
Roosevelt, Theodore, *An Autobiography*, Charles Scribner's Sons, New York, 1920.
Sibert, W. L. and Stevens, John F., *The Construction of the Panama Canal*, D. Appleton and Co., New York, 1915.
Siegfried, André, *Suez and Panama*, Jonathan Cape, London, 1940.
Stevens, John F., *An Engineer's Recollections*, McGraw-Hill Publishing Co., New York, 1936.

Wyse, L. Napoléon-Bonaparte, Reclus, A. and Sosa, P. S., *Canal Interocéanique 1877–1878*, A. Lahure, Paris, 1879.

PERIODICALS

Abbot, H. L., *Atlantic Monthly*, Vol. 86, No. 518 (Dec. 1900).
Abbot, H. L., *Forum*, Vol. 26, No. 3 (Nov. 1898).
Bigelow, P., *Independent*, Vol. 60, No. 2979 (Jan. 1906).
Cornish, V., *Geographical Journal*, Vol. 33, No. 2 (Feb. 1909).
Goethals, G. W., *National Geographic Magazine*, Vol. 20, No. 4.
Engineering, Vol. 89 (1910).
National Geographic Magazine, Vol. 22, No. 2.
Gorgas, W. C., *Medical Record*, Vol. 73, No. 7 (Feb. 1908).
Menocal, A. G., *American Society of Civil Engineers, Proceedings, Papers and Discussions*, Vol. 32, Nos. 2 and 4.
Panama Star and Herald, Panama C.Z.
Reclus, A., *Geographic*, Vol. 41, No. 1 (Jan. 1924).
Reed, C. A. L., *American Medical Association Journal*, Vol. 44, No. 10 (March 1905).
Shonts, T. P., *National Geographic Magazine*, Vol. 16, No. 12 (Dec. 1905), Vol. 17, No. 2 (Feb. 1906).
Slosson, E. E. and Richardson, G., *Independent*, Vol. 60, Nos. 2989–94 (March to April 1906).
Stevens, John F., *Engineering News-Record*, Vols. 114–15 (Spring and Autumn 1935).
Waldo, F. L., *Engineering Magazine*, Vol. 26, No. 4 (Jan. 1904), Vol. 30, No. 3 (Dec. 1905), Vol. 31, No. 3 (June 1906), Vol. 32, No. 5 (Feb. 1902).
Wallace, J. F., *Engineering Magazine*, Vol. 29, No. 6 (Sept. 1905), Vol. 30, No. 2 (Nov. 1905), Vol. 30, No. 6 (March 1906).

INDEX

Abbot, Henry Larcom, 64, 75, 79, 159, 160, 262
Africa, 129, 258
Aizpuru, Rafael, 77
Amador, Guerrero Manuel, 110-14
Amazon, 24
American Contracting and Dredging Co., 58, 82; *see also* Huerne, Slaven and Co.
American Medical Association, 141
Amsterdam, 36
Ancon, 121, 188, 237
Ancon Hill, 237, 239
Ancon (S.S.), 253-6
Andes mountains, 23
Anglo-Dutch Co., 78, 83
Antigua (working force), 143
Appleton, Nathan, 80
Argentine, 215
Arizona, 147
Arizona Railroad, 128
Army and Navy Commission, 117; inefficiency of, 118-20; ridicules Gorgas, 121, 122, 129, 258; asked to resign, 123, 131; fails to provide food, 145; mentioned, 149
Arosemena, Pablo, 80, 113
Artigue, Sonderegger et Compagnie, 60, 62, 73, 82-5, 91
Assam, 210
Athens, 143
Atlantic Ocean, 36, 56, 58, 77, 78, 91, 106, 113, 162, 181-3, 189, 201, 205, 223, 224, 253-5, 257, 261
Atlantic Division, 173-201
Atrato River, 265

Baihaut, Charles, 86, 102
Balboa (town), 137, 140, 229, 231, 233-6, 239, 253, 255
Balboa docks, 228

Balboa Point, 228
Balboa, Vasco Nuñez de, 17, 18, 116, 268, 269
Bangs, Anson M., 166
Baratoux, Letellier et Compagnie, 82, 85
Barbacoas, 34
Barbados, 143
Barcelona, 36
Barrès, 99
Bas Obispo, 47, 50, 54, 66, 91, 150, 152, 185, 187, 204
Bas Obispo Cut, 208
Baudelot, 97
Bergerac, 95
Bertrand, Marcel, 64
Bierd, William G., 157, 170
Bigelow, John, 80, 81
Bishop, Joseph Bucklin, Secretary to Isthmian Commission: opinion of French records, 35, 40, 41; describes Colon, 56, 57; opinion of French dredges, 181; describes construction of Gatun Dam, 187, 188, 204; describes slides in Culebra Cut, 207; mentioned, 218
Bitter Lake, 44
Blanchet, Gaston, 40-2, 44
Blois, 95
Blondin, 102
Blythe, Samuel G., 215
Bogota, 19, 109, 110; government, 109
Bohio, 60, 79, 91, 116, 184, 253
Bonaparte, Napoléon, 19
Bordeaux, 95
Boston, 36
Bourges, 95
Boyd, Frederico, 113
Boyer, Leon, 86, 262
Brazil, 129
Brest, 95

British Columbia, 215
Brunet, Joseph, 97
Brussels, 36
Bryce, James, 218
Bucyrus management, 154; *see also* Excavating equipment
Bulletin du Canal Interocéanique, Company magazine: founded, 33, 34; describes de Lesseps' visits to isthmus, 34, 81; provides publicity, 36; describes Colon, 40; compares Panama to Suez, 46, 47; denies disease, 47, 48, 50; describes work on canal, 53, 54, 63, 66, 67
Bunau-Varilla, Philippe: patriotism, 41, 42, 69, 76, 254, 260; work in Culebra Cut, 67, 68, 73–5, 153, 183, 256; views on yellow fever, 76, 77; role in secession of Panama, 77, 110–15, 259; in charge of Artigue, Sonderegger and Co., 82–4, 91; champions temporary lock canal, 88–90, 159, 160, 265; works to sell French canal to United States, 105, 107, 108; mentioned, 39, 94, 95, 171, 217, 257, 260, 262
Burr, William Hubert, 118, 160

Caledonia Bay, 265, 267–9
California, 57, 137, 229
Camp Elliot, 66
Canal Record, Company magazine: describes *Ancon* and *Culebra*, 178, 179; describes floods, 182, and Gatun Dam, 185, 186, and spillway, 190; describes Gamboa dyke, 202, and drainage of Cut, 211, and pipelines in Cut, 213; praises Bucyrus shovels, 215; 217; describes Cut at night, 218–21, and meeting of steamshovels; 222, 223, and Naos breakwater, 228, and use of hydraulic jets, 229, 230; describes *Corozal*, and *Gopher*, and work on Pacific terminal, 235, 236; describes berm-cranes, 241, and chamber-cranes, 243, and lock gates, 247 and electric locomotives, 250; describes opening of canal, 255
Canal Zone, 29, 105, 115, 118, 121, 142, 143, 169, 170, 179, 207, 209, 234, 255, 259, 268

Cannon, Joseph G. (Speaker of House of Representatives), 172, 257
Caribbean Sea, 18, 23, 34, 106, 171, 177, 179, 186, 190, 195, 200, 255, 268
Carpenter, Admiral, 80
Carroll, Charles L., 121, 122
Carter, Henry Rose, 130
Cathedral Plaza, 40
Central America, 18, 19, 23, 30, 31, 33, 38, 39, 107, 110, 113, 129
Central American Republics, 77
Central Division, 173, 201–24, 228, 230
Cette, 95
Chagres basin, 107
Chagres River: floods, 26, 27, 33, 34, 48, 51, 60, 78, 169, 182, 224; collapse of Barbacoas bridge, 34; crosses French canal, 27 times, 36; attempts to measure floods, 41, 79, 159, 262; efforts to dam or divert (French), 54, 184, 258 (American), 162, 184–7, 190–3; harnessed to form lake, 198, 201–4, 209, 211, 212, 253, 256; mentioned, 83, 106, 181, 196
Chagres valley, 34, 36, 44, 53, 54, 56, 60, 62, 63, 82, 91, 181, 184–6, 188, 198, 201, 204, 256
Chambre des Députés, 49, 58, 96, 100
Chamé, 234; beach, 234; Point, 239
Chartres, 95
Chicago, 36, 124
Chilibre River, 41
Clavenad, 56, 60, 62, 63, 67
Clermont-Ferrand, 95
Cocarde, La, 99
Cocoli, 237; River, 252; valley, 245
Colombia, 28, 97, 109–12, 115, 260; working force, 143
Colombian government, 107–10, 114, 117
Colon, 19, 23, 31, 34, 36, 40, 43, 46–8, 50, 53, 56, 57, 62, 75, 77, 80, 82, 91, 97, 106, 116, 120, 121–4, 127, 130–2, 137, 150, 170, 182, 253, 267
Comacho River and Diversion, 211
Compagnie Nouvelle du Canal de Panama, 107, 109, 111, 114, 115, 184
Compagnie Universelle du Canal Interocéanique: launching of, 33, 37; construction work at Panama, 40, 41, 48–51, 54, 57, 58; shareholders'

meetings, 46, 47, 80; reaction to disease, 46, 47, 85–7; financial difficulties, 87, 90–5; liquidation, 96–8, 99, 100, 102, 105, 106
Compagnie Universelle pour l'Achèvement du Canal Interocéanique, 98
Companyo, Dr., 43
Congo, 24
Congrès International d'Études du Canal Interocéanique, 30, 164
Corozal, 237, 239
Corozal (S.S.), 231–3, 236
Cottu, Henri, 100, 101
Couvreux, Abel, 39, 40, 43–5, 48–50, 53–5, 63
Crédit Foncier, Le, 107
Cristobal, 116, 140, 145, 146, 148, 169, 170, 173, 177, 180, 182, 190, 195, 213, 253, 255
Cristobal (S.S.), 254
Cromwell, William Nelson: appointed counsel to *Compagnie Nouvelle*, 107; champions Panama rather than Nicaragua, 108–10; 111; legal work for *Compagnie Nouvelle*, 115; part played in Wallace's resignation, 124, 125; persuades Stevens to take position of chief engineer, 127; tribute to, 260; mentioned, 105, 257
Cuba, 130, 143
Cucuracha, 91
Culebra, 47, 50, 54, 63, 68, 69, 75, 81, 83, 122, 150, 156, 168, 182, 205, 213, 221
Culebra Cut: French plan near-vertical slopes, 39, 48, 65, 205; complex geology, 41, 64–6, 205–7, 209; slides, 64, 74, 205, 209, 222, 227; techniques of excavation in (French), 67, 72, 73, 91 (American), 119, 125, 127; use of dredges in, 89, 91, 223; use of Railroad to remove soil from, 150–2, 156; vast scale of excavation, 172, 205; final breaching of, 223, 224; first passage by canoe, 253; mentioned, 69, 83, 105, 128, 162, 169, 170, 173, 183, 192, 201–3, 210, 211, 225, 228, 229, 236, 256
Culebra Mountain, 81
Cuna Indians, 189, 268, 269
Cutbill, de Longo, Watson and Van Hattum, 72; *see also* Anglo-Dutch Co.

Darien, 17, 269; hills, 267; rivers, 256; valley, 257
Davis, George W., 118, 121, 160
Delahaye, Jules, 99
Denormandie, 97
Department of Machinery, 153, 154, 157, 158
Diablo Hill, 91, 138
Dijon, 91, 95
Dingler, Jules: appointed chief engineer, 54; his plan for canal approved in Paris, 55; his work on isthmus, 56, 57, 60, 63, 75, 153, 217; appoints Bunau-Varilla, 69; tragic death of his family, 76; invalided to France, 76; tribute to, 261; mentioned, 257
Dirks, Jacob, 35
Drumont, Edouard, 93, 98
Duval, Miles P., 81, 165, 166, 183, 258

Earthquakes, 108
Ecuador, 143
Eiffel, Alexander Gustave, 81, 91, 92, 101
Empire (Emperador), 40, 46, 47, 50, 54, 63, 66, 84, 91, 150, 156, 212, 220, 224
Endicott, Mordecai T., 124
Engineering News, 185
Ernst, Oswald H., 124
Europe, 19, 47, 56, 76, 92, 110, 143; southern European workers, 262
Excavating Equipment:
　Dredges: French, 44, 53–5, 57, 58, 72, 82, 105, 117, 159, 180; Americans rebuild and pay tribute to, 181; American, 44, 106, 135, 154, 176, 181, 183, 223, 224, 229, 235; mentioned, 18
　dipper-dredges, 231, 235
　ladder-dredges, 60–2, 176, 180, 183, 186, 230, 231, 233
　pipeline dredges, 177, 180, 230–3
　suction-dredges, 45, 177, 178, 179, 185, 186, 187, 193, 194
　Ancon, 177–80, 231, 233
　Badger, 233
　Cardenas, 235

278   INDEX

Excavating Equipment—*continued*
 Comte de Lesseps, 57–60
 Corozal, 231–3, 236
 Culebra, 179, 231, 236
 Gopher, 70, 183, 233, 234
 Mole, 70, 71, 181, 233, 235
 Nathan Appleton, 57, 58, 60
 Prosper Huerne, 57, 58, 60
 Dump-cars: Decauville, 92, 105, 117; Lidgerwood, 135, 150, 156–9, 176, 187, 188, 210, 214, 229, 256
 Locomotives: French, 44, 55; American, 154, 156, 158, 159, 187, 217, 220, 221
  Baldwin, 156
  Brook, 156
  Cook, 156
  Electric towing, 248, 250–2, 254
  Porter, 244
 Steam-shovels: French lightweight, 44, 55; American idle through derailments, 125, 127; Stevens puts faith in, 154; large numbers ordered, 158, 159; 183, 187, 188, 194, 196, 204; technique of excavating in Culebra Cut, 210, 214–17, 220–2; meet at bottom level of Cut, 222, 223; mentioned, 218, 229, 230, 235
  Bucyrus: best type for excavation, 154; mentioned, 155, 158, 187, 215, 229
  Marion: Taft awards contract to, 154, 158, 166
 Trackshifters, 154, 157, 158
 Unloaders, 150, 154, 157, 158, 175, 239

Fallières, Clemont, 100
Ferdinand of Castile, 17, 18
Finlay, Carlos, 28, 130
Folks River, 53, 57
Fontane, Marius, 100, 101
France, 33, 36, 40, 42, 62, 63, 76, 94–6, 100, 105, 114, 115, 160, 254, 258, 260
French records, 41, 117

Gaillard, David du Bose: in charge of Central Division, 173, 201; troubled by slides, 168, 222, 256, 262; creates Gatun Lake, 203, 205; deals with water in Culebra Cut, 209–12; techniques of excavation in Cut, 212–14, 216; death and tribute to, 222, 262
Gamboa, 26, 36, 47, 50, 54, 79, 87, 201, 211, 214, 216, 223, 224
Gamboa dam, 161, 201–3, 205, 223, 224
Gatun, 36, 40, 46, 47, 50, 54, 82, 153, 173, 177, 181, 182, 184, 186, 194–6, 198, 199, 201, 204, 224, 225, 243
Gatun Dam: de Lépinay's original plan for, 31, 32, 258, 259; adopted by United States, 162–4; Stevens's defence of, 161; filled with soil from Limon Bay, 180; controversy over its design, 183–6, 227, 261; attempts to block Chagres during its construction, 186, 187, 191–3; construction of, 187, 188, 195, 198–200; completion of, 200, 235; mentioned, 173, 176, 190, 201, 204, 236, 256
Gatun Lake, 116, 173, 190, 201–5, 224, 237, 252, 253, 256, 257
Gatun locks: description of, 185, 186; assembly of material for building, 188, 189, 195; excavation of site, 193, 194; concreting, 195, 196; gates, 198; system of filling and emptying, 248, 249; passing vessels through, 248, 250; towing locomotives, 250, 251; first passage through, 254; too small for modern needs, 265; mentioned, 190
Gatun Spillway, 116, 188–93, 198, 204, 256
Gatuneille River, 41
Guadeloupe, 143; working force, 143
Gaulois, Le, 38, 102
Gauthier, 99
Geographical Society, 30
Gerig, William, 181
Germain, Henry, 94, 95
Germany, 254
Ghent, 36, 39
Goethals, George Washington: opinion of French records, 41, 117; describes French excavation in Cut, 72, 73; unsympathetic to Gorgas, 140–2, 168; his opinion of Jackson Smith, 147; describes plan for high-level canal, 162–4, and method of its construction, 171, 172; appointed

chief engineer, 167; Mrs. Gorgas's description of, 167, 168; relationship with Stevens, 168–70; divides work into three divisions, 173; improves terminal facilities, 182, 183; his character and efficiency, 194, 222; describes blasting in Cut, 213, 214; tribute to his work, 259, 260; mentioned, 177, 201, 205, 211, 254, 255, 257, 258
Gold Hill, 214, 221, 222
Gorgas, Mrs. William Crawford (*née* Marie Doughty), 123, 167, 168, 258
Gorgas, William Crawford: appointed Chief Sanitary Officer, 28; praises French hospitals, 43; estimates number of French deaths, 68; ridiculed by Army and Navy Commission, 118, 121; his experimental work in Havana on connection between mosquitoes and disease, 120, 130, 131; given free hand by Stevens, 129; his successful battle against yellow fever, 129–34; his partially successful battle against malaria, 134–41; relationship with Goethals, 142, 168; first passage of canal by canoe, 253, 254; tributes to his work and character, 141, 171, 172, 258; death, 258; mentioned, 126, 142, 180, 257, 259
Gorgona, 50, 54, 63, 84, 156
Granada (working force), 143
Greece (working force), 143
Grunsky, Carl Ewald, 118
Gunnell, F. M., 78

Hains, Peter C., 124
Harding, Chester, 173
Harrod, Benjamin Morgan, 118, 124
Haut Obispo Hills, 211
Havana, 120, 121, 130, 131
Hay, John, 109, 111, 113, 114
Hay-Bunau-Varilla treaty, 114, 115, 260
Hay-Herran treaty, 110, 113
Hayes, Rutherford B., 106
Hecker, Frank Joseph, 118
Herran, Thomas, 109
Hersent, H., 39, 40, 43–5, 48–50, 53–5
Hill, U. L., 222

Hodges, Harry Foote, 222
Hospitals, 75, 80; Ancon, 43, 63, 69, 120, 133, 134, 183; Colon, 43; Limon Bay, 63
Howarth, David, 62, 255, 257, 268
Hue, 97
Huerne, Slaven and Co., 53, 57, 58, 60; *see also* American Contracting and Dredging Co.
Hutin, Maurice, 63, 67–9

Idaho, 147
Illinois, 124
India, 215
Independent, The, 128
Indian guides, 17, 18, 128
Issoudun, 98
Isthmian Canal Commission (First), 120, 129, 131, 148, 153, 171
Isthmian Canal Commission (Second), 28, 35, 124, 144–6, 166, 170, 171, 189, 207, 259
Italy, 230; working force, 143

Jacob, 82
Jacquet, 86
Jadwin, Edgar, 173
Jamaica, 112; government, 97; working force, 143
Johnston, William Edward, 33
Journal des Débats, 38
Judson, 173

Key West, 106
Kimball, William W., 42
Kirk, J. S., 222
Knox, Philander C., 161

La Boca, 54, 72, 91, 92, 116, 179, 233, 234
La Chesnaye, 98, 101, 102
Lafayette (U.S.S.), 40
Las Cascadas, 66, 212
Las Cruces, 256
Laveran, Dr., 135
Lazear, 28, 130
Lee, Storrs, 186
Le Mans, 95
Lépinay, Adolphe Godin de: puts forward scheme at *Le Congrès International* for high-level canal with

Lépinay—*continued*
  locks, 31, 32; his scheme accepted 27 years later by United States, 164; plans to dam Chagres, 184; tribute to, 257–9; mentioned, 198, 255
Le Prince, Joseph, 123, 131, 134, 137, 140, 253, 254
Lesseps, Charles de, 37, 38, 55, 83, 93–95, 100, 101, 262
Lesseps, Comte Ferdinand de: builder of Suez, 19, 28, 30, 32, 33; inability to cope with Chagres floods, 26, 204, 256; personality, 30; insistence on sea-level canal, 31, 38, 51, 87, 160; idealistic dream of "oceanic Bosphorus to unite nations", 33, 34, 257, 262; visits isthmus, 34–6, 79–81; launches *Compagnie Universelle*, 37, 67, 68; difficulty in excavating Culebra Cut, 63, 64, 67, 68, 72, 91; attempts to run lottery, 85–7, 94; financial difficulties, 92, 93, 95, 96; retires to La Chesnaye, 98; prosecution and trial, 99–101; death, 102; his canal sold to United States, 115; tribute to, 257; mentioned, 39, 40, 42, 43, 47, 49, 56, 57, 67, 68, 76, 82, 88, 90, 105–7, 116, 117, 125, 170, 171, 173, 211, 260–2
Lesseps, Comtesse de (*née* de Bragard), 102
Lesseps, Jules de, 37
Lesseps, Victor de, 37, 100
Lévy-Crémieux, 94
Liberté, La, 38
Libre Parole, La, 99
Limon Bay, 32, 40, 42, 43, 47, 54, 56–8, 60, 78, 82, 112, 171, 173, 175, 176, 179, 180, 200, 227, 231, 255
Livermore Laboratory, 265
Liverpool, 36
Lobnitz and Co., 70, 231
Locks, 31, 32, 86–92, 97, 121, 159–62, 166, 170, 173, 201, 225, 227, 236, 248, 249, 257–9; *see also* Gatun, Miraflores and Pedro Miguel
London, 36, 102
Lorient, 95
Lyons, 36, 95

MacDonald, Donald F., 207, 209
MacDonald, D. J., 222
Mack, Gerstle, 30, 44, 64, 77, 84, 87, 98, 101, 109, 120
Madrid, 36, 143
Magellan, Straits of, 106, 160
Magoon, Charles E., 124
Malaria: isthmus an endemic centre, 26; discovery of connection with mosquitoes, 28; incidence among labour force, 29, 46, 48, 62, 63, 136; Blanchet dies of, 41; French hospitals not screened against mosquitoes, 42, 43; French deaths from, 68, 69; Bunau-Varilla and, 75, 76, 78, 117, 128, 189; Gorgas's battle against, 120–3, 129, 134–42
Maltby, 173
Mamei, 63
Mandinga River, 211
Manzanillo Bay, 56, 175
Marchiafara, Dr., 135
Markel, Jacob E., 145
Marseilles, 95
Martinique, 35, 143; working force, 143
Maryland Steel Co., 177, 231
Masambi River, 211
Matachin, 53, 54, 63, 66, 68, 91, 211
Mexico, 143, 265
Middle East, 31
Mindi, 182, 187, 214
Mindi Hills, 58, 177, 181, 185
Miraflores, 91, 92, 152, 225, 227, 236, 239, 241, 243, 245, 247, 252
Miraflores channel, 230
Miraflores Lake, 237, 252
Miraflores locks: Taft insists on resiting, 166, 225–7; Williamson excavates by hydraulic jet, 229, 237; dredges work on, 233, 235, 236; chamber-cranes, 242, 243, 246; concreting, 245; gates, 247; filling and emptying, 248, 249; towing locomotives, 250–2; too small for modern needs, 265; 253
Moissenet, Dr., 100
Moluccas (Spice Islands), 18
Momotombo (volcano), 108
Moniteur des Chimères, 34
Monkey Hill, 53
Montana, 128, 147

Morgan, John Tyler, 106, 107, 265
Mulatupo, 268

Nancy, 95
Nantes, 82, 95
Naos breakwater, 228, 231, 235, 243
Naos Island, 228, 235
Napoleonic War, 18
Nashville (U.S. cruiser), 112
Nelson, Wolfred, 42, 56
New Granada, 19
New Mexico, 147
New Orleans, 124, 142
New York, 36, 40, 106, 107, 111, 124, 142, 146, 166, 188, 195
New York *Sun*, 108
New York *Times*, 184, 223
New York *World*, 35
Nicaragua, 31, 106–9, 160; government, 108
Nicaragua canal, 106–8, 260
Nicaragua Lake, 106, 108, 265
Nicaraguan Canal Association, 106
Nicolay, Helen, 43
Nîmes, 95
Noble, Alfred, 160
Nombre de Dios, 188, 195
North America, 259

Obispo Diversion, 211, 253
Obispo River, 41, 72, 211; watershed, 36
Ohio, 154
Oliver, William J., 166
Oregon (U.S. battleship), 106
Out West, 112
Oyster Bay, 160

Pacific, 17, 34, 54, 87, 91, 106, 113, 137, 162, 176, 189, 201, 223, 224, 227, 233, 235, 236, 253, 255, 257, 268
Pacific Division, 69, 173, 225–52
Padilla (Colombian warship), 113
Paolo Horqueta, 91
Panama (S.S.), 171
Panama Bay: terminus of canal, 32, 54, 69, 173, 225, 227; convalescent home in, 43; excavation of channel through, 69, 70, 85, 89, 227–9; climate and tides, 227; mentioned, 35, 128; *see also* Naos breakwater

Panama Canal: Saavedra's suggestion for building, 18, 269; comparison with Suez, 30, 37, 39, 47, 50–2, 80; de Lesseps' determination to build at sea-level, 31, 86–8; de Lépinay's proposal for, 31, 32; original French plan, 36; scale and difficulty of work, 44, 172; diversity of French equipment used in construction, 45; Dingler's plan accepted, 55; disease, 75, 130, 137, 138; efforts to preserve French canal, 105–7; comparison with Nicaragua, 106–8; value of French canal to Americans, 116, 117; chaos under Army and Navy Commission, 118–123; Stevens's preparations, 127–9; composition of labour force, 142–4; reliance of canal on railroad, 148–153; equipment used by Americans, 153–9; sea-level or high-level?, 160–162, 164; to be built by Commission or contractors?, 165–7; Goethals "Tsar over all", 169, 170; excavation in Atlantic Division, 173–200; excavation in Central Division, 201–24; excavation in Pacific Division, 225–52; first passage by canoe, 253, 254; first crossing by ship, 254; official opening, 255; description of transit, 255–7; mentioned, 23, 28, 39, 53, 54, 57, 58, 60, 62, 64, 69, 70, 73, 75, 77, 83–5, 90, 91, 96, 98–101, 109, 124, 142, 146, 147, 168, 170, 173, 253, 258, 262, 265

Panama Isthmus: Balboa sights Pacific from, 17; Saavedra suggests strait through, 18; geology and climate, 23–8; floods, 26, 27, 210; centre of yellow fever and malaria, 26, 28, 29, 48, 63, 69, 75, 76, 122, 123; de Lesseps' visits, 33–7, 80, 81; first French engineers arrive, 39; French surveys, 40–2; French buildings unscreened, 42–4; differences between Panama and Suez, 51, 52; slides, 64, 65, 207, 209; first U.S. engineers arrive, 116; initial chaos under Army and Navy Commission, 118–22; Gorgas eliminates disease from, 120–3, 129–42; housing

Panama Isthmus—*continued*
and feeding working force, 142–147; sea-level canal or high-level, 159–64; proposals for nuclear excavation, 265–7; mentioned, 38, 46, 50, 53, 54, 55, 57, 58, 77, 85, 86, 90, 92, 97, 98, 100, 105, 106, 108–13, 117, 124, 125, 126, 128, 148, 149, 153, 165–71, 176, 188, 213–15, 223, 225, 256, 257, 259, 261, 262

Panama, La, 93, 100

Panama or Nicaragua?, 108

Panama Railroad: Wyse obtains concession from, 28; used for disposal of excavated soil, 45, 147–53, 176, 239; American control of, 68, 77; French failure to use, 75; built by Trautwine, 78; finances contractors, 97; assists secession of Panama, 110; assets, 116; early inefficiency, 122, 125, 147; death of construction workers, 129, 148, 180; Stevens's re-organisation of, 147–53, 212; staff petitions Stevens, 171; flooded, 182; efficiency of new staff, 149, 217; Shonts and, 262; mentioned, 35, 92, 145, 157, 235, 254, 256

Panama Railroad Company, 188, 254

Panama *Star and Herald*, 91, 92, 168–70

Panama Steamship Company, 145

Panama town: climate, 24, 39; terminus of canal and railroad, 31, 40, 146, 150; visited by de Lesseps, 34–6; site of hospitals, 43; disease and lack of sanitation, 100, 116, 123, 131–3; facilities as port, 148, social centre, 225; mentioned, 46, 48, 77–9, 127, 234, 237, 267

Paraiso, 47, 50, 54, 92, 150, 156, 213; Cut, 219

Paris, 33, 36, 48, 50, 101, 115

Paris canal congress, 91

Parsons, William Barclay, 118, 160, 166

Pedro Miguel, 205, 214, 216, 224, 225, 227, 236, 237, 241, 243, 245, 252

Pedro Miguel locks: Eiffel plans locks at, 91, 92; Taft insists on re-siting, 225, 227; difficulties arising from site, 236, 237; construction of, 237–241; berm-cranes, 243, 244; concreting, 244, 245; gates, 247; filling and emptying, 248–9; towing locomotives, 250–2; first passage through, 254; too small for modern needs, 265

Pelée, Mont, 108

Père-Lachaise, 102

Perico Island, 54, 69, 70

Periguex, 95

Perpignan, 95

Philadelphia, 36

Philip II (of Spain), 18

Philippe, 78

Philippines, 124

Pittsburgh, 121, 122, 234

Plowshare programme, 265, 267

Porto Bello, 175, 188, 195, 255

Portugal (working force), 143

Prestan, Pedro, 77

Prinet, 101

Provost de Launay, 99

Quartermaster's Department, 140, 142

Raggi, 45

Randolph, Isham, 160

Reclus, Armand, 40, 41

Reed, Walter, 28, 130

Reinach, Baron Jacques de, 94

Reine-Blanche (French warship), 77

Rennes, 95

Rheims, 36

Rio Grande Diversion, 237

Rio Grande River, 41, 70, 85, 212, 213, 231, 237, 252, 258

Rio Grande valley, 36, 54, 60, 69, 72, 225, 229, 245, 257

Ripley, Joseph, 160

Robinson, Tracy, 58

Rocky Mountains, 23, 128

Rodman, Captain (U.S.N.), 254

Rodrigues, José Carlos, 35

Rome, 143

Roosevelt, Theodore, fosters secession of Panama, 109–15; appoints and supports Gorgas, 120, 129, 141; and Army and Navy Commission, 123, 124; and Stevens, 127, 160, 167; supports high-level canal, 159, 160, 162; brings in Army to construct canal, 167; influence on building of canal, 259, 260; mentioned, 105, 118, 166, 257

Rosenberry, J. V., 222

Ross, Dr., 28
Ross, Sir Ronald, 135
Roubaix, 95
Rousseau, Armand, 42, 85, 86

Saavedra de Céron, Alvaro de, 18, 263, 269
Saint Étienne, 95
Saint Germain, 31
Saint Lucia (working force), 143
San Blas, 31, 265, 267
San Francisco, 36, 57, 106
San Juan River, 106
San Miguel, 17; Gulf of, 268
San Pablo, 91, 92
Sapoa River, 31
Sardanilla River, 211
Saturday Evening Post, 171, 215
Saville, Caleb M., 193
Schildhauer, Edward, 250
Sens, 95
Shonts, Theodore Perry, 124, 127, 129, 153, 154, 166, 167, 262
Siberia, 215
Sibert, William Luther: in charge of Atlantic Division, 173; builds Toro and Manzanillo breakwaters, 175, 176, 255; diverts course of Chagres, 186, 187, 191–3; describes attempt to buy sand from Cuna Indians, 189, 268; designs Gatun spillway, 190, 191; work on Gatun locks, 194–6; and Gatun Lake, 203, 204; describes work in Culebra Cut, 210, 211; tribute to, 261; mentioned, 182, 257
Siegfried, André, 93, 95
Slaven, Henry B. and Moses, A., 57–60, 82
Slides: description of, 64, 66; first French experience of, 66, 67; Bunau-Varilla and, 67, 68, 73–5, 83, 84, 89, 91; French held up by, 73, 79; cause subsidence in Gatun Dam, 184, 188, Gatun locks, 194, and Naos breakwater, 228; geological explanation of, and effect on Culebra Cut, 205–9; diversion channels accentuate, 211; mentioned, 222
Cucaracha slide, 168, 209, 222–4, 230
Culebra slide, 207, 227, 235, 262
La Pita slide, 209

Las Cascadas slide, 209
Smallpox, 48
Smith, "Square-foot" Jackson: in charge of housing and feeding, 142; administrative ability, 143, 147; builds houses on principle one square-foot for every dollar of pay, 144, 145; builds subsistence depot, 145, and mess halls, 146; provides good cheap meals, 147; clash of personality with Goethals, 147; dismissed, 147, 257; tribute to, 261
Société de Géographie de Paris, 28, 258
Société des Dépôts et Comptes Courants, 85
Société des Travaux Publics et Constructions, 82, 84
Soldado, 60
Sosa Hill, 176, 225, 237, 255
Sosa, Lope de, 41
Sosa, Pedro, 32
South America, 110, 113, 259
South-East Asia, 24
Spain, 18, 19, 106; government, 143; working force, 143
Spaniards, 17
Spanish-American War, 106
Spillway Hill, 190
Stearns, Frederic P., 160
Stevens, John Frank: appointed chief engineer, 127; character and background, 128, 129, 165; quoted, 48, 75, 119, 144, 146, 227; relationship with Roosevelt, 127, 167; relationship with Gorgas, 129; restores order on isthmus, 128, 129, 261; appoints and supports Smith, 142, 145, 147; opinion of Panama Railroad, 147, 148; improves terminal facilities, 148, 182; reorganises railroad, 149–53; supervises ordering of suitable top-quality equipment, 153–9, 180; supports high-level canal, 159–64, 259; dispute over contracts, 165–7; resigns, 167; transfers power to Goethals, 167–9; farewell to, 170–2; tributes to, 172, 257, 258; supports earth dam at Gatun, 184, 185, 256; designs electric railway, 195, 196; describes Gatun Lake, 203, 204
Suez Canal, 19, 30–3, 36, 37, 39, 43, 47, 50–2, 69, 80, 87, 88, 96, 102

INDEX

Sullivan and Cromwell, 107; *see also* Cromwell, William Nelson
Sutherland, third Duke of, 80

Tabernilla, 56, 63
Taft, William Howard, 124, 125, 127, 129, 147, 154, 166, 167, 184, 225, 227, 255, 259
Technical Commission, 31, 50, 53, 55, 58
Tehuantepec, 31, 265
Telfers Island, 53, 57, 58, 177
Teredo (drill-barge), 234, 235
Texas, 147
Tiger Hill, 53
Toro Point, 173, 175
Totten, George Muirson, 35
Tours, 95
Trautwine, John Cresson, 78
Tribunal Civil de la Seine, 97
Trinidad (working force), 143
Trinidad River, 41, 54; valley, 203

United Kingdom (working force), 143
United States: supplies equipment to de Lesseps, 56; fosters secession of Panama, 77, 110–13; interest in purchasing French canal, 105, 106, 109, 115; declares war on Spain, 106; and Hay-Herran treaty, 109, 110; and Hay-Bunau-Varilla treaty, 113, 114; Wallace returns to, 124, 125; recruiting of labour force from, 142, 143, 149; supplies equipment for American canal, 180, 231; and nuclear excavation, 265, 267; mentioned, 58, 119, 134, 147, 167
United States Army, 130, 167–70, 173, 176, 228, 254
United States government, 44, 97; plans for canal through Nicaragua, 106–8; and secession of Panama, 111; and Wallace's resignation, 125; awards contracts, 154; negotiates with Cuna Indians, 189
United States Navy, 111, 254, 255, 265
United States (working force), 143

Versailles, 95
Vienne, 95
Vigia, 182
Vignaud, Barbaud, Blanleuil et Compagnie, 82, 84
Volcanoes, 108, 205
Vulcan (drill-barge), 234, 235

Walker, John G., 118, 121
Wallace, John Findley: parsimony in ordering equipment, 44, 156; dissatisfied with French dump-cars, 45, 218, 256; relationship with Army and Navy Commission, 118, 119; favours sea-level canal, 121, 160; brings his coffin to Panama, 124; resignation, 124, 125, 169; failure to build houses and lay track, 145, 149; mentioned, 127, 148, 165
Washington, 109–11, 113, 114, 118, 119, 123, 124, 153, 154, 161, 166, 167, 250
West Indians, 141, 143, 144, 146, 262
West Indies, 129, 143
West Point, 201
Williamson, Sydney B., 173, 227–9, 234, 235, 237, 243, 245, 247, 252
Wilson, Woodrow, 202, 223–5, 227
Wood, Leonard, 142, 147
Wyoming, 147
Wyse, Lucien Napoléon-Bonaparte: arrives in isthmus, 19; fails to make accurate survey, 23, 24, 26, 35; negotiates concession, 28; puts plans to de Lesseps and *Congrès International*, 30, 31; challenged by Godin de Lépinay, 31; negotiates extension of concession, 97; tribute to, 260, 261; mentioned, 40, 41, 257

Yellow Fever: isthmus an endemic centre of, 26; incidence among labour force, 29, 46, 62, 69, 75, 125; connection with mosquitoes, 42, 120, 130, 131; failure to screen houses against mosquitoes, 42, 43; attitude of the *Compagnie Universelle* to, 48; Bunau-Varilla and, 75, 76, 117, 128, 135; Gorgas's research in Havana, 120, 130, 131; Gorgas ridiculed by Army and Navy Commission, 121–3; Wallace's fear of, 135; Gorgas's successful campaign against, 129–34, 141, 142; mentioned, 262

Zurcher, Philippe, 64

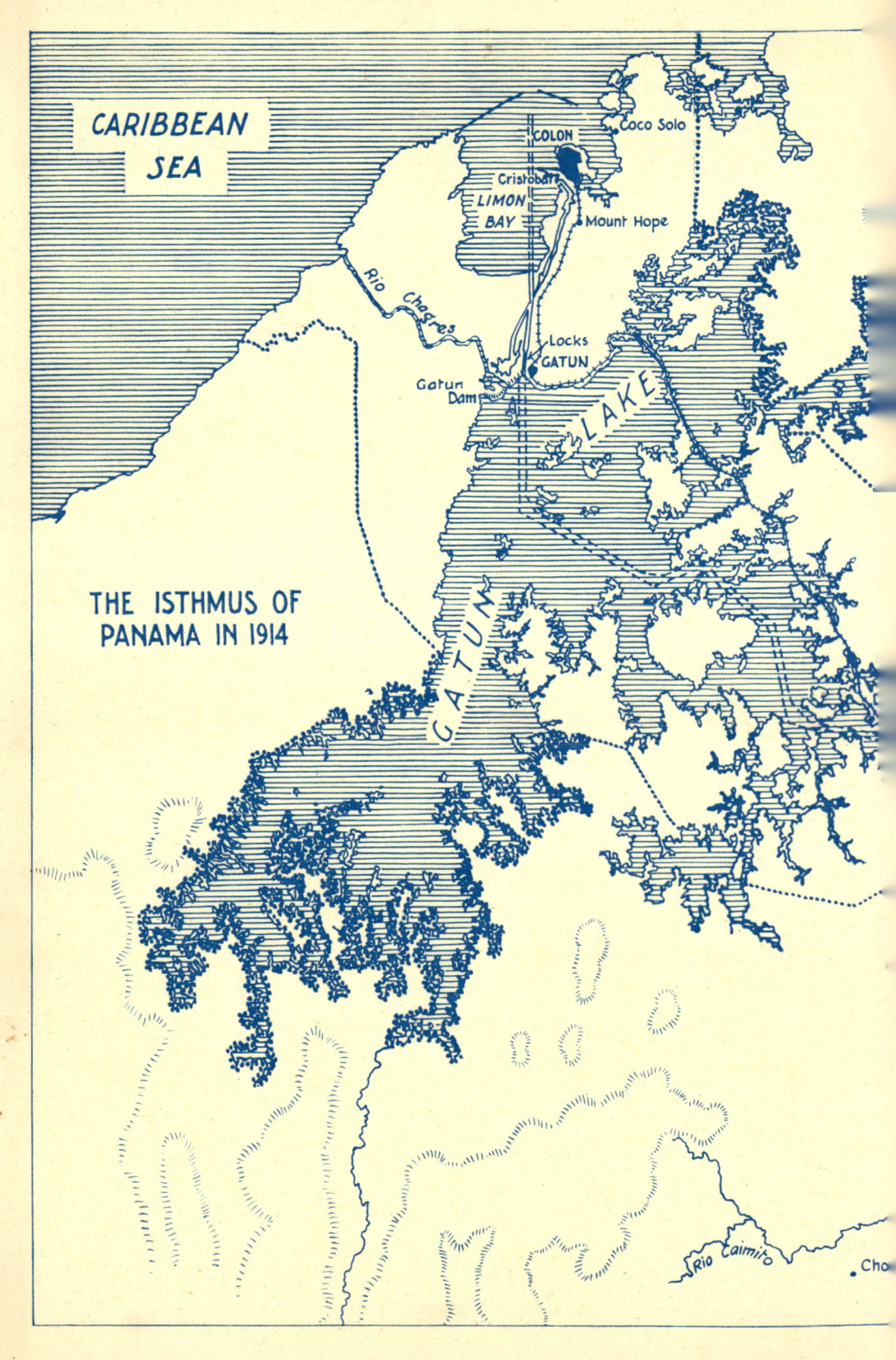